PV

**The Working Class in American History**

*Editorial Advisors*
David Brody
Alice Kessler-Harris
David Montgomery
Sean Wilentz

*A list of books in the series appears at the end of this volume.*

# On the Line

# ON THE LINE

## Essays in the History of Auto Work

edited by
**Nelson Lichtenstein and Stephen Meyer**

UNIVERSITY OF ILLINOIS PRESS
Urbana and Chicago

Library of Congress Cataloging-in-Publication Data

On the line : essays in the history of auto work / edited by Nelson
  Lichtenstein and Stephen Meyer.
     p. cm. — (The Working class in American history)
    Bibliography: p.
    Includes index.
    ISBN 0-252-01539-8 (cloth : alk. paper). ISBN 0-252-06015-6 (paper :
  alk. paper)
    1. Trade-unions—Automobile industry workers—United States—
History.  2. Automobile industry and trade—United States—History.
3. Industrial relations—United States—History.  4. Automobile
industry and trade—United States—Management—History.
I. Lichtenstein, Nelson.  II. Meyer, Stephen, 1942–  .
III. Series.
HD6515.A805 1989
331'.04292'9073—dc 19                    88-2372
                                                      CIP

*To Daniel
and
to Margo*

# Contents

# 1

# Introduction: The American Automobile Industry and Its Workers

## NELSON LICHTENSTEIN

"The automobile industry," Peter Drucker wrote in 1946, "stands for modern industry all over the globe. It is to the twentieth century what the Lancashire cotton mills were to the nineteenth century: the industry of industries." Forty years later, Drucker's assessment remains equally valid, but now as much because of the industry's uncertain future as of its historic triumph. Though its relative economic bulk has diminished of late, the production of motor vehicles still holds a cultural and ideological importance that makes this endeavor central to understanding the way twentieth-century society works. Thus, if this industry, once labeled "capitalism's favorite child," is now entering an extended era of reorganization and crisis, its travail is in large measure synonymous with that of American capitalism itself. When his company still teetered on the edge of bankruptcy, Chrysler president Lee Iacocca rightly asserted, "My problems are the problems of the country."[1]

In the United States the automobile industry looms so large for three reasons. The first is sheer size. By the mid-1920s, an industry which had hardly existed twenty years before had already assumed a central place in the American economy. In 1929 it accounted for almost 13 percent of the value of all manufactured goods, 15 percent of all steel went into motor vehicles, and 80 percent of all rubber into tires. Almost 400,000 workers were directly employed by the industry, with millions more indirectly dependent on its fortunes: perhaps one in six employed Americans.[2] With almost two million residents Detroit had become the nation's fourth largest city, a metropolis which a visiting European car designer declared, "an earthly

1

Paradise, the color of smoky gray."[3] During World War II the industry built few cars, but its converted factories produced more than a
quarter of all war materiel bound for the armed forces. In the postwar
years the American automobile companies entered their high noon
of industrial maturity. They spread a new generation of modern factories across the land, brought automation to the national consciousness, and doubled car and truck production to about ten million a
year. The Big Three automakers—General Motors, Ford, and Chrysler
—were always among the ten largest manufacturing companies. In
fact, General Motors had been first for more than forty years and Ford
usually third behind Standard Oil of New Jersey. When the latter
briefly dethroned GM after the first oil shock in 1974 it seemed as if
an earthquake had rocked the industrial landscape.[4]

Second, the automobile industry has transformed the texture of
American life. In their 1925 study, *Middletown*, Robert and Helen
Lynd found the automobile "an accepted essential of normal living," and by then it was already the most important force reshaping
the physical landscape. Automobiles destroyed the crossroads market town, urbanized much of rural America, and by supplanting all
competing forms of transport helped throw a ring of suburbs around
the soon to be neglected core of many larger cities. More than any
other technical artifact, the automobile has come to symbolize physical mobility, social status, and freedom itself. The product of mass
production themselves, automobiles so reshaped access to goods and
services that they became the foundation for a vast mass consumption
market. Although some observers have postulated the emergence of
a pervasive "car culture" obliterating many social norms of an earlier
generation, automobiles also became one of the most visible indexes
of status and class. Working-class Americans saw car ownership as
a great symbol of respectability and advancement; this may explain
why so few relinquished them even in the darkest years of the depression. To more prosperous Americans, ownership of a particular
model drew a line between themselves and those below, advertising
their rank on a scale instantly visible to every schoolchild.[5]

Finally, the automobile industry has played a paramount role in
shaping and reshaping our ideas about production itself. We begin, of
course, with Henry Ford's assembly line, which assumed mythic proportions even as it was first deployed in 1913 and 1914. Ford himself
called the machinery of mass production the "New Messiah," and his

vision of a fully integrated, continuous flow production process became the standard emulated by manufacturers worldwide. With Ford as a model, car firms displayed a remarkable capacity to generate novel production techniques and diffuse them rapidly from one company to another. The automobile firms were among the first to market a sophisticated product on a large scale, to develop modern forms of corporate organization, and to employ large numbers of workers on highly mechanized and fragmented operations. In the Soviet Union during the 1920s "Fordizatsia" was a watchword for up-to-date technique even in those sections of the country where the motor vehicle was still unknown.[6]

In its purest form, "Fordism" lasted only until the mid-1920s when even Henry Ford recognized that a changing market would not accommodate the endless production of a standard model on a super specialized assembly line. Led by General Motors, the industry inaugurated an era of relatively flexible mass production, which still relied on a predominantly unskilled workforce, but adapted factory production techniques to the annual model change and a greatly expanded product mix. After World War II the industry sought to "automate" its facilities, at first through deployment of massive transfer machines, but more recently and more successfully, by reliance on computer-aided design, numeric control of machine tools, and installation of computer controlled robots that gradually depopulated many manufacturing and assembly operations.[7]

Because it did so much to create a new world of work, the automobile industry has played a vanguard role in defining the relationship between labor and capital in twentieth-century America. One phase encompassed the era from 1914, when Ford introduced the five-dollar day, until 1937, when during the sit-down strikes of that winter—certainly the most significant labor conflict of this century—workers organized into the United Auto Workers (UAW) forced General Motors and other major auto companies to recognize their union. For two generations thereafter the big auto corporations and this union established much of the pattern that the rest of American manufacturing would follow: periodic renegotiation and improvement in the pay and benefits of a growing workforce, a careful delineation of the power and prerogatives of management and union at the shop floor level, and the incremental deployment of automation technology. Much auto work remained dehumanizing and difficult, but now a "civilized relationship" seemed to replace the once bitter conflict which had divided top leaders of the UAW and the large auto corporations.[8]

Since the mid-1970s change in all these realms has accelerated: the auto companies have shrunk their workforce, demanded greater control over job assignments, and increased their commitment to a new and more flexible generation of computer guided machine tools and assembly systems. At the same time the UAW found it could no longer rely on the industry's historically high productivity growth to make the incremental wage and fringe benefit advances its members had come to expect. After 1973, two sharp recessions, greater competition from low-wage foreign labor, and a more adverse political climate at home threw onto the defensive a union once widely recognized as the most powerful and progressive of all American labor organizations.

In the 1970s the failure of the American automobile companies to compete successfully with their Japanese and West German rivals forced many industry observers to reassess what had once been considered an unalloyed success story. Emma Rothschild offered an early broadside in her *Paradise Lost: The Decline of the Auto-Industrial Age*, which decried the "pattern of industrial inertia" that had come to characterize an industry faced with "social obsolescence." Her attack on Fordism as an increasingly inefficient production system was soon sustained, even from within the halls of the Harvard Business School; here William Abernathy and a number of likeminded associates argued that the industry's characteristic devotion to capital intensive, high-volume production stifled innovation and actually reduced productivity in the increasingly competitive market environment of the late postwar era. This critique was further advanced by Charles Sabel and Michael Piore who held that Fordism itself lay at the heart of the crisis faced by late twentieth-century capitalism. An extreme division of labor, a socially rigid structure of authority, and a UAW commitment to a detailed set of work rules and job controls had combined to sap the efficiency and flexibility of the industry.[9]

The social and economic structures required of assembly line production have also shaped the study of auto workers themselves. In the 1950s industrial sociologists cautiously reaffirmed one of Marx's original insights: even in the midst of the high-wage postwar boom, the industry's minute subdivision of labor and its reliance on machine paced production still generated an "alienated" workforce. In their now classic studies, sociologists Robert Guest, Eli Chinoy, and Robert Blauner found auto workers to be the archtypical worker of the mid-twentieth century. Chinoy's portrait of men trapped by the assembly line, dreaming they might one day escape, proved particularly poignant in the mid-1950s. The sociologists' rediscovery of the essential relationship between the work process and worker consciousness pointed the way forward, but the plant-centered focus of most industrial sociologists of this school prevented them from casting their work in any larger and more dynamic historical or political framework. The assembly line, the labor-management relationship, the resulting consciousness of the workforce all seemed timelessly fixed in an economy grown wealthy and mature in the early postwar era.[10]

It took more than a decade for historians of American labor to appreciate the importance of work process in a study of the labor history of the industry. By then a new exploration of the social history of the working class was well underway, largely as a result of the considerable impact of historians such as E. P. Thompson and Herbert Gutman who helped revitalize labor history by reintroducing human agency and consciousness into the study of class relations.[11] Gutman and Thompson helped take the study of labor history out of the hands of the economists and sociologists and return it to historians. But of even more decisive importance for students of twentieth-century industry, and of auto work especially, was the appearance in 1974 of Harry Braverman's *Labor and Monopoly Capital: The Degradation of Work in the Twentieth Century*. Braverman broke new ground by alerting historians and sociologists to the social context within which the technology of production was embedded. The work process was a function not of some abstract logic of production but rather of the managerial drive to more effectively control and deskill a sometimes recalcitrant workforce. For the first time Frederick Taylor, the influential founder of "scientific management," seemed to loom as importantly as Henry Ford or UAW President Walter Reuther in setting the industry's labor relations pattern.[12]

It soon turned out, of course, that Braverman's insights could only be applied with some caution: the deskilling process was neither as uniform as Braverman had projected, nor were workers simply ciphers in this process. There was much debate over the extent to which craft skills were actually eroded in mass production industry, and much discussion of when and why managers chose particular work control strategies. For example, Stephen Meyer's work on the origins of labor management at the Ford Motor Company demonstrated that automobile industry Taylorism was as much a political and social phenomenon as it was a technical and economic one. To successfully deploy assembly line production techniques Ford managers thought it necessary to homogenize the culture as well as degrade the skill of the several thousand immigrant workers at Ford's Highland Park factory. More recently, sociologist David Gartman has used the work of a number of neo-Marxist scholars to argue that the corporate search for control of the work process required constant innovation, both technical and bureaucratic, to manage a resistant workforce. Less successful, however, may be his effort to distinguish between what he calls "neutral production techniques," which promote greater quality and simple efficiency, and those work process innovations "biased" by the capitalist ownership of the means of production. But the culture and technique of a particular stage in the evolution of capitalist production is more nearly a seamless web, in which the design and deployment of a particular machine represents the outcome of a complex process that so thoroughly incorporates a whole set of social and technical conflicts as to make distinctions between repressive and nonrepressive functions meaningless.[13]

The attention now focused on the social dynamics of the shop floor work environment meant that a new history of the United Automobile Workers would soon be written. In the older schema, the years before 1937 were seen as a dark age of speed up, authoritarian management, and low wages; but once the workers rebelled and the UAW was organized, auto workers and their employers inaugurated an era of stable, if not conflict free, collective bargaining.[14] In contrast, historians of the 1970s and 1980s saw much more complexity and ambiguity in the rise of the UAW. Peter Friedlander's detailed history of the unionization process at a Detroit parts plant demonstrated the narrowness of the active trade union base there, the slow progress won by this cadre, and the importance of ethnocultural identification in determining a worker's whole world view, including of course, his or her attitude toward the union. Instead of finding the union the product of a mass movement, Friedlander discovered that the local he studied consisted of a handful of radicals who won over a passive majority, many of whom were still linked to the peasant cultures of their

East European homeland. In the process they built a union, but they also established the preconditions for its later bureaucratization.[15]

Ethnic conflict and accommodation were also central to the work of Elliott Rudwick and August Meier whose *Black Detroit and the Rise of the UAW* found the cleavage between black and white workers virtually unbridgeable in the UAW's early days. Like Friedlander, they also found the union's leadership cadre the key players in resolving these ethnic tensions, but in the UAW of the 1940s this required the suppression of the union's white majority whose reluctant acquiescence was only won after the federal government itself backed up UAW and civil rights movement demands that the production lines integrate. Although Meier and Rudwick end their study with the alliance forged by the leadership strata of the black community and the UAW in the mid-1940s, racial and ethnic tensions in organized auto plants hardly diminished over the next generation, and when they next exploded, in an upsurge of nationalist militancy in the late 1960s and early 1970s, a more firmly entrenched UAW leadership found itself generally opposed to this new movement.[16]

Just as the UAW seemed incapable of transcending the cultural and ethnic divisions within the workforce, so too did the new history of the union take a more measured view of the degree to which the union has contested management power in reconstructing the shop floor work regime. David Brody has argued that although collective bargaining itself codified a region of union power, it also generated a restrictive "contractual net" to contain and repress spontaneous and independent shop floor activity. Similarly Nelson Lichtenstein found in the postwar era an elaboration of a wide array of institutional obstacles to the exercise of worker power at the departmental and local level. But he weighed more heavily than Brody the accommodationist politics and policy of the international union which often put top UAW leaders in an adversarial relationship with the union's local units.[17]

This collection sheds new light on many of these issues. It brings together essays from the fields of sociology, history, industrial relations, and economics, but all have this in common: they find the dynamic relationship between workers, managers, and the production process central to understanding the history of the organization of work in the auto industry. They are bound together by both their

historical perspective and a sensitivity to the condition and the consciousness of auto workers and auto industry managers in a given
social context. The essays are arranged in a chronological order, but
they are also part of a more general dialogue about the nature of work
and production that ranges across the history of the industry in the
twentieth century.

The first three essays consider the origins and essential features of
what has come to be known as the Fordist system of mass production.
In a comparative study of the early years of the British and American
auto industries, Wayne Lewchuk found that the transatlantic deployment of the same production technology can nevertheless lead to the
evolution of very different industrial relations systems. Of utmost
importance is the subtle interplay between a preexisting workplace
culture, management expectations, and the character of the market
for both labor and manufactured products. In Detroit auto manufacturers began with a relatively "clean slate"; factories were nonunion,
semiskilled labor plentiful, the craft tradition weak. Fordism therefore flourished in the United States, but in Great Britain the managerial effort to introduce a high-volume, continuous flow production
system foundered. It was not simply a question of Britain's failure to
develop a mass market, for in the early years of the industry, when
economies of scale could still be achieved at low output levels, some
British firms did build simple utility vehicles.

Instead, Lewchuk found that the strong union tradition among
skilled metal workers, who continued to play an organic role in the
organization of shop floor production, made British managers reluctant to adopt those American methods, including machine paced production and close supervision, a hallmark of the Ford system in Detroit. In Britain a species of worker self-management, largely keyed
to a wage incentive system, partially accommodated the powerful
working-class desire for autonomy and control on the shop floor;
from a management viewpoint, it substituted as a mechanism for coordinating production and fulfilling tasks which in American firms
were performed by lower level management.

Managerial domination of the labor market proved one of the decisive reasons American manufacturers were able to reshape the
production process with such ease. Thomas Klug's study of the
Employers' Association of Detroit (EAD) demonstrates the extent to
which the labor market itself proved a "terrain of struggle" between

workers and employers during the first three decades of this century. Manufacturers were all too aware of the symbiotic relationship between the control of skilled labor within their factories and the need for a well-managed, open-shop labor market on the outside. Full deployment of assembly line production would only become possible when employers were sure they could readily draw upon a new immigrant workforce of unskilled, highly mobile employees. Employers experimented with a number of strategies to achieve this end. At first they sought to manage this workforce with an Americanization program that emphasized cultural assimilation and paternalistic social control, but the labor shortage of World War I undermined employer unity and forced the EAD to call directly upon the federal government to help manage its workforce. Statist solutions were made unnecessary, however, by the recession of 1920–1921. Thereafter, a policy of high wages and harsh factory discipline successfully reinforced management authority until a new and greater economic crisis again deprived them of unfettered labor market control.

Finally, Stephen Meyer explores the implications of the idea, most recently advanced by David Noble, that innovations in the technology of production represent a "social choice" that reflects the values of their inventors and the interests of management.[18] Meyer argues that one of the key features of Fordism was a "transfer of skill" from worker to manager embedded in the techniques of the production process itself. In this essay he takes issue with those scholars, including Michael Piore and Charles Sabel, who have postulated that the emergence of new production technologies has opened the door to a system of "flexible specialization" under which a reskilling of the workforce might be possible. Instead, Meyer demonstrates that classical Fordism actually ended in the late 1920s when General Motors inaugurated the annual model change and a full range of cars "for every purse and purpose." But despite the fact that GM President Alfred Sloan's new market strategy emphasized a decentralized and flexible form of mass production, and despite the emergence of increasingly sophisticated forms of automation technology in the postwar era, the organization of the production process continued to operate on Fordist premises that generate an increasing number of fragmented and monotonous jobs.

Trade unionism in the American automobile industry has had as its chief aim the amelioration of this harsh factory regime, and the next group of essays examines the extent to which unionism has in fact proved an effective counterweight to managerial power at the shop floor level. In his study of the unionization process at Dodge Main, Steve Jefferys demonstrates that the unusually powerful shop floor organization there arose after union activists captured the Chrysler company union, transforming its departmental representation structure into a strong shop steward system that "legitimized" the frequent exercise of union power at the point of production itself. For more than twenty years these workers commanded a remarkable degree of de facto authority, not only because of Chrysler management's failure to recast itself in the General Motors mold but also because of the democratic autonomy sustained by the Dodge Main UAW local. The destruction of this militant tradition came only in the late 1950s when a deep recession gave Chrysler and the national leadership of the UAW the opportunity to bring conditions at the Dodge Main plant into conformity with the industrial relations practices of the rest of the automobile industry.

But the distribution of shop floor power was never merely the product of shifting economic conditions. In his social history of automobile industry foremen, Nelson Lichtenstein demonstrates that the allegiance of this crucial strata in the factory hierarchy depended as much upon union power and ethnic consciousness as it did upon management design. Confronted in the early 1940s by both a militant shop stewards movement and an erosion in the power of the anti-Catholic, Masonic job trust that had once controlled entry to the supervisory ranks, many foremen rejected their traditional identification with management and cast their lot with a CIO-oriented Foreman's Association of America (FAA). The FAA challenged key elements inherent in the Fordist division of authority; but with their shop floor disciplinary power now at stake, top management fought back on both the legal and industrial front, smashing the new foremen's union in 1947 but never entirely regaining the undivided allegiance of this social strata.

Yet the cost was high. Just as Chrysler's postwar victory made governance of the shop floor at that corporation rigid, so too did the auto industry's successful effort to maintain the loyalty of lower level management reemphasize the hierarchical character of the factory regime in the U.S. auto industry. Despite much company propaganda about the need for "teamwork" and "human engineering,"

lower level supervision came to function, in the words of one foreman, as "puppets on a string" even as their numbers proliferated in
the early postwar years.

Ruth Milkman's study of the industry's defeminization at the end
of the Second World War also demonstrates the way in which the
social upheaval generated by unionization and wartime conversion
of the industry constituted a potential turning point in the history of
Fordism. Although women constituted as much as 25 percent of the
industry workforce during the war, they remained segregated in an
expanding but nevertheless rigidly defined set of female jobs. In most
plants there were actually very few tasks the average woman did not
have the physical capacity to master, but the capital intensive character of the industry made the substitution of cheap female labor for
the more traditionally well-paid males unnecessary in management
eyes, especially in view of the intense resistance such a policy would
engender from male workers organized in the militant UAW. Women
workers were therefore purged from auto factory employment roles
after the war, and sexist hiring and layoff policies were institutionalized for a generation.

Milkman's reexamination of "Rosie's" brief sojourn in the wartime
auto factories is particularly telling because it shows the subtle relationship between both industry structure and worker consciousness
in determining the character of the workforce from which the auto
corporations drew. For the most part women auto workers did not
share an ideology of collective advancement during the 1940s, nor
did they see themselves as part of a social movement with an inherent claim on industry jobs. All this stood in sharp contrast to the
rising tide of racial militancy which helped legitimize the large employment gains black workers made during the war. By 1945 the latter
were entrenched within the production workforce of most Northern
factories, and a long struggle to win entrance to the skilled trades
and the lower ranks of management had begun. Although civil rights
seemed a social issue the UAW had to address, a serious discussion of
women's status in the industry would have to wait a quarter century
more.

The last two essays evaluate the extent to which a mature Fordist
organization of production continues to shape not only the character
of the workforce and the nature of labor-management conflict but
also the fate of the auto industry itself. Jonathan Zeitlin and Steven

Tolliday's comparative study of post–World War II labor relations raises the whole issue of how one measures union power inside the factory. They argue that in the postwar years shop steward control of the factory work environment in Great Britain, which reached its apogee between the mid-1950s and the early 1970s, was far more limited and precarious than commonly supposed. Control over the production process was most efficacious when brought to bear in setting piecework pay rates and manning schedules. But shop floor power of this sort was often internally divisive, did not form part of a wider union strategy, and was possible only because of the relatively decentralized character of both the British car firms and their trade unions.

In the United States, of course, shop stewards themselves had little direct authority, not only because of the relative financial strength and determination of American management but also because of the centralized bargaining regime the UAW felt it necessary to construct if it were to confront successfully the Big Three auto makers. But Tolliday and Zeitlin hold that American auto workers nevertheless exercised a degree of job control unionism in some ways greater than that of the British, especially if one looks at the situation in terms of the relative constraints each national union movement imposed upon management. Challenging the work of those historians like Brody, Lichtenstein, and Jefferys, who have recorded a gradual expansion of managerial prerogatives, these authors argue that the UAW turned the extreme Taylorism of the American industry to its own advantage, by codifying work rules, negotiating an elaborate grievance procedure, and insisting upon a rigid seniority schedule to determine in-plant promotions and layoffs and thereby to severely limit management flexibility and plant efficiency.

The implications of this argument are many, but perhaps the most important bears upon the contemporary struggle waged between many local unions and the auto companies over management efforts to negotiate wholesale changes in seniority rules and job definitions. Are such factory work rules, often labeled antiquated in the popular press, in fact outmoded in light of contemporary competitive and technological developments, or are they minimal job rights especially necessary in the absence of the kind of vibrant shop steward organization described by Jefferys in Chrysler's early years?

Steve Amberg offers a historical reading of this question by examining in some detail the experience of Studebaker-Packard, whose labor relations and marketing strategy seemed to deviate from the American norm until a new management group tried to make it conform to General Motors practice. Until then Studebaker had survived by adopting a management strategy that closely resembled true "flexible specialization." This relatively small firm prospered by combining an informal system of union-management accommodation with a "niche" marketing program that banked heavily upon the skill and loyalty of its South Bend, Indiana, workforce. By examining the role played by Studebaker unionists, top UAW leaders, and the Eisenhower administration, Amberg makes clear that this alternative to Fordism would only have been possible in a political environment that provided some measure of national economic planning and community participation in heretofore private business decisions. Although these alternatives were briefly glimpsed at that time, none proved viable, and the company adopted a survival strategy that would become all too familiar in the 1980s: wage cutbacks, unilateral workrule changes, and merger with a stronger company. In the late 1950s this "triumph of industrial orthodoxy" generated an intense round of shop floor conflict, market failure, and eventual bankruptcy.

For the last fifteen years the U.S. automobile industry has been undergoing a major reorganization, prompted by the unpredictable price of oil, the appearance of powerful competitors from abroad, and the stagnation of the domestic economy. Some argue that we have therefore reached a point where Fordism, as a production system and labor relations strategy, has finally outlived its historical moment. Mass markets have begun to fragment, while robotization and computer-aided manufacture have reorganized labor requirements to such a degree that reskilling the workforce, even democratizing the work process, may be taking place. Meanwhile, competitive pressures have simultaneously reduced the ability of even powerful unions like the UAW to make uniform wage and working conditions in the principle auto companies (and even in individual plants) that serve the U.S. market, thereby making auto workers open to a more cooperative relationship with management.[19]

Structural change in the industry has certainly been greater than at any time since the 1920s, but one should greet with some skepticism the notion that auto work itself is on the verge of a major transformation. Employers have long sought the maximum flexibility in the deployment and pay of their labor force, while workers have tried to infuse their daily routine with a rights consciousness legitimizing their struggle and thwarting the exercise of managerial power beyond certain socially defined limits. Thus far contemporary experiments in work reorganization, such as the quality circles set up in many big auto plants or the more elaborate team production effort designed for GM's highly robotized Saturn plant in Tennessee, have at best an ambiguous character. These management sponsored initiatives have been implemented at a time when labor was weak and demoralized. Although they embody much rhetoric of "participation," in practice they often seem designed to return auto work to conditions reminiscent of the 1920s. Thus at its new Saturn facility GM is prepared to offer employment guarantees and salary wages to a large proportion of its workforce, but the virtual absence of a UAW shop floor presence and the deployment there of "team leaders" and the implementation of a "pay for knowledge" scheme seem a throwback to an earlier era when the pace and pay of auto work was policed by an ever vigilant corps of foremen and working straw bosses.[20]

Automobile manufacturing has long attracted the attention of scholars of industrial society because production there so graphically displays the social antagonisms between labor and capital. Despite all the contemporary discussion of robotization and "non-adversarial" labor relations, little seems to have altered the essential features of this conflict. As a number of the authors in this collection make clear, this antagonism does not generate any uniform response from either workers or managers, but it does provide the basic social framework for the conflict and accommodation that have taken place throughout the history of this industry. The character of automobile work will in all likelihood remain the product not only of market forces and technological change but also of the social consciousness and political choices auto workers and auto managers bring to the production process.

## NOTES

1. Peter F. Drucker, *The Concept of the Corporation* (New York, 1983), 149; Edward D. Kennedy, *The Automobile Industry: The Coming of Age of Capitalism's Favorite Child* (New York: Reynal and Hitchcock, 1941), 314; Robert B. Reich and John D. Donahue, *New Deals: The Chrysler Revival and the American System* (New York: Times Books, 1985), 2.

2. John B. Rae, *American Automobile Manufacturers: The First Forty Years* (Philadelphia: Temple University Press, 1959).

3. As quoted in Emma Rothschild, *Paradise Lost: The Decline of the Auto-Industrial Age* (New York: Random House, 1973), 169.

4. Brock Yates, *The Decline and Fall of the American Automobile Industry* (New York: Vintage, 1983).

5. A vast literature exists on this subject, but see especially Joseph Interrante, "The Road to Autopia: The Automobile and the Spacial Transformation of American Culture," in David Lewis and Laurence Goldstein, eds., *The Automobile and American Culture* (Ann Arbor: University of Michigan Press, 1980), 89–104; James J. Link, *The Car Culture* (Cambridge: MIT Press, 1975); Warren James Belasco, *Americans on the Road: From Auto Camp to Motel, 1910–1945* (Cambridge: Harvard University Press, 1981); and Paul Barrett, *The Automobile and Mass Transit* (Philadelphia: Temple University Press, 1983).

6. Keith Sward, *The Legend of Henry Ford* (New York: Rinehart, 1948), 49.

7. See especially David A. Hounshell, *From the American System to Mass Production, 1800–1932* (Baltimore: Johns Hopkins University Press, 1984); and Harley Shaiken, *Work Transformed: Automation and Labor in the Computer Age* (New York: Holt Rinehart, 1984).

8. William Serrin, *The Company and the Union: The "Civilized Relationship" of the General Motors Corporation and the United Automobile Workers* (New York: Knopf, 1974).

9. Rothschild, *Paradise Lost*; William Abernathy, *The Productivity Dilemma: Roadblock to Innovation in the Automobile Industry* (Baltimore: Johns Hopkins University Press, 1978); Michael Piore and Charles Sabel, *The Second Industrial Divide: Prospects for Prosperity* (New York: Basic Books, 1984); see also William J. Abernathy, Kim B. Clark, and Alan M. Kantrow, *Industrial Renaissance: Producing a Competitive Future for America* (New York: Basic Books, 1983).

10. Robert Guest, *The Man on the Assembly Line* (New Haven: Yale University Press, 1952); Eli Chinoy, *Automobile Workers and the American Dream* (New York: Beacon Press, 1955); and Robert Blauner, *Alienation and Freedom* (Chicago: University of Chicago Press, 1964).

11. See, for example, Michael Frisch and Daniel Walkowitz, *Working Class America: Essays on Labor, Community and American Society* (Urbana: University of Illinois Press, 1983), especially the introductory essay.

12. Harry Braverman, *Labor and Monopoly Capital: The Degradation of Work in the Twentieth Century* (New York: Monthly Review Press, 1974); and for the last decade's work see Richard Price, "Theories of Labour Process Formation," *Journal of Social History* 14 (1983): 91–110.

13. David Stark, "Class Struggle and the Transformation of the Labor Process," *Theory and Society* 9 (1980): 89–130; Stephen Meyer III, *The Five Dollar Day: Labor Management and Social Control in the Ford Motor Company, 1908–1921* (Albany: State University of New York Press, 1981); David Gartman, *Auto Slavery: The Labor Process in the American Automobile In-*

*dustry, 1897–1950* (New Brunswick: Rutgers University Press, 1986). On the culture of machinery design see Merritt Roe Smith, *Harper's Ferry Armoury and the New Technology* (Ithaca: Cornell University Press, 1976); and David Noble, *Forces of Production: A Social History of Industrial Automation* (New York: Knopf, 1986).

14. Jack Stieber, *Governing the UAW* (New York: John Wiley and Sons, 1962); Sidney Fine, *Sit-Down: The General Motors Strike of 1936–1937* (Ann Arbor: University of Michigan Press, 1969).

15. Peter Friedlander, *The Emergence of a UAW Local, 1936–1939* (Pittsburgh: University of Pittsburgh Press, 1975).

16. August Meier and Elliott Rudwick, *Black Detroit and the Rise of the UAW* (New York: Oxford University Press, 1979). Ethnic and racial succession has typically generated conflict between the newcomers who initially occupy the poorest jobs and the generation which came before who now control the lower level management posts and run the union. Such a conflict accounts for the volatility of many urban auto factories in the late 1960s. See James A. Geschwender, *Class, Race and Worker Insurgency: The League of Revolutionary Black Workers* (New York: Cambridge University Press, 1977); and Dan Georgakas and Marvin Surkin, *Detroit: I Do Mind Dying* (New York: St. Martin's Press, 1975).

17. David Brody, *Workers in Industrial America: Essays on the Twentieth Century Struggle* (New York: Oxford University Press, 1980), 173–214; and Nelson Lichtenstein, *Labor's War at Home: The CIO in World War II* (New York: Cambridge University Press, 1982); and Lichtenstein, "UAW Bargaining Strategy and Shop-Floor Conflict in the U.S., 1946–1970," *Industrial Relations* 24 (Fall 1985): 360–81.

18. David Noble, *America by Design: Science, Technology and the Rise of Corporate Capitalism* (New York: Knopf, 1977) as well as his *Forces of Production*.

19. Harry Katz and Charles Sabel, "Industrial Relations and Industrial Adjustment in the Car Industry," *Industrial Relations* 24 (1985): 295–315; and the editors' introduction in Steven Tolliday and Jonathan Zeitlin, eds., *The Automobile Industry and Its Workers: Between Fordism and Flexibility* (Cambridge: Polity Press, 1986). See also Alan Altshuler, Martin Anderson, Daniel Jones, Daniel Roos, and James Womack, *The Future of the Automobile: The Report of MIT's International Automobile Program* (Cambridge, Mass.: MIT Press, 1984).

20. For contrasting views of such management sponsored work reorganization schemes, Mike Parker and Jane Slaughter, *Choosing Sides: Unions and the Team Concept* (Detroit: Labor Notes, 1988); and Stephen Wood, "Technological Change and the Cooperative Labour Strategy in the U.S. Auto Industry" (Paper presented at the conference on "Trade Unions, New Technology, and Industrial Democracy," University of Warwick, June 1986) should be read against Harry Katz, *Shifting Gears: The American Automobile Industry in Transition* (Boston: MIT Press, 1986).

# 2

---

# Fordism and the Moving Assembly Line: The British and American Experience, 1895–1930

## WAYNE LEWCHUK

As a production technique and industrial relations strategy Fordism is today encountering criticism of truly global proportions. In Japan, Sweden, and West Germany vehicle makers have deployed a variety of new production techniques and labor-management schemes designed to make mass production more flexible and assembly line work less dehumanizing. Likewise, in the United States, the social and economic crisis through which the automobile industry passed in the early 1980s has opened the Fordist system, with its rigid divisions of labor, hierarchical management structure, and fixation on a mass market, to a spirit of self-examination and innovation far greater than at any time since it was pioneered by Detroit's vehicle makers from 1911 to 1920.[1]

Thus, it is fitting that we reexamine the origins of this system in the early years of the century and the factors causing its enthusiastic adoption by American management but rejection by British management. In the United States a unique set of social forces and historical conditions made Fordism an effective managerial response to the labor relations crisis created by the enormous expansion of automobile industry employment in the years just prior to World War I. In particular, the Fordist system was based on the assumption that a workforce could be found, or created, which would accept higher wages in return for high-effort norms and unilateral managerial control of shop floor decision making. The hostile attitude of American employers and legislators toward unions, the relative defenselessness of a largely immigrant workforce, and the shift in American values from that of earlier "Yankee individualism" to a more consumer-oriented culture, all played a role in Fordism's American success.[2] In contrast, British managers did not believe that labor would either accept or could be forced to tolerate a system trading high wages for more effort and less shop floor autonomy. Through their unions and political channels, British labor demanded the reform of shop floor life along more democratic lines. Unable to break with the social and institutional traditions of the nineteenth-century labor movement, in which skilled workers played an organic role in the organization of shop floor production, British managers found the rigid management system embodied in Fordism both impractical and inefficient.[3]

Labor market conditions played a role in shaping acceptance or rejection of the Fordist system, but they were not, as some scholars postulate, the crucial variables in determining the outcome. Such an approach, which argues that the shortage of skilled labor in the United States forced the Ford Motor Company to experiment with new production systems, exaggerates the difference between the workforce skill profile found in the early British and American auto factories. It oversimplifies the complex process of institutional innovation by focusing our attention on the skill displacing methods employed by Ford rather than the social control mechanisms at the heart of the Fordist revolution. As we shall see, Fordism's main objective was not to fit labor demand to labor supply but rather to monitor the effort bargain of an expanding factory payroll and extract from the available workforce the maximum level of effort.[4]

Nor was Fordism simply the product of a mass market. It is true that this system emerged in the context of rapidly expanding demand for a cheap, standardized automobile. However, Ford's very high levels of output were not absolutely necessary to make his model of factory reorganization a viable management strategy. As we shall see, many elements of the Fordist system began reducing costs at annual sales levels in the low thousands, well within the reach of a number of British firms. Thus, their decision to adopt an alternative managerial system cannot be explained merely by differences in the scale of their respective national car markets.[5]

Although the changing character of labor and product markets provided the economic context in which Fordism emerged, its birth must be understood as an important chapter in the social struggle brought on by the spread of large scale factory production in the late nineteenth century. It advanced management's "frontier of control" a quantum leap, evolving out of but also moving beyond Frederick Taylor's scientific management movement. The Fordist revolution was made necessary not by the use of skill displacing machinery or the extreme division of labor but by the failure of these new machine systems, introduced between 1909 and 1913, to increase substantially managerial control of the effort bargain. To work, Fordism required a further reorganization of production departments along flow principles, a large wage increase to halt labor turnover, and a new labor relations system that curbed the independent authority of foremen and other low-level supervisors.[6] Successfully deployed by a self-confident group of American entrepreneurs, this Fordist ensemble would encounter stiff resistance on the very different social terrain existing in early twentieth-century Britain.

## Fordism and the Ford Factories in Detroit

The labor environment of Detroit was an important factor shaping the Fordist strategy. A booming, open-shop city, Detroit attracted a large number of immigrant workers and often experienced labor shortages in the years before World War I. Despite these tight labor market conditions, a strong union movement did not emerge until the 1930s. The Employers' Association of Detroit sought to regulate competition for factory labor and crush unions that tried to operate in the city. The association fought its first major battle with the International Association of Machinists in 1901, and by 1907 it had all but eliminated Detroit trade unions.[7] But the failure of unionism did not mean that Detroit employers were without a labor problem. Despite the aggressive labor recruitment drives of the Employers' Association, which attracted 20,000 workers to Detroit in 1910, local industry was unable to meet the demand for skilled and unskilled labor, forcing many firms to "pirate" the labor supply of their competition. By 1912 the situation had reached a crisis and under the direction of the association, Detroit employers called a truce. They halted competitive advertising for local labor and established a new fund to advertise for labor outside Detroit.[8]

Within the context of this tight, but union free, labor environment, the Detroit automobile producers grew and innovated. The organization of the early vehicle factories differed from Fordist factories in two important ways. First, in the manufacturing departments machines were organized functionally in contrast to the later adoption of line organization based on the kind of component being produced. Under the functional system components had to be transported between departments for successive machine operations. Second, these early auto factories assembled components and chassis on stationary trestles, and parts for each vehicle had to be delivered to each assembly stand. In the early years gangs of workers were given the responsibility for assembling an entire component or even vehicle; at a later stage the task was divided between a number of gangs, and gangs moved between assembly stations performing their tasks.[9]

The first real breakthrough into flow production in the assembly department came not at Ford, but rather at the neighboring EMF Company, whose two key managers had come from Ford. W. E. Flanders, one of the founding partners of EMF in 1908, had earlier been recruited by Ford to oversee the expansion and administration of the firm's manufacturing operations. But Flanders's stay with Ford was short, and when he left he took with him Max Wollering, who had been responsible for setting up and managing Ford's first venture into engine manufacture in 1906. EMF began production in August 1908 and in three years produced over 23,000 vehicles. Just prior to Studebaker's purchase of the firm in 1911, Flanders and Wollering installed a mechanized assembly line to boost chassis output to 100 per day. This first line had about thirty work stations, controlled by a clerk who recorded the order and completion time of each task. The entire line would then be moved forward. Wollering gave the following description of this first line: "We kept pushing them and then we thought we'd try to pull them [chassis]. We took two elevator drums, put a couple of motors on them with cables, and had proper hooks attached to the cable that would grasp the front axle of the car to tow it along."[10] This powered assembly line preceded Ford's first assembly line by at least two years. Why then did Ford delay the adoption of this system until late 1913?

Was it possible that Ford was not a sufficiently large producer to justify the capital expense of an assembly line and machine reorganization? This is unlikely as neither the cost of adopting the new system of factory organization nor the required level of output appears excessive. The first line at Highland Park in 1913 was 150 feet long and

**Table 2.1.** Output and Employment, Ford Motor Company, 1906–1913

| Year | Output | Employment |
|------|--------|------------|
| 1906 | 8,729 | 700 |
| 1907 | 14,887 | 575 |
| 1908 | 10,202 | 450 |
| 1909 | 17,771 | 1,655 |
| 1910 | 32,054 | 2,773 |
| 1911 | 69,762 | 3,976 |
| 1912 | 170,068 | 6,867 |
| 1913 | 195,954 | 14,366 |

Sources: A. Nevins, *Ford: The Times, the Man, the Company* (New York: Charles Scribner's Sons, 1954), 451; M. Wilkins, *American Business Abroad* (Detroit: Wayne State University Press, 1964), 436.

employed about 140 assemblers. It was a primitive affair designed to hold but five or six chassis.[11] The actual capital outlay in assembly departments was very small. As late as 1919 the Ford chassis assembly department accounted for only $3,490 worth of machinery, and in 1922 the entire capital outlay in the chassis department was less than $40,000.[12] Moreover, the net effect on the firm's capital requirements was probably negative because the assembly line permitted a reduction both in the number of partially finished vehicles one needed to hold in stock and in floor space.

Estimates of the scale of operation needed to make Fordism economically efficient suggest that, in manufacturing departments, a machine could be fully employed on a single piece with a yearly output of about 6,000. Machine specialization was necessary to allow machine departments to move to line organization and flow production. In the assembly areas an output of about fifty per day appears necessary to take advantage of assembly line production. In both cases, smaller savings could be had at lower levels of output.[13] Ford had easily exceeded these scale requirements by 1909 when annual output reached 17,771.

To understand why and when Ford moved to adopt assembly line methods one must look at the rapid growth in both output and employment. The relevant, and one might say spectacular figures, are presented in Table 2.1.

Ford's rapid expansion created two related problems. First, as the demand for output increased, the existing stationary method of assembly reached an upper bound beyond which production costs increased.[14] Second, as the workforce expanded, the existing institutions for monitoring and enforcing effort norms broke down. Ford faced a labor problem that was insoluble without a radical reorganization of production. The Fordist system, introduced in 1913, would successfully deal with both problems.

Under the stationary system of production, mobile trucks carried the stock along the rows of assembly stands dropping off necessary items. Eventually Ford required over 100 chassis assembly stations spread over two rows 600 feet long to meet production.[15] In machine departments, components had to be trucked between departments for successive machine operations. By 1913 congestion created by the transportation of parts stymied further expansion.[16]

The problems generated by the growth of employment are rather more complex but directly related to our thesis regarding the different behaviors of American and British management. Because Ford did little actual manufacturing in the early years, his workforce was surprisingly small. Total employment did not reach 1,000 until 1909, after which it grew rapidly. Meanwhile, other area vehicle producers employed significantly larger workforces: in 1910 EMF/Studebaker employed 5,700, Packard 4,640, Buick 4,000, and Cadillac 3,500.[17] Thus at Ford the rapid expansion of the workforce after 1910, in conjunction with the extreme division of labor, created a labor problem more keenly felt than by other local employers.

Until about 1905 or 1906, Ford shops had been run within a paternalistic framework, feasible given the relatively small size of the workforce but also necessary given Ford's dependence on skilled workers whose value to the firm gave them an implicit voice regarding how tasks were to be performed. Ford could be found regularly in the shops where he knew all the workers and the workers knew him as Henry or Hank. Work attitudes were described as cooperative, and all were enthusiastic about mounting production levels.[18] A movement away from this friendly paternalistic environment took place in 1907 and 1908 when employment grew too large for Ford to maintain personal contact with each worker. He was forced to delegate most responsibility for labor relations to low-level supervisors, now responsible for hiring, firing, and setting pay rates.[19] Labor problems were aggravated by the stationary system of assembly and the functional organization of machine departments, thus making it difficult for foremen to monitor individual workers or enforce effort norms.[20] In an attempt to keep productivity high, Ford introduced a profit sharing program in 1908 and resorted to crude time studies of labor tasks. Wollering described the system at Ford Manufacturing in 1907: "I had studies made on the various manufacturing operations. . . . We would get a man whom we had confidence in and who knew what he was doing as to whether it was a lathe or a screw machine or a grinder. He knew the fundamentals of it and he would take a stop-watch and operate the machine himself to get a fair idea of what could be done."[21] Work study was also begun in the foundry: "We [management] had to go out and make them to prove our point. We worked hard to do it and we did it. Of course, after we did it the other boys had to do it. This is essentially what I was doing back in 1908. I was setting work standards."[22]

By 1913 the rapid growth in employment levels introduced new strains on the system, although further division of tasks and the resulting reduction in average skill requirements opened up new avenues for monitoring and enforcing the effort bargain. Labor turnover reached massive proportions: 400 percent per annum at Ford, at least twice the rate of other vehicle plants at this time. Absenteeism was also on the rise with an average 10 percent of the workforce missing each day. In the words of one writer, "They are conducting a continuous, unorganized strike."[23] The tight labor market, high levels of worker mobility (due to the low level of skill needed to perform most jobs), and autocratic foremen all contributed to Ford's labor problem. Ford responded by creating a centralized employment office, establishing a new wage grade system, and curbing the authority of foremen to hire, fire, or promote the workers they supervised. Low-level supervisors could refuse to employ a worker in their department, but the employment office now decided whether the worker should be fired or simply transferred.[24]

By weakening the control low-level supervisors exercised over hiring and firing, top management also reduced their ability to enforce effort norms. Figures supplied by Stephen Meyer point to a drastic fall in the rate of unit productivity improvement. In 1911 labor productivity increased 41 percent, but in 1912 it grew only 15 percent and in 1913 a mere 4.7 percent.[25] The simplification and routinization of work, a process completed at Ford by early 1913, had thus failed to resolve the company's labor problem. The stationary system of production proved increasingly less efficient with the higher levels of output, while the existing management infrastructure could not effectively discipline the soaring number of workers.

Fordism resolved these problems. The company introduced the assembly line and flow production within months of the adoption of the new labor relations system, and the five-dollar day was adopted just three months later. Over a period of less than twelve months Ford had altered the entire basis of production in his factories. A contemporary Ford manager observed, "We are trying to make you do things with a mechanical pace setter; that is my own version of this thing . . . I never thought that would take too kindly with the average working man. He didn't like to be put on a tread mill, you know, that was the idea."[26] The success of the new strategy depended upon labor's willingness to accept regimentation, unilateral managerial control of shop floor decisions, and higher effort norms in exchange for the chance to earn relatively high wages. It is beyond the scope of this paper to explain in detail why American workers were willing to accept this bargain. In part they had little choice; the lack of trade unions and the vulnerability of immigrant workers forced many to accept Ford's offer. The rise of a consumer-oriented society certainly played a role. Moreover, many members of the Detroit workforce held the characteristically "peasant" dream of one day returning to Poland, Italy, Ontario, or Kentucky with a nest egg large enough to rebuild their shattered agrarian lives on native soil.[27]

## History of British Motor Vehicle Production, 1895–1913

The British motor vehicle industry has been criticized, as have most British industries in this period, for slowness to adopt American mass production techniques. Several scholars have argued that the vehicle makers were slow to expand, concentrated exclusively on luxury products, and continued to employ inefficient craft methods of production.[28] The evidence concerning the slow rate of expansion is clear. In 1907 Britain was the only major producer of motor vehicles unable to supply domestic demand.[29] The evidence concerning the industry's product mix is less conclusive. The luxury producers—Rolls Royce, Daimler, and Napier—were leading firms. But careful scrutiny of the models offered by other firms in the industry suggests that at least until 1906, and again after 1912, the British industry produced a large volume of less expensive models destined for the utility market. Firms such as Sunbeam, Singer, Vulcan, and Vauxhall produced mainly for this utility market before 1906, and after 1912 Humber, Rover, and Standard expanded rapidly on the strength of their small car lines. Further evidence of the extent to which British producers were supplying the small car market can be found in Daimler's turn-of-the-century decision not to produce an inexpensive model. The firm argued that there were already too many British small car producers in the market. The years 1906 to 1911 did witness a shift from small cars toward the luxury models. Former small car firms, such as Vauxhall and Sunbeam, concentrated on the larger models, but this trend was reversed in 1912 when low priced American producers threatened an invasion of the British market.[30]

The British auto industry made a larger shift to skill displacing, mechanized production methods than has usually been recognized. The failure of Britain to develop a mass market did limit the length of production runs and made some forms of mechanization less economical. However, the need for accurately machined components encouraged mechanization, particularly in the engine and chassis departments where the tastes of the British consumer were less of a factor. British vehicle producers' close ties with British cycle makers aided their shift to mechanization. The cycle trade had been slow to adopt the repetition methods pioneered by the American firms in the 1880s, but the next decade witnessed a rapid conversion. The professional journals reported a large demand by the cycle makers in 1896 and 1897 for repetition machinery, and contemporary reports suggest that by 1900 firms such as Rudge, Rover, Humber, and Northfleet had made the conversion to repetition production with unskilled labor. In his study of the British cycle trade, A. E. Harrison concluded, "it cannot be confidently asserted that the British techniques of cycle manufacture were markedly inferior, though nearly all the major developments of the 1890s in automatic and semi-automatic, and labour saving cycle-making machinery emanated from the U.S.A."[31]

The cycle trade's experience with repetition production was quickly absorbed by the young vehicle industry. As early as 1897 contemporary reports suggest that in Midland, where there was a concentration of vehicle makers, rapid progress was being made in the use of new machine techniques and the employment of unskilled labor.[32] Reports of the first Daimler factory indicate that a large stock

of American machines was installed and careful attention was paid
to machine organization to minimize transportation. By 1899 Daimler further added to the machine stock, including self-sequencing
lathes, multiple head boring machines, and milling machines. The
latter were particularly important because they replaced lathes as
the work horses in repetition machine shops, making it possible for
the firm to employ a high percentage of boy labor. In 1899, when the
adult workers called in the Amalgamated Society of Engineers over
the issue, one in four machine operators was a boy, and in the turning
department over half the operators were boys.[33]

Daimler was not the only plant moving in the direction of repetition production with less skilled labor. At Humber, "Advantage
has been taken of the long experience which Humber have had in
the employment of labour saving tools for the production of bicycle
parts, and it would be difficult to find a better regulated machine
tool shop, or one with a greater output for its size. The machines
are all worked at their maximum capacity, high speed steel being
employed throughout . . . limit gauges and micrometer working are
universal."[34] Advances were also made at the Belsize works in Manchester, described by the *Motor Trader* as the Anglicized embodiment
of American methods and organization.[35]

By 1914 the lessons of American repetition production had been
widely absorbed by the British vehicle producers. In that year, a management consultant argued that "in the motor trade . . . a large portion of the workers were either turret hands who do not do much
more than pull certain handles, or milling machine hands who only
put work in a fixture and let it go, having the speed and feed set for
them, and jig drillers."[36] Similarly L. A. Legros, president of the Institute of Automobile Engineers, argued that by 1911, "the tendency
in the bigger factories is to diminish the amount of responsibility left
to the individual worker in respect to the employment of . . . shop
knowledge."[37]

Most scholars have underestimated the extent to which repetition methods and less skilled labor were employed because the rate
of change from craft to machine production differed so markedly
throughout the factory. Most body production and the final assembly of the luxury models remained a craft operation until after World
War I. But the majority of manufacturing operations on the engine
and other components had been converted to repetition methods by

a much earlier date. The *Automobile Engineer's* description of the Daimler works in 1907 reveals the uneven rate of technical progress:

> It is a curious fact that although the firm under discussion wasted many pounds in hand fitting parts, yet the engine erecting was carried out on a totally different system. . . . There was exceedingly little which was hand fitted on any of the engines . . . any part, which during the operation was found to be of a size other than that necessary, had to be returned to the machine shop and replaced with one which would fit . . . very few of the engine gangs possessed a file or other instrument which could be used for fitting in the ordinary sense of the word.[38]

Another factor receiving little attention in studies of the British vehicle industry is size of the workforce. It is certainly true that the production scale of the British firms lagged well behind those of the leading American producers. Output levels of 1,000 were considered large in the pre-1914 years, and Humber's output of 2,500 was considered exceptional.[39] But these low production runs are deceiving. Many American producers concentrated on assembling components purchased from outside suppliers, and even when these firms began to increase the level of in-house manufacturing the large component suppliers continued to play an important role. When Ford began manufacturing engines in 1906, he still purchased the more complex components from external suppliers. As late as 1913, 84 percent of the cost of the Ford Model T represented the cost of material and components purchased from outside suppliers, while less than 7 percent of costs represented labor employed by Ford.[40] The extensive use of component suppliers allowed Ford to produce over 17,000 vehicles in 1909 with less than 1,700 workers. On the other hand the early British producers both manufactured and assembled their products and hence required large workforces. By 1906 Argyll employed 3,000; Daimler had 2,000 in 1906, jumping to 4,500 in 1910 and 5,000 in 1913; and Humber employed 5,000 by 1908, and Wolseley 4,000 in 1913.[41] Thus in the critical pre-1914 period, when car producers were formulating strategies for the new industry, British managers had to oversee a far more complex production process than did the American assemblers. The latter had merely to create institutions to coordinate a much simpler production process and then gradually adapt them as they moved into manufacturing areas.

The vigor of the prewar union movement in Britain made it more difficult for management to monitor these large factory workforces relative to the American scene where heavy industry remained virtually unorganized until the late 1930s. Between 1910 and 1926 British unionism was more clearly on the offensive than in any other period of its development.[42] Membership advanced from 2.5 million in 1910 to almost 8.5 million a decade later. Officially recorded strikes, which had averaged 500 a year in the previous decade, escalated to three times that number in 1913; and, after a lull caused by the wartime "industrial truce," rose to a new peak in 1920.[43] Moreover, a radical, syndicalist mood suffused this growing movement; as British workers became increasingly disenchanted with parliamentary politics they turned with greater enthusiasm to direct action, shop steward organizations, and a demand for "workers' control."

Such an aggressive posture deeply affected British management, especially in the engineering industries, where a powerful shop stewards movement had arisen during the First World War. As labor became more vocal in its demand for a democratic form of industrial organization, British management came to realize that such radical views were widely and deeply held. In Birmingham, a group of employers suggested that the end of the war would require, "the surrender by Capital of its supposed right to dictate to Labour the conditions under which work shall be carried on."[44] As late as 1921 the chairman of the board of directors of the Daimler Company complained to his stockholders that labor has been "convinced that the conditions of which they complain result from the greed and fraud of the wealth owning section of the community. They have been taught, and now sincerely believe, that because labour is necessary to the creation of all wealth that, therefore, all wealth is created solely by labour."[45]

Faced with the specter of a highly politicized, potentially revolutionary working-class movement, a section of the British managerial elite recognized that a simple reassertion of capital's "right to manage" would prove unnecessarily confrontational and instead sought to channel and deflect this movement onto safer terrain. The so-called Whitley Councils, which proposed the postwar establishment in each industry of permanent joint bodies of employers and union officials, represented British capital's most well publicized effort to restore "orderly" industrial relations to the shop floor, while at the same time accommodating and deradicalizing the pervasive demand for a working-class voice in the management of industry.[46] Whitleyism left little mark once the postwar industrial crisis had passed, but this did not mean that British managers now felt free to reorganize the factory work regime in any fashion they chose. At the shop floor level especially, the managerial innovations adopted by their American counterparts seemed seriously at odds with both the craft tradition of the engineering workers and the syndicalist impulse so recently manifest throughout the British labor movement. Instead, British employers opted for an industrial relations strategy which provided indirect control of the labor process via an incentive wage payment system. Labor would be allowed to retain a degree of autonomy over the pace of work and technique at the actual point of production, but only because this very limited element of "workers' control" would occur within a piece rate system in which management alone set the rate schedule. Thus the chairman of the British Higher Productivity Council argued in 1919, "The whole point is that workmen now say that they want a share of the control of business and this scheme [incentive payment systems] gives them the share that they want."[47]

Incentive pay also proved popular in the United States, but the limited information we have suggests that it played a different role there, largely because bonus levels rarely reached the British norm of 50 to 100 percent.[48] The relatively high bonus earnings possible in Britain meant that incentive payment systems not only checked labor effort but also encouraged labor to perform some minor tasks of factory coordination needed to insure steady output. Under such schemes, where the bonus represented up to half of all earnings, workers had a direct monetary incentive to look after their own parts supply problems and ensure that basic maintenance was performed on the machines being used.[49] As Steven Tolliday and Jonathan Zeitlin argue in their contribution to this volume, "the line between job control and self-supervision was thin."

Daimler is an interesting case in point. Despite the extensive use of American machines, factory coordination and productivity were very poor in the early years. After much investigation the firm formalized the managerial hierarchy, reduced the number of low-level supervisors, and adopted first straight piecework and then the Premium Bonus system. P. Martin became factory manager in 1901; he wanted to replace the "driving" system of supervision with a system he called "induction." The Premium Bonus system was the key to this strategy. Under this scheme, management set minimum work norms, and workers earned a bonus once these production criteria were met. The critical factor though, and the one Martin stressed, was that the worker would not receive the entire savings in labor cost generated by higher output levels. Instead the savings would be divided, usually fifty-fifty, between firm and worker. Martin argued that since unit labor costs would fall automatically as output rose, management would have less incentive to cut piecework prices and labor could increase output and earnings without any fear of a future price reduction.

Martin's managerial reforms operated at two levels. On the one hand, he strengthened management by introducing a more comprehensive costing and planning system and the beginnings of a work study department. On the other hand, he weakened managerial control on the shop floor by having workers perform some of the basic co-ordination tasks and by giving labor some say in setting effort norms. As Martin told the 1906 meeting of the Institute of Automobile Engineers:

> Instead of the staff driving the workers for output, the workers drive the staff to supply them with material, and jobs are finished off by virtue of fresh ones pushing them out. . . . The usual driving system is absolutely reversed. The staff, and everybody connected with the company is kept on the jump all the time to keep the man supplied with material, so that he can earn more wages; and I think the greatest advantage of the bonus system is to be found in that very fact.[50]

This system of induction was only beginning to emerge in the pre-1914 period. It is easy to see how such a system might be attractive to managers operating factories more complex than those in America and where the labor force was less willing to accept autocratic managerial control of the labor process. This trend toward granting workers limited control over effort norms while management controlled the effort bargain through incentive pay stands in direct contrast to the Fordist system. Thus, it was not predominantly the skill content of their jobs that distinguished British workers from their American brothers and sisters. Rather, the British workforce was unique in its ability to ward off direct managerial control of effort norms and its ability to retain a voice in how work was to be done within the relatively narrow management constraints. In the final section of this paper I will examine how the induction system spread through the British vehicle industry and provided an alternative to American managerial strategies.

## Fordism in Britain, 1913–1930

Fordism spread to Britain in 1911 when Ford began producing cars at its Manchester plant. Initially, knocked-down kits were shipped from Detroit and reassembled; however, the cost of shipping bulky components such as bodies and gasoline tanks led Ford to begin manufacturing in Britain a year later. Ford proposed to manufacture these components under conditions similar to those found in its plants in Detroit. New employees hired as handymen were expected to perform any task management requested. A 1915 description of the plant confirmed that many of the jobs were designed for unskilled labor: "All parts are machine cut to templates and jigs, and little indeed is left to be done by hand, except actual putting together. The processes in the department of this factory are almost automatic, little being left for hand work beyond the insertion of screws."[51]

Ford's unwillingness to recognize existing labor customs and practices or grant any measure of control over the production process to individual workers or to the unions generated a rash of small strikes as early as 1912. Toward the end of that year, the United Kingdom Society of Coachmakers shut down the body plant for twenty-two weeks in opposition to the "American System." "We are now engaged in a struggle with the Ford Motor Company," declared the leadership of the union, "who are hoping to Americanise our Trade here, by claiming the right to employ who they like upon our work and the work of other skilled Trades, and to entirely ignore Trade Unions."[52] This strike received little more than moral support from the other unions in Manchester, and chassis assembly continued during the stoppage using bodies imported from Detroit.

Despite the strike's failure, wages rose rapidly at Ford's Manchester plant. When P. Perry, the British managing director, first arrived on the scene, he viewed the existing hourly wage of four and one-half pence per hour a starvation rate. When the coachmakers strike began, the minimum hourly rate was 5 pence per hour, but this soon rose to 6 pence and over the next few months was allowed to drift up to 10 pence per hour. These increases all took place before Ford introduced the five-dollar day in Detroit, after which a further 5 pence per hour profit-sharing bonus was added to the Manchester wage.[53] The combination of high wages, employer resistance to trade unions, and the reduced skill demands, which made workers easily replaceable, all but eliminated labor resistance to the new system of production and allowed Ford to press forward with the Americanization of the Manchester plant. In September 1914, the firm installed a mechanized assembly line, less than twelve months after Ford had adopted a similar line in Detroit.[54]

Although British workers and their unions were initially hostile to the American system, the tripling of wages at the Manchester plant between 1912 and 1914 may well have altered their viewpoint. Both the reminiscences of former workers and the lack of organized agitation in the nonunion Ford plants over the next thirty years suggest that British labor was at least sympathetic to the deal Ford offered. On a number of occasions union officials indicated they were willing to make concessions in return for Ford style wages. For example during the 1925 negotiations between the Engineering Employers Federation and the unions, the following exchange took place:

> Chairman EEP: "Do you think for one moment your men would submit themselves to the principle of Henry Ford?"
> Union reply: "They do it . . . our people seem quite well satisfied. It is true that for a period they did not take to it, but today they are quite satisfied with their employment."[55]

Moreover, British unionists, perhaps not fully understanding the contradiction between the American system of management and their own desire for democratic shop floor decision making, advocated the Americanization of their country's industry. J. T. Brownlie, the leader of the Amalgamated Society of Engineers, the strongest union in the vehicle industry, pushed for the modernization of British industry on the American model amidst the labor turmoil of 1919.[56] And two years later the Trades Union Congress also condemned British factory organization and pointed to American factories as a model: "The British engineering industry is, with few exceptions, badly organised from one end to the other. Therefore compared with many American establishments, and even with the best in this country, the great majority of British engineering workshops are badly laid out, often badly lighted, inadequately equipped, and, many of them, wastefully managed."[57]

But leading managers of British vehicle factories viewed American managerial innovations differently. Arrol Johnston's T. C. Pullinger argued against American methods and the rigid managerial control they entailed and in favor of "kindly and sympathetic" treatment of labor.[58] A. W. Reeves from Crossley argued:

> An important factor to the author's mind, and one which appears to be entirely ignored in the wonderful systems on the other side of the Atlantic, and among many idealists on this side, is that of the personal or human element. Anyone with any knowledge of the independent and, it must be confessed, awkward spirit, characterising the workers of say the Northern Midlands, would hesitate before applying the extreme methods of the latest American Scientific Management, well knowing the futility of the task.[59]

Managers of this viewpoint emphasized cooperation between labor and management and self-regulation of effort norms rather than the direct managerial control through machine pacing and close supervision used under Fordism.[60]

A detailed examination of the Austin managerial strategy reveals that it carried the pre-1914 Daimler system of "induction" into the interwar period; much evidence suggests that British managers saw this strategy as an alternative to the Fordist system. By the 1920s Austin was a mass producer and had achieved the level of output needed to adopt full-scale Fordism. Production reached 9,500 in 1924, rose to 25,000 in 1926, and exceeded 40,000 after that.[61] Some changes in the production process were made, but the system adopted differed significantly from American Fordism. Assembly lines were installed after 1924, but they remained relatively simple and unmechanized until the late 1920s. More important, Austin's system of labor relations was vastly different from Ford's. In the tradition of the Daimler induction system, the Austin workers were placed on incentive payment systems and were allowed to earn bonuses, often exceeding 100 percent. Self-regulation rather than direct control seemed to be the organizing principle at the Austin shops.[62]

Austin's observation of Fordist methods during visits to the United States certainly influenced his labor relations strategy, but not on terms that American automobile manufacturers might have approved. What impressed Austin about the Ford factories was not the use of sophisticated machinery but rather the amount of labor effort forthcoming from the workforce. He was impressed that, "everybody in the establishment seemed to be trying to do their best."[63] This led him to argue that if Britain were to compete with the United States it needed an improved spirit among labor, not new machine meth-

ods. The Austin focus on organization and shop floor social relations, rather than changes in production technology, was also evident
among the leading managers of his firm. The works director held the
view that "good organization and an indifferent plant achieve better results than a good plant and indifferent organization," and the
head of the costing department argued that "the obvious difficulty
at the moment is the lack of confidence as between employer and
employed."[64] Evidently the Austin factory was facing labor and coordination problems similar to those found in the Ford works in 1913,
but Austin proposed resolving his problems in a very different way.

Control over labor and the coordination of shop floor activity were
to be achieved by a novel payment system called "Bonus on Time."
Under this scheme prices were set in units of work time rather than
money. At the end of each week workers tallied their time credits and
multiplied this by their base rate to determine their final pay. Costing
department head P. Keene suggested that the system worked because
with "such a basis, many economic problems become common to
both employers and employed, and interests flow in one direction.
. . . The reason why the system of control became really efficient
was that they inculcated into the whole staff a maximum idea of
personal responsibility to the firm itself whereby they and the firm
were likely to prosper."[65] Indirect managerial control over labor was
enhanced by the custom of paying workers a base rate that was on
average 25 percent lower than they could expect in other Midland
shops and then allowing them to earn above average bonus rates.
To Keene, the efficiency of the payment system was obvious. "The
remuneration he [the worker] is able to obtain through savings is a
sufficient incentive to the worker to make large output effective with
the minimum of supervision."[66] Indeed, Austin managers argued that
their system was an alternative to American production methods:

> There are still a few employers who object to piecework on principle.
> Their stand-point is that an efficient management ought to be able to
> get the same results at an agreed rate of wage without having to pay
> more money to encourage the men to work harder. . . . Some form of
> extra wage must be paid to a man if he is expected to work harder. The
> only alternative is to pay a high wage similar to the Ford system, and
> insist upon task achievement. The obtaining of results by this system
> could not be regarded with favour by an Employers Federation, as the
> advantage would be to one particular firm only. When every other con-
> cern came into line, the status quo would be again obtained, and a circle

of rising wage competition would begin. . . . The daily task system at fixed wages may perhaps, be workable in American, or even Continental factories, but the necessary . . . driving works policy would not be acceptable either to English Labour or Management.[67]

Those British managers who favored the Fordist system were severely criticized by their colleagues. Thus Mr. Cole of the Employers Association ridiculed one Rover executive: "Captain Wilks, to my mind is suffering from some rather ill-digested views with regard to Capital and Labour. He is a great admirer of Mr. Ford and American methods. His idea is that everybody should receive a high day rate and then be compelled to work as hard as possible and if they do not they are to be fired out."[68] Likewise, G. Rushton, of the Associated Equipment Company, was diagnosed as having "Forditis" when he put elements of the Ford system into practice. After Associated Equipment installed moving assembly lines and high fixed day wages in the late 1920s, the London Engineering Employers Federation threatened to expel the firm from its ranks unless Associated Equipment made changes in its production system. The Employers Federation argued that "the essential difference between his [Rushton] Southall scheme, and schemes in operation at Walthamstow and at other federation firms was a payment in anticipation [of output], whereas the scheme approved by the Association were payments made after the results had been assured."[69] Thus, British management could not envision a production system without a direct link between wages and output as a check on labor behavior and as an aid to factory coordination. The Fordist notion that both could be embodied in the system of machine operation did not suit the particular needs or the general world view of British managers. Even when British workers voiced an interest in a Fordist effort bargain, British management remained suspicious. The managerial debacle associated with the industry's shift to measured day work in the late 1960s, which contributed to the collapse of the last of the British mass producers, BLMC in 1975, suggests that management's reluctance to directly control shop floor organization may have been well founded.

## Conclusions

The failure of the Fordist system to gain more than a foothold in the British vehicle industry confirms the overriding importance of social and political relations in determining the organization and technology of factory work. In the United States Ford's ability and willingness to rationalize production and increase supervision were predicated not so much upon the existence of an automobile market markedly larger than that in Britain nor relative wage rates favoring the use of less skilled workers; rather they were based upon the availability of a fragmented workforce with little tradition of organized resistance to management authority, a workforce willing to tolerate rigid managerial control of effort norms in return for relatively high wages. In contrast British managers, whose complex manufacturing operations necessitated careful shop floor coordination, were confronted with a labor movement whose traditions were hostile to labor control methods inherent in American Fordism.

A species of worker self-management, largely keyed to a wage incentive system, proved the durable solution to this managerial dilemma. Initially, such incentive wage schemes were designed to control effort norms, but in the British context they came to have a larger social function. They partially accommodated the powerful working-class desire for autonomy and control at the point of production, and from a management viewpoint they served as a substitute mechanism for improving factory coordination and fulfilling tasks which in American firms were performed by foremen or building superintendents. For the British workers, their desire for job control had been converted by management into a potent system of self-regulation. Thus, despite transatlantic similarities in production technology and product, this unique managerial outlook created a twentieth-century factory regime in the British vehicle industry which differed substantially from that of their counterparts in the United States.

## NOTES

1. See E. Rothschild, *Paradise Lost: The Decline of the Auto-Industrial Age* (New York: Vintage, 1973); R. B. Reich, *The Next American Frontier* (New York: Times Books, 1983); W. J. Abernathy, K. B. Clark, and A. M. Kantrow, *Industrial Renaissance* (New York: Basic Books, 1983); M. J. Piore and C. F. Sabel, *The Second Industrial Divide, Possibilities for Prosperity* (New York: Basic Books, 1984).

2. The production methods Ford employed have been extensively stud-

ied. See S. Meyer III, *The Five Dollar Day: Labor Management and Social Control in the Ford Motor Company, 1908–1921* (Albany: State University of New York Press, 1981); D. A. Hounshell, *From the American System to Mass Production: 1800–1932* (Baltimore: Johns Hopkins University Press, 1984); W. Gartman, "Auto Slavery: The Development of the Labor Process in the Automobile Industry of the United States: 1897–1950" (Ph.D diss., University of California, San Diego, 1980); J. Russell, "The Coming of the Line: The Ford Highland Park Plant, 1910–1914," *Radical America* 12 (1978): 29–45; A. Nevins, *Ford: The Times, the Man, the Company* (New York: Scribner, 1954). On the shift to a consumer-oriented society see D. T. Rodgers, *The Work Ethic in Industrial America, 1850–1920* (Chicago: University of Chicago Press, 1974). See also J. O'Connor, *Accumulation Crisis* (New York: Blackwell, 1984), 68–79.

3. On attitudes to Fordism in Europe see C. Maier, "Between Taylorism and Technocracy: European Ideologies and the Vision of Industrial Productivity in the 1920's," *Journal of Contemporary History* 5 (1970): 27–51. See also P. Fridenson, "The Coming of the Assembly Line to Europe," in W. Krohn, E. T. Layton, Jr., and P. Weingart, eds., *The Dynamics of Science and Technology* (Dordrecht: D. Reidel, 1978). On the history of British labor see K. Burgess, *The Challenge of Labour* (London: Croom Helm, 1980); R. Charles, *The Development of Industrial Relations in Britain, 1911–13* (London: Hutchinson, 1973); G. Brown, *Sabotage* (Nottingham: Spokesman Books, 1977); B. Holton, *British Syndicalism, 1900–1914* (London: Pluto Press, 1976); and J. Hinton, *The First Shop Stewards Movement* (London: Allen and Unwin, 1973).

4. For arguments concerning the possible impact of American social factors on American technology see E. S. Ferguson, "The Americanness of American Technology," *Technology & Culture* 20 (1979): 3–24.

5. See C. F. Sabel, *Work and Politics: The Division of Labor in Industry* (Cambridge: Cambridge University Press, 1982). On levels of output employed see L. V. Spencer, "Conveyor Systems Aids Big Production," *Automobile* 35 (July 20, 1916); *Ford Times* 8 (April 1915): 299; W. Klann, Rough Draft Reminiscences, 112, Ford Motor Company Archives, Henry Ford Museum, Dearborn, Mich.; Nevins Selected Research Papers, Acc. 572, Box 21, Ford Archives. For an interesting British view that the principles of Fordism were applicable at relatively low levels of output see F. G. Woollard, *Principles of Mass Production* (London: Iliffe and Sons, 1954), 15–48.

6. For a history of American managerial methods see A. Chandler Jr., *The Visible Hand: The Management Revolution in American Business* (Cambridge, Mass.: Harvard University Press, 1977); D. Nelson, *Managers and Workers: Origins of the Factory System in the United States, 1880–1920* (Madison: University of Wisconsin Press, 1975); D. Noble, *America by Design* (Oxford: Oxford University Press, 1977). For a survey of the evolution of American managerial throught see M. Rose, *Industrial Behaviour, Theoretical Development since Taylor* (Harmondsworth: Allen Lane, 1975).

7. G. Heliker, "Detroit Labor: 1890–1910," Acc. 958, Ford Archives; D. Montgomery, *Workers Control in America* (Cambridge: Cambridge University Press, 1979), 55.

8. Nevins, *Ford*, 513–18; Heliker, "Detroit Labor: 1890–1910," 35; G. Heliker, "Detroit Labor, 1900–1916," 8, Acc. 958, Ford Archives.

9. H. L. Arnold and F. L. Faurote, "Ford Methods," *Engineering Magazine* 47 (1914): 673; Litogot, "Reminiscences," 7, Ford Archives; Dickett, "Reminiscences," 13–14, Ford Archives.

10. Max Wollering, "Reminiscences," 43, Ford Archives; E. K. H., "Factory Transportation II," *Machinery* 11 (November 1917): 117–19; A. R. Erskine, *History of the Studebaker Corporation* (Studebaker Corp., 1924), 33.

11. Litogot, "Reminiscences," 7; Arnold and Faurote, "Ford Methods," 673.

12. Department Appraisals 1919, Acc. 73, Ford Archives; Plant Accounts, Highland Park, Acc. 571, Ford Archives.

13. Spencer, "Conveyor System Aids Big Production"; G. D. Babcock, *The Taylor System in Franklin Management* (New York: Engineering Magazine Company, 1917), 125. In 1927, A.E.C. operated an assembly line in England with a planned output of eighty to one hundred chassis per week. See EEF Membership Files, A.E.C., Interview, March 21, 1927, EEF Archives; and "The Work of the Associated Daimler Company," *Automobile Engineer* (January 1928): 9–11.

14. For a similar thesis arguing that machine innovation might be caused by the need to increase output levels rather than productivity see E. P. Duggan, "Machines, Markets and Labor: The Carriage and Wagon Industry in Late Nineteenth Century Cincinnati," *Business History Review* 51 (1977): 308–25.

15. H. L. Arnold and F. L. Faurote, "Ford Methods," *Engineering Magazine* 47 (1914): 673; Litogot, "Reminiscences," 7; Dickett, "Reminiscences," 13–14.

16. Litogot, "Reminiscences," 7; Klann, "Reminiscences," 10.

17. Nevins, *Ford*, 532.

18. A. M. Wibel, "Reminiscences," 52, Ford Archives; Nevins, *Ford*, 271.

19. G. Heliker, "Detroit Labor: 1900–1916," 25.

20. See Gartman, "Auto Slavery," 149.

21. Wollering, "Reminiscences," 26.

22. Klann, "Reminiscences," 7.

23. Meyer, *Five Dollar Day*, 82–83, 85.

24. Ibid., ch. 5. See also G. Heliker, "Detroit Labor: 1900–1916."

25. Meyer, *Five Dollar Day*, 72.

26. Wibel, "Reminiscences," 18.

27. Russell, *Coming of the Line*, 30–31. See also Sabel, *Work and Politics*.

28. Most generalizations about vehicle producers during this period stem from S. Saul, "The Motor Industry in Britain to 1914," *Business History* 5 (1962): 22–44. For a more sympathetic treatment of mass production in Britain in the nineteenth century see A. E. Musson, "J. Whitworth and the Growth of Mass Production Engineering," *Business History* 17 (1975):

109–49. For a more recent study of vehicle builders during this period see R. Church, *Herbert Austin* (London: European Publications Ltd., 1979).

29. *Motor Trader* (October 7, 1908).

30. Data on the model lines of various firms were obtained from various issues of *Motor Trader* and W. C. Bersey, *The Motor Car Red Book* (n.d.). On Daimler see, Simms Papers, University of London, files 16/10 and 16/119/i; Daimler Board of Directors, Minute Books, February 2 to March 14, 1899, February 11, 1901, June 11 and January 29, 1902. Sixth Annual General Meeting, Daimler Company, November 27, 1902. On the trend toward larger models after 1906 see J. D. Siddley's column in the *Times Engineering Supplement* (1905 and 1906).

31. A. E. Harrison, "The Competitiveness of the British Cycle Industry," *Economic History Review* 22 (1969): 294. See also *Engineer* (June 18, 1897): 620; J. Newton, "Looking Backward," *Rudge Record* (1909); "Repetition Bicycle Plant," *The Cycle Referee* (February 16, 1899, supplement); "The Firms You Do Business With," *The Cycle and Motor Trades Review* (June 7, 1906): 541. See also *Rudge Record* (October and December 1908).

32. "The Engineering Strike," *Engineer* (August 27, 1897): 207.

33. ASE Minute Books, Coventry, July 12–26 and August 15, 1899. See also Simms Papers, University of London, file 16/33; "The English Motor Industry: Description of the Plant and Practice of the Daimler Company Works," *The Cycle Referee* (January 19, 1899, supplement): ii–xiv.

34. "The Humber Works (Beeston)," *Engineer* (September 4, 1903): 232–35.

35. *Motor Trader* (October 8, 1913): 101, (September 7, 1910): 1036, (August 7, 1912) and (December 10, 1911).

36. Owen Linley, "Manufacturing on a Medium Scale," *Motor Trader* (July 8, 1914).

37. L. A. Legros, "Influence of Detail in the Development of the Automobile," *Proceedings Institute of Automobile Engineers* (October 11, 1911): 5–6.

38. "Erecting Shop Methods," *Automobile Engineer* (July 1912): 216.

39. Saul, "Motor Industry"; *Motor Trader* (March 7, 1906).

40. Model T cost books, Acc. 125, Ford Archives. See also Wollering, "Reminiscences," 7–13.

41. *Royal Commission on Motor Cars*, 1906, cmd. 3081, 153–54; *Motor Trader* (July 4 and August 15, 1906, and March 18, 1908); St. John Nixon, *Daimler 1896–1946* (London: G.T. Foulis, 1946), 112. On the reluctance of British firms to supply components to British motor vehicle producers see R. Church, *Herbert Austin*, 186; G. Maxcy, "The Motor Industry," in P. L. Cook and R. Cohen, eds., *Effects of Mergers* (London: Allen and Unwin, 1958), 360.

42. See S. Meacham, "The Sense of an Impending Clash: English Working-Class Unrest before the First World War," *American Historical Review* 77 (1972): 1343–63; J. White, "1910–1914 Reconsidered," in J. E. Cronin and J. Schneer, eds., *Social Conflict and the Political Order in Modern Britain*

(London: Croom Helm, 1982); J. E. Cronin, "Coping with Labour: 1918–1926," in Cronin and Schneer, eds., *Social Conflict*. On the history of trade unionism in Britain see K. Burgess, *The Challenge of Labour* (London: Croom Helm, 1980). On the history of unskilled unions in manufacturing see R. Hyman, *The Workers Union* (Oxford: Clarendon Press, 1971); J. Hinton, "The Rise of a Mass Labour Movement: Growth and Limits, " in C. J. Wrigley, ed., *A History of British Industrial Relations: 1875–1914* (Brighton: Harvester, 1982).

43. Statistics taken from R. Hyman's foreword to C. Goodrich, *The Frontier of Control* (London: Pluto Press, 1975), vii.

44. Cited in Cronin, *Coping with Labour*, 113.

45. Coventry Record Office, Acc. 594, box file 8, B.S.A., General Meeting, April 11, 1921, 9.

46. For details on the impact of Whitleyism see R. Charles, *The Development of Industrial Relations in Britain, 1911–35* (London: Hutchinson, 1973).

47. Letter from Howe to EEF, October 29, 1919, P(13)5, EEF Archives. On the response of labor and capital to early twentieth-century political unrest in other countries see C. S. Maier, "Between Taylorism and Technocracy: European Ideologies and the Vision of Industrial Productivity in the 1920s," *Journal of Contemporary History* 5 (1970): 27–61.

48. On British bonus levels see Coventry District Engineering Employers Federation, Board Minutes, February 27, 1922, July 27, 1931; Local Conference, December 22, 1919, P(5)49, EEF Archives.

49. On the impact incentive payment systems can have on labor see M. Burawoy, *Manufacturing Consent* (Chicago: University of Chicago Press, 1979).

50. P. Martin, "Works Organisation," *Proceedings Institute of Automobile Engineers* 1 (1906): 126.

51. *Automobile Engineer* (July 1915): 189; Ford Motor Company, "Historical Notes," 1912, Ford Archives, Warley.

52. *UKS Quarterly Journal* (July 1913). See also M. Wilkins and F. Hill, *American Business Abroad, Ford on Six Continents* (Detroit: Wayne State University Press, 1964).

53. Wage rates supplied by the Ford Motor Company, Dagenham. See also *Special Edition of the Ford Times* (1914) and the *Automobile Engineer* (1915).

54. Despite Ford's success in Americanizing his British plants, he had much more trouble producing a product acceptable to British consumers. Austin and Morris were more successful, and it was not until the late 1930s that Ford began to erode their market share. On the reasons for this see R. Church, "The Big Three: Competition, Management and Marketing in the British Motor Industry, 1922–1939," in B. Supple, ed., *Essays in British Business History* (Oxford: Oxford University Press, 1977).

55. Special Conference, May 1, 1925, EEF Archives. On British labor attitude toward the Ford operation see *Manchester Evening News* (June 1978).

56. Conference EEF and ASE, July 24, 1919, 29, EEF Archives.

57. "Comments on the Present Economic Position of the Engineering and Allied Industries," 23–24, TUC Archives.

58. T. C. Pullinger, "Opening Address," *Proceedings Institute of Automobile Engineers* 12 (1917/1918): 432.

59. A. W. Reeves and C. Kimber, "Works Organisation," *Proceedings Institute of Automobile Engineers* 11 (1916/1917): 375.

60. See the piece by Tolliday and Zeitlin in this volume where they argue that after World War II British workers were somewhat freer than American workers regarding direct managerial control but found themselves unable to turn this control in their own favor due to constraints imposed by the piece-work wage system and the lack of solidarity among workers.

61. Church, *Herbert Austin*, 84.

62. See C. R. F. Engelbach, "Some Notes on Re-Organisation of a Works to Increase Production," *Proceedings Institute of Automobile Engineers* 23 (1928). Mechanized lines were adopted in 1928.

63. Third Annual Meeting of the Institute of Automobile Engineers, as reported in *Proceedings Institute of Automobile Engineers* (1924/1925): 7.

64. For statements by Engelbach and Keene see Ward Papers, MRG1, Organisation Section, W/8/29–34/13/476, 2–14, housed at the Business History Unit, University of London.

65. Ibid.

66. Ward Papers, W/8/29–34/476, P. Keene to MRG 1, December 2, 1930.

67. "Piece Work in the Toolroom," W(3)129, February 1, 1934, 26–28, EEF Archives.

68. Cole Memo, September 10, 1930, P(20)5, EEF Archives; Membership Files AEC, Memo W. L. Bayley to A. C. Bayley, March 18, 1927, EEF Archives.

69. Membership Files AEC, "Failure to Obey Rules," 4, EEF Archives.

# 3

## Employers' Strategies in the Detroit Labor Market, 1900–1929

### THOMAS KLUG

The managerial revolution of the late nineteenth and early twentieth centuries transformed the relationship between workers and employers in the United States, not only at the point of production but also in the recruitment and purchase of labor. Although the advent of the assembly line, the minute subdivision of labor, and shop floor conflict between managers and workers have captured the interest of many historians, less attention has been directed to the labor market itself as a terrain of struggle between capital and labor. Of course, some scholars have investigated the evolution of internal labor markets in large firms: the development of personnel departments and the formulation of bureaucratic rules to govern hiring, dismissal, promotion, transfer, layoff, and job classification. But the internal labor markets that appeared around the time of the First World War hardly exhaust the strategies by which Detroit employers structured their employment practices in the early twentieth century.[1]

For in Detroit, as elsewhere, managers recognized that their ability to set the terms under which workers sold their labor in large measure determined the success of their business enterprises. And they understood that the maintenance of effective control over this external labor market was no simple feat. Faced with various manifestations of worker resistance, competition among a handful of large employers for the same workforce, and the social impact of the rapidly expanding auto industry itself, the manufacturers of Detroit found that control of their sources of labor required constant change and experimentation during the first three decades of this century.

Detroit was, of course, synonymous with the automobile in these

early years, and it was then that the growth of the industry caused unprecedented problems for employers, including periods of great labor
shortage, extraordinary levels of labor turnover, and escalating wage
rates. Indeed, the high wages paid by automobile firms attracted tens
of thousands of workers to Detroit. In 1910, when Detroit had become
the auto capital of the world, the 15,000 to 25,000 workers in the city's
automobile and automobile body and parts factories constituted 18 to
30 percent of all manufacturing workers. By early 1920, 160,000 wage
earners in the Detroit area were employed by twenty-one automobile
and automobile body and parts companies. Ford and General Motors
alone gave work to 83,000. Eight years later, Ford, General Motors,
and Chrysler employed 200,000 out of 285,000 industrial workers on
the payrolls of sixteen automobile and auto-related corporations in
the district. From a mere 4 percent of all industrial workers in 1904,
at the end of the 1920s the fate of one-half to two-thirds of all manufacturing wage earners in the Detroit area was tied directly to the
fortunes of the automobile industry.[2]

From the late 1890s through the 1920s, Detroit employers deployed
five distinct, but sometimes overlapping, strategies to manage their
rapidly growing urban labor market. Before the appearance of the
automobile factories, employers cut deals with the business agents
of local trade unions with the intent of stabilizing the recruitment
of skilled metal workers. This initial accommodation enabled craft
unions to maintain wages, establish an elaborate set of work rules,
and control entrance to their trades. In the early 1900s, however,
a broad alliance of metal-working manufacturers formed the Employers' Association of Detroit, and under the banner of the "open
shop" they inaugurated a campaign to circumvent union power. With
this new strategy of unrelenting opposition to organized labor, Detroit manufacturers gained direct and unfettered access to the labor
market, reduced the amount of employment information reaching
workers, and minimized competition among employers for skilled
workers. A third strategy evolved after 1910 when employers focused
their attention on organizing internal labor markets within their separate firms. By this time, the development of mass production techniques had begun to irreversibly transform Detroit's job structure, and
the institutional and social control features of the emerging internal
labor markets aimed at disciplining and motivating the transient mass
of young, semiskilled production workers. Through enterprise-level

internal labor markets, employers hoped to overcome the unwelcome instability caused by the interconnected evils of labor turnover, labor radicalism, and the breakdown of working-class discipline.

The extreme labor shortage of World War I intervened exactly at the point when employers were becoming serious about controlling labor mobility. To meet the new situation, Detroit employers edged toward a fourth strategy: political control of the labor market, in large measure designed to prevent self-destructive wage competition among manufacturers. In 1918, as federal agencies and local patriots purged dissenters and sabateurs from factories, industrialists brought Detroit's municipal authorities to organize the conscription of labor on behalf of the war effort. But this could only be a temporary measure during the wartime crisis; the policy of political control shifted in the 1920s to a fifth and in some ways more brutal strategy that took advantage of the oversupply of unskilled labor in that decade. Relatively high hourly wages combined with a migratory labor force, seasonal production, and irregular employment established the conditions for effective economic control that underpinned the decade's apparent prosperity and stability.

## Accommodation with the Skilled Crafts

In the late 1890s, just as automobile companies began to appear in Detroit and other cities, many American employers reached an accommodation with unionized skilled craftsmen. In the metal trades, a sector of vital importance to the development of the automobile industry, the foundry interests, represented by the Stove Founders' National Defense Association (SFNDA) and the National Founders' Association (NFA), and the machine shop owners organized into the National Metal Trades Association (NMTA); they experimented with collectively bargained national trade agreements with such unions as the Iron Molders and Machinists. The correlate of union recognition by employers was usually the closed (or union) shop, where employers would employ only union workers. Although only a few employers of iron molders formally agreed to the exclusive employment of union men, many foundries were de facto closed shops. The reason, according to economist F. W. Hilbert, was that the Iron Molders Union "had so thoroughly organized the trade that nearly all the best molders are in the Union, and whenever a founder increases his force, it must be with union men." [3]

The closed shop did have some practical advantages for organized employers. It gave privileged employers access to a critically short supply of skilled labor on which they depended to run their shops. In addition, by threatening to choke the labor supply of uncooperative businessmen, closed-shop deals helped employers' organizations suppress cutthroat price competition in the product market. Collective bargaining and the closed shop could, therefore, serve as strategies for organizing and disciplining the employers' ranks—a consequence some labor leaders applauded with the expectation that once employers spoke with a unified voice, they would naturally align themselves in favor of trade agreements and force recalcitrant, antiunion businessmen into line.

Trade agreements certified the fact that important sectors of the late nineteenth-century labor market in the United States were incorporated into the network of rules and practices of craft unions. Indeed, craft unions, such as those in the metal trades, resembled internal labor markets which over a wide geographic area administered the movement, compensation, and employment standards of workers. Labor organizations maintained their own selection mechanisms and criteria by which they admitted workers into their "brotherhoods," screening out those deemed undesirable. Typically, admission to a trade required a period of apprenticeship designed not only to limit the overall size of the skilled labor supply and teach workers the mysteries of the craft but also to imbue workers with a sense of loyalty to the union. [4]

Unions often policed the craft tradition of the tramping artisan. Former automobile body worker Arthur Rohan recalled that tramping was common and widespread among skilled trimmers. "Fellows who were making top money," Rohan recalled,

> might work for six months and then they would not have any orders and they would drift on to the next place that might have an order for several hundred bodies. There was quite a bit of migration from job to job. So you would be wandering on to the next place and usually one floater would get in first and then he would write to the others. There was a clique around the country who were always willing to move for one reason or another, so you would drift into another town. [5]

Extensive, yet loose and informal, movement among trimmers may have been a hindrance to the development of a union, as Rohan believed. But workers' mobility within the confines of an organized craft's labor market helped forge a communication system among scattered locals, thereby strengthening a union. Organized trades issued members union cards and dues stamps, documents that functioned as passports for travel within a craft's labor market. Monthly union publications provided locals with the names of workers who had lost their union cards, died, or abused tramping privileges.[6]

Tramping was also a strategy to spread unemployment by giving job priority to residents who had families. Young bachelors, cast upon the migration stream, would journey to their craft's locals in other cities in search of work or food and a night's lodging. The practice had the advantage of reserving work in a given area for those less able to travel. And if out-of-work tramps honored their union commitments, they not only retained the privileges of membership in the organization (at a bare minimum, they could always expect an inexpensive funeral paid by the union), but they also deprived employers of that "reserve army of the unemployed" so useful in strikebreaking or wage erosion.

Employers' flirtation with collective bargaining did not last long. With the notable exception of the stove industry, the experiment with trade agreements in the metal trades collapsed after 1900; the Murray Hill agreement between the NMTA and machinists disintegrated in 1901, and in 1904 the NFA broke off all relations with the iron molders. Employers had realized that the closed shop made them susceptable to disruptions in production and labor supply caused by jurisdictional disputes among rival unions. Employers also lamented that the closed shop made them dependent upon union business agents, the so-called "walking delegates" who were the local administrative chieftains in their trade. Although the closed shop gave employers access to skilled labor, it was a labor market terrain where rights and power belonged to union workers and union functionaries. Not unexpectedly employers saw trade union membership increase after they negotiated industrywide agreements. From 1897 until the economic slump of 1904, union membership increased from 440,000 to over two million workers, and the frequency of strikes and lockouts accompanying these gains occurred at a rate not surpassed until the struggles of 1919–1920.[7]

In Detroit, union organizing efforts also advanced in the early 1900s. More than 8,000 workers, representing about one-fifth of Detroit's industrial workers, belonged to forty-four union locals in 1901. Two years later their numbers increased to 13,794 workers in sixty locals, and in February 1904 Employers' Association secretary John J. Whirl estimated that 12,000 out of the city's 65,000 wage workers (or 18.5 percent) belonged to trade unions. Union membership was also concentrated. Over one-third of the workers in the metal trades were members of trade unions. Twelve metal trades unions alone accounted for 36.8 percent of the organized workers in 1901, of which the most important were the iron molders, coremakers, metal polishers, patternmakers, and machinists. The heavy concentration of unionized workers in the metal trades, out of which the early Detroit auto industry emerged, corresponded to the primacy in the economy of the machine shop and foundry sector, then the city's second largest (after the construction of railway cars) with seventy-four establishments employing 5,933 wage earners. By 1910 a network of automobile companies, body makers, foundries, and machine shops took the lead, employing one-third of the 86,000 industrial wage earners in the Detroit area.[8]

At the turn of the century, some metal trades unionists worked for a few of Detroit's largest firms. Three stove companies employed 3,500 workers, including many of the 1,178 members of Iron Molders' Union No. 31. More than 500 people worked at the Detroit yards of the Detroit Shipbuilding Company. The American Car and Foundry Company, the city's single largest employer and a manufacturer of railway cars, employed 2,200. Around this handful of big firms was a highly competitive sector of small- and medium-size machine shops and foundries. They too required skilled workers to produce an assortment of nuts and bolts, boilers, pipes, valves, plumbing hardware, and components for marine engines. But after 1897 competitive conditions in the product marketplace drove these employers to make a determined stand against organized labor.[9]

## The Open-Shop Offensive

Given similar circumstances throughout the United States—an aggressive labor movement and heightened competition among metalworking companies—it was not surprising that almost everywhere

employers quickly lost interest in collective bargaining. In Detroit
metal trades employers organized the Employers' Association of Detroit (EAD) in December 1902. Henry Leland, a pioneer in the nascent
automobile industry, led employers toward a coordinated antiunion
stance. An old-time machinist from New England, Leland had relo-
cated to Detroit in 1890 and was general manager of Leland & Faul-
coner Manufacturing Company, a supplier of engines and other parts
to the Cadillac Motor Company of which he was also a director. The
EAD's earliest members represented machine shops, brass works, and
foundries allied with such national organizations as the NMTA and the
NFA, both of which Leland had a hand in organizing in the late 1890s.
Among the list of seventy-five charter signatories were the automobile firms of Olds, Ford, Cadillac, and Blomstrom. The establishment
in 1910 of a separate Automobile and Accessories division within the
EAD marked the auto industry's "coming of age" in Detroit.[10]

The EAD declared war against Detroit's trade unions in 1903. Employers believed that the brief accommodation with labor unions
in the late 1890s and early 1900s had gained them few benefits.
Trade agreements had not produced labor peace. Rather, strikes became more frequent, and unions gained additional recruits. Nor did
closed-shop deals necessarily cheapen the costs of production. As
employers saw it, the power of skilled workers under closed-shop
conditions prevented proprietors from increasing the daily output
per worker, introducing new labor-saving machinery, and employing cheaper nonunion and less skilled workers. These methods of
reducing production costs were especially critical to employers in
the highly competitive machine and jobbing branches of the foundry
business which faced very real shortages of skilled foundry workers,
many of whom preferred to work for the more remunerative and stable stove companies.[11]

As part of their open-shop offensive, employers insisted on their
right to get what they considered a fair day's work out of their men
and to pay workers on the basis of their individual worth. Many of
Detroit's brass manufacturers, Chester M. Culver of the EAD recalled,
"had formerly worked at the bench and knew what was reasonable
to expect" in terms of daily output. Their estimation of what constituted a fair day's work conflicted with the systematic restriction of
output practiced by skilled workers and embodied in unilaterally set
union work rules. The control exercised by unionized skilled workers

in the workplace had gone so far, according to the EAD's John J. Whirl, that "in some of our industries the proprietors were merely the financial agents to purchase the supplies, pay the wages, and sell the manufactured products." Whirl explained, "As to the operations of the factory, they had no more real control than if they were in no way connected with it. It was for them to find out the costs of production as arranged by organized labor, and then make the selling price sufficient to leave them a profit."[12]

Against the entrenched union labor markets, open-shop employers counterposed the doctrine of free contract, insisting on their right to hire any worker whether union member or not. Because of their crucial role in the production process, skilled workers had compelled employers to obtain craftsmen from union labor markets and prevented employers from bringing unapprenticed workers into their shops. Unwilling to tolerate union control over important segments of the skilled labor pool, open-shop employers violated union job rationing rules and work practices with impunity. They introduced into workplaces labor-simplifying machinery and less skilled and unapprenticed workers straight from the external labor market. Although technical and business necessity forced employers to continue relying on some unionized tradesmen, employers dealt with them as individual employees instead of with union business agents who represented workers collectively. Employers also imposed their own unilaterally determined criteria for evaluating pay and work performance and for managing the hiring, disciplining, and dismissal of workers. On all fronts, therefore, antiunion employers insisted on the projection of their property rights into areas of employment and shop practice where management had seldom ventured before the twentieth century. In the process, employers collectively began to organize and police their own labor market in Detroit.[13]

As the next stage in the development of an employer-dominated local labor market, the EAD established a Labor Bureau in 1903. At the time of the Bureau's appearance the Detroit labor market was relatively unfettered except by unions, and plant-level personnel activities were quite unsophisticated, with foremen in charge of most day-to-day employment and production matters. Without their own employment offices, companies themselves could not systematically recruit, select, hire, promote, or transfer workers. Although the staff of the EAD's Labor Bureau performed a variety of functions, including occasional strikebreaking, its ordinary tasks involved the much more mundane business of attracting workers to the doors of the Bureau located in downtown Detroit, channeling them through a records filing system, and undertaking a preliminary selection and occupational arrangement of applicants. Final selection—or hiring—took place at the factory level. Of course, plant managers and foremen always had the right to reject workers even if they came recommended by the EAD, and companies were perfectly free to hire workers who did not come to them through the Labor Bureau.[14]

The Labor Bureau represented a collective, bureaucratic method of hiring labor designed to weaken workers' bargaining power. At the heart of this ambitious effort were the selection criteria and techniques of the Bureau's staff. Joseph Bryce, a journalist who observed the Labor Bureau firsthand, testified that employers expected workers to meet certain standards if they wished to obtain jobs through the EAD. "Good character, experience, and the ability to do the work required are all requisites for the securing of a job through this bureau." However, "the unclean, ignorant or bleary-eyed whiskey or cigarette users are given scant attention." What enabled the EAD Labor Bureau to raise its selection criteria to a full-blown method was an elaborate recordkeeping system. As early as December 1902, Henry M. Leland had envisioned a bureau that would keep "an accurate record of each metal worker in the employ of the members regarding his last place of employment, his proficiency or the excellence of his mechanical ability, and other information regarding his general character, habits, etc." Employers could rely on the Bureau to select and recommend dependable men to the shops. In 1907, John Whirl praised the Bureau as "our greatest element of strength to cope with the professional labor disturber." According to Whirl, workers approved by the Bureau were "less susceptible to the influence of those whose mission is to make trouble." The records maintained by the Bureau let employers attach identities to ordinarily nameless and characterless workers. As one employer observed, "when you take into your employ every fellow who calls at the door of your shops, you usually know nothing whatever about him. He may be a mischief maker, he may be a spy, he may be a good man. But if you call upon our commissioner [of the Labor Bureau] you are sure to get a safe man."[15]

Obvious blacklisting possibilities existed with this system. As early as February 1904, the Labor Bureau had records on 16,000 union and nonunion workers. By 1906 the Bureau had 40,000 names, 100,000 in 1909, and just over 180,000 in 1912. From the start, unionists distrusted the EAD's Labor Bureau. Workers complained that they had to fill out forms asking about their nativity, where they were previously employed, and why they left their last place of work. According to Ed Heathfield, a business agent for the Metal Polishers' Union, workers failed to see the need for these probing questions and believed that by answering them they might blacklist themselves from future employment in Detroit. In 1907 one key issue in a strike at the Detroit Stove Company by union iron molders involved the kinds of questions the company asked for its employee files. The molders maintained that the compilation of personnel files was the company's initial step toward the declaration of an open shop.[16]

Through the Labor Bureau, the EAD also recruited workers for specific firms. Employers frequently made their labor requirements known to the association, and the EAD responded by placing employment advertisements in newspapers, both locally and throughout the country. One 1907 EAD ad notified readers of positions for "a few good machinists, electricians, molders, coremakers, plumbers and fitters, polishers and buffers, wood and metal patternmakers, boilermakers and helpers, handymen and laborers, and boys for shop work." Another advertisement in 1911 called for "Automobile Men —chassis assemblers, crankshaft grinders, engine and motor assemblers, general machinists, fox, speed, and monitor hands."[17]

EAD leaders repeatedly warned employers not to individually and openly advertise for labor. Employers stood to gain nothing by staging a public bidding war for labor. Internecine conflict threatened employers' solidarity and led to uncontrolled wage escalation, increased labor turnover, and the breakdown of workforce discipline. And advertising alerted trade unionists to companies susceptible to pressure. The EAD preferred to concentrate in the hands of company officials and Labor Bureau clerks accurate information about the supply, demand, and wages for labor. As a result employers steadily eroded workers' independent knowledge of conditions in the general labor market.

The Labor Bureau at times became essential to the management policies of Detroit companies. In early 1914, for example, Ford Motor Company raised its daily minimum wage from $2.34 to $5.00 for workers who met certain personal and productive standards fixed by the firm. When thousands of workers rushed to the Detroit area and descended on the Ford plant in the Detroit suburb of Highland Park, the company and the EAD struck an agreement to meet this potentially serious crisis. The chief worry of other employers was that high wages at Ford would lead their own skilled workers to quit or press for wage increases to match Ford's level of compensation. Through EAD mediation, Ford agreed to accept both skilled workers and some categories of semiskilled labor only through the Labor Bureau. EAD manufacturers were less concerned about unskilled common labor. The most immediate threat to the open shop, they believed, came from skilled workers who could press more easily their natural bargaining advantages.[18]

According to the plan negotiated between Ford and the EAD, workers who wanted jobs first had to go to the Labor Bureau and fill out a brown card. If approved by the EAD, this card, containing personal and work-related information, was then sent to the Ford plant which, in turn, might send back to the EAD a white card which the applicant would present the next day at a specified plant gate. In this manner the Labor Bureau prevented Ford from hiring other employers' skilled tradesmen, thus checking the migration of craftsmen among the Detroit factories. Instead, the EAD preferred to meet Ford's demands with skilled labor drawn or pirated from other cities. Years later one author recalled that "plants elsewhere were reluctant to welcome visitors from Detroit through fear that labor recruiting might result."[19]

The EAD's response to strikes similarly demonstrated the value of the Labor Bureau in temporarily managing the flow of labor between Detroit's various shops and plants. On June 17, 1913, a strike began among toolmakers at plant #3 of the Studebaker Corporation, then the city's second largest automobile manufacturer. With leadership provided by members of the Industrial Workers of the World (IWW), the majority of the plant's 3,500 workers quickly followed suit, thereby initiating the first mass strike in the American automobile industry. The EAD quickly mapped out a strategy to contain the Wobbly-led insurgency. At the outset the Detroit Police Department began arresting agitators who tried to extend the conflict to other automobile factories. Next, strikers who wanted to go back to work at Studebaker were told to register with the Labor Bureau. This drew the men away from Studebaker's employment office and compelled

strikers to undergo an initial screening by the Bureau. Finally, other
EAD firms agreed to close their employment offices for a short time,
thereby preventing strikers, particularly scarce toolmakers, from finding similar jobs elsewhere in Detroit and also putting a stop to Wobbly
infiltration into other plants. These strikebreaking tactics successfully localized the strike at the Studebaker factory, neutralized toolmakers' job mobility, and reinforced employers' steadfast opposition
to unionization.[20]

The 1913 campaign by the IWW to organize a revolutionary union
in the automobile industry drew together two ominous trends that
led employers to further structure the labor market. First, and most
obviously, the IWW assault awoke employers to the spread of labor radicalism throughout the United States and the vulnerability of
modern heavy industry to strikes and unionization. Yet, the strike at
Studebaker—following an unsuccessful six-week battle by the Wob-
blies against the rubber corporations of Akron—did not take Detroit's
open-shop guardians entirely by surprise. As John Whirl of the EAD
cautioned employers in early 1912, "there is at this time more rest-
lessness, more aggression among the workmen in Detroit and elsewhere than there has been for several years."[21]

Second, the radical threat appeared at a time of growing public
anxiety about the consequences of mass immigration and labor turnover—twin aspects of worker mobility which connected international
migration streams with local labor markets. Elite opinion makers
worried that the proliferation of unassimilable foreign colonies in the
midst of American cities generated an assortment of political, social,
and economic ills ailing the country. From 1910 to 1914, over two-
thirds of the 5.1 million immigrants who entered the United States
were of the "new" immigration from eastern and southern Europe.
Demographic trends in Detroit reflected the national pattern. After
1900, Detroit's population increased 350 percent to nearly one million in 1920. One-third of all inhabitants were foreign born, and by
1920 85 percent of Detroit's inhabitants had been born abroad or
had at least one immigrant parent. The 1920 Census of Occupations
indicated that Detroit's industrial working class was largely immigrant. The foreign born made up 44 percent of those employed in the
manufacturing sector, with only one of five industrial workers native-
born whites. Among the automobile factories, 51 percent of the
64,000 laborers and semiskilled operatives were foreign born. An-

other 20 percent were native born, but of foreign or mixed parentage. In an early 1917 survey at Ford Motor Company, then the district's single largest employer, 60 percent of the labor force consisted of immigrants, three-quarters of whom originated in eastern and southern Europe.[22]

An epidemic of labor turnover among American industries paralleled the migration of millions into the United States. Before World War I, annual turnover rates of over 200 percent were not uncommon. Packard Motor Car Company suffered nearly 200 percent turnover in its workforce in 1913. That same year, Ford Motor Company had to hire more than 52,000 workers to maintain a force of about 13,600 at its new Highland Park plant—an annual rate of 382 percent. In 1916 the turnover rate among fifty-seven plants in Detroit averaged 252 percent. The turnover phenomenon led industrial managers to examine its costs and specific causes for the first time. In 1914 one employment manager estimated that it cost a company an average of $35 to break in a new employee. George Grant, the EAD secretary, put the figure at $100 per worker. Managers found turnover most frequent among the thousands of young men who worked as semiskilled machine operators and assemblers. The mass production jobs that managers and engineers had designed in the automobile industry enabled companies to tap a broad labor pool. But semiskilled workers were also most prone to job-hopping, especially at peaks in the business cycle when workers moved between a succession of plants and standardized jobs.[23]

For all employers, labor turnover signified more than an economic loss; it reflected resistance, even aggressiveness, on the part of many workers. For example, in 1914, an employer of mostly young Polish women complained, "the worst thing about them is that they are so independent. They work practically the time they want to, for they often leave and go to a show in the afternoon without saying anything to their employer about it." Worse, "they quit for the least reason." In the summer of 1917 the general manager of the Detroit Steel Castings Company reported, "all classes of labor [are] extremely independent and unreliable." For this reason, "it has been impossible to get either a full day's output from the men or to insist as thoroughly on quality as is desired." He added, "the habitual attitude of men today seems to be, 'If you don't like the way I am doing the job, give me my money.' "[24]

## The Rise of Personnel Management

To combat labor radicalism and what they saw as excessive worker mobility, Detroit employers sought to organize enterprise-level internal labor markets administered by welfare, employment, or personnel departments and a new cadre of managers. This strategy reflected the ascendance in Detroit of a network of automobile companies and economically dependent parts suppliers who saw that the rapid development of the city's automotive-based economy depended on the utilization of large numbers of semiskilled and unskilled workers. As the first step toward building the new system personnel managers rearranged the lines of managerial authority within companies and, in opposition to foremen, asserted their singular right to hire, fire, and discipline workers. As employment specialists, personnel managers insisted that only they comprehended the long-term labor needs of companies. Abusive foremen drove workers out of the plants, and the shortsighted pecuniary interests of financial executives stood in the way of rational employment and welfare policies required to retain workers. Companies with centralized employment departments in charge of selecting, placing, transferring, and disciplining workers took on less replacement labor than companies without. Hayes Manufacturing Company, for example, reported a 50 percent decline in labor turnover in the first year of the operation of its department and a 30 percent increase in output per worker.[25]

Welfare capitalist reforms were a second method of reducing worker mobility. Ideally, welfare programs—from company-sponsored baseball teams, libraries, and lunch rooms to bonus wage plans, group insurance, and English-language classes for immigrant workers—provided employees with economic and social benefits and gave them an incentive to remain with a company during business cycle peaks when labor turnover was most severe. Besides providing workers with incentives to stay with a firm, company welfare programs also reflected an ambitious attempt by employers to cultivate the model "steady employee." The type of employee preferred by manufacturers was a thrifty family man and a homeowner. He spoke English, ate "American food," and did not drink, gamble, or frequent saloons with his work mates. Chalmers Motors, Dodge Brothers, Packard Motor Car, Studebaker Corporation, and Timken-Detroit Axle were just a few of the companies that undertook welfare

work in the Detroit area in the 1910s. Of course, the most systematic attempt to develop a welfare program occurred at Ford Motor
Company. Ford's Five-Dollar Day and the programs administered by
the company's Sociological Department became world famous as an
example of what successful open-shop employers could do for loyal
and efficient employees.[26]

Some welfare reforms, such as the "Americanization" of immigrant workers, directly contributed to the formation of company internal labor markets by bolstering the authority of personnel managers and bureaucratizing employment methods. The organization of
English-language and civics classes served as a major point of contact between middle-class Americanizers and personnel managers.
Educators, public office-holders, social workers, ethnic leaders, and
employers viewed Americanization as a panacea for reducing labor
turnover, lessening workplace accidents attributed to the failure of
immigrants to understand the supervisors' orders, and combating labor radicalism by inculcating conservative tendencies in the immigrant masses. In 1915, when an Americanization campaign began in
Detroit, Americanizers joined with company executives and personnel managers to encourage, and sometimes compel, adult immigrant
workers to attend evening-school English classes as the first step
toward their assimilation.[27]

The citywide Americanization movement of 1915 led many companies to make the first census of their labor forces. To their surprise,
employers discovered "colonies" of non–English-speaking workers
within their plants "large enough to have a powerful influence on industrial and social life, even if they had never become a 'problem' or
a body of strikers within the plant." Americanizers urged companies
to either create or revamp their employee records system to make
information readily accessible to the coordinating body, the Americanization Committee of the Detroit Board of Commerce.[28]

Americanization at Packard Motor Car Company, however, demonstrated the practical difficulties in establishing welfare programs and,
indirectly, the obstacles in this period to the organization of company-
level internal labor markets. In September 1915 about one-third of
Packard's 1,200 "foreigners" enrolled in public evening-school English classes, but many students failed to attend consistently the
twice-a-week class after a tiring day on the job. To improve the situation, Packard devised a system to monitor the progress of its im-

migrant workers. For motivation the firm had foremen and inter-preters notify employees that their job security depended on steady class attendance. Packard and public school officials kept track of the achievements of workers by having evening-school instructors issue attendance cards to pupils at the end of every week. Workers gave the cards to their foremen who, in turn, handed them over to the company's welfare department. Clerks in that office checked the cards against a master list which grouped workers by department. One Packard executive, Harvey Saul, explained to the Americanization Committee that the master list only contained the number of foreign workers per department, not their actual names. If twenty foreigners were listed but only fifteen cards were turned in, "we put it up to the foremen to find out who the five men are that have not handed in cards."[29]

The system described at Packard mirrored the balance of forces inside the company. Although middle-class groups from outside the factory had won company executives and welfare department managers to the idea of Americanizing the foreign born, the same was not true of foremen and immigrant workers. Given the power they wielded as the shop floor organizers of production, foremen were a force to be reckoned with by all proponents of social and economic reform—whether Americanization or scientific management. At best, Packard officials formally coopted these supervisors into the Americanization movement, leaving the prodding and monitoring of immigrant workers almost entirely dependent on the initiative and willingness of foremen to comply with the program. That two-thirds of Packard's "foreigners" did not enroll in evening-school classes, and those who did were known only anonymously by the welfare department, suggests managers' reluctance to insist too strongly on Americanization for fear of alienating workers and, thereby, increasing turnover rates.

The United States' mobilization for war in 1916 gave personnel managers a historic opportunity to expand their authority into plant operations. Labor turnover became a critical issue—and soon a national emergency—as orders for war material poured into American factories. Welfare secretaries, employment managers, and personnel specialists met frequently under these wartime conditions and established the basis for the personnel management profession in the United States. They called for the expansion of personnel depart-

ments to reduce labor mobility, the development of written job speci-
fications and physical and aptitude examinations, and the restriction
of the right of foremen to discipline workers.[30]

Although the war arrived at an opportune moment for personnel
managers, it was not entirely a blessing for employers more generally. In October 1917 manufacturers in Detroit began to experience
a critical shortage of skilled metal workers, particularly tool and die
makers; and by the spring of 1918, the EAD reported an acute shortage
of all grades of factory labor. EAD officials complained that the military draft had depleted the local labor pool. In April 1918, 123 firms
notified the EAD that they needed immediately 1,821 skilled workers,
4,620 semiskilled, 2,645 unskilled, and 4,235 women workers; in
other words, a total of 13,321 were in demand. To make matters
worse, the companies estimated that over the next six months they
would require another installment of 22,177 workers.[31]

The EAD made some attempt to restock the Detroit labor market
with workers from outside Detroit. In May 1918 the association obtained two field men from Packard and Studebaker and sent them
searching for spare labor. In every place they looked, however, labor was in short supply and high demand. As an indication of how
bad things had become, Chester Culver, the new general manager of
the EAD, told his executive board that employers were fighting over
the bottom of the barrel of the labor market. Culver in fact tracked
down a rumor that skilled workers were available in Cincinnati. "We
immediately communicated with that point," Culver said, "and received a report that if there were any men of that kind unemployed,
they do not know where they were." Culver's contact in Cincinnati
remarked that a moment earlier "he had observed two employment
men fighting over two negroes in the street in front of his office." [32]

Thrown back on its own home turf, the EAD had to guard and
develop the Detroit labor pool, fending off outside raiders like the
General Electric Company (which attempted to paste advertisements
for labor in the city's street cars), and help smooth the transition of
companies to the employment of women and black migrants from
the South. To prevent a drain on the local labor market, the EAD even
offered to assist a Detroit firm assemble a labor force of workers living
outside the Detroit area for construction of a new military training
camp in Battle Creek, Michigan.[33]

The EAD's difficulties increased as the wartime labor shortage shredded solidarity among the district's employers. Early on, the EAD warned employers of the trouble that would result from the increased number of want ads placed by companies in local newspapers. As the EAD staff knew from experience, public advertising for labor by individual firms inevitably fragmented the precarious unity among employers. Fearing the consequences of unrestrained competition, the EAD mediated an agreement in April 1918, whereby companies promised to cease advertising as long as the shortage continued.[34]

More damaging to employers' ranks than labor advertising were the raiding practices of some companies. Agitated department store managers protested to the EAD about the pirating of their women workers by manufacturing firms. In September 1917 the EAD also received complaints about the raiding activities of the Fisher Body Company, which had rehired painters and trimmers fired only a few months earlier for union activities. The heightened bargaining power enjoyed by such skilled body workers enabled them to sustain the wartime organizing drive of the Automobile Workers Union (AWU). Apart from the AWU, locals of the Machinists, Patternmakers, and Iron Molders likewise made significant gains during the war.[35]

For employers, neither the EAD Labor Bureau nor company personnel departments could resolve the wartime labor crisis. For the Labor Bureau to succeed as an employers' tool first a surplus of labor had to be directed to its doors. That precondition was obviously absent during the war. And as agents of rival companies, personnel managers could do little to bring about a coherent and rational labor policy among employers despite the EAD's best efforts to reinforce cooperation. Thus, the increased leverage of all workers resulting from the tight labor market spelled doom to both labor market strategies employers had formulated before the war.

## The State and Wartime Labor

In near desperation, Detroit employers turned to the state for assistance in a new strategy of establishing political control over the labor market. With the EAD's encouragement, the Federal Justice Department spawned local branches of a semiofficial auxiliary known as the American Protective League (APL). Each branch consisted of respectable and trustworthy patriots (like the EAD's general manager, Chester Culver, a lieutenant in the outfit) who volunteered to monitor foreign-born workers, deter industrial sabotage, and collect information for local police departments. By the end of the war, the Detroit APL unit had enrolled 4,000 volunteers under the command of Frank Croul, a manufacturer and former police commissioner. At its plant in Highland Park, the Ford Motor Company assigned 100 APL operatives to forty-five departments and shops. Seventeen agents worked in the company's employment department where they screened job applicants. In that capacity, APL volunteers monitored the behavior of workers, recommending the names of the least dependable to the local draft board.[36]

The APL could detect troublemakers and agitators among the employees of an industrial plant, but it could not deal with the "slackers" and "loafers" whose very existence troubled employers throughout 1918. The EAD believed these men refused to work until employers offered higher wages and surrendered to other demands such as the establishment of the closed shop, a view confirmed by Harvey Watson, business agent for the Electrical Workers' Local 58. "There is no shortage of mechanics in Detroit at this time," Watson declared, "and if Mr. Leland [then head of Liberty Motors] would only pay the wage and grant the conditions that American-spirited employers do in this city, he will have no difficulty in filling his shop with competent mechanics in all lines." The message was clear: employers would have to pay dearly to secure labor. But to do so meant jeopardizing the foundations of open-shop rule.[37]

To resolve this intractable dilemma, the EAD endorsed a hardline policy which entailed the suppression of workers' constitutional liberty to contract and negotiate in the labor market. Although in September 1918 the U.S. House of Representatives rejected the conscription of labor, Detroit employers prepared for a local solution. On October 8 the EAD proposed an ordinance to the Detroit Common Council. The scheme, called the Municipal War Work Card Plan (and by the Detroit Federation of Labor, the "War Loafing Ordinance"), was the brainchild of James M. Teahen, an officer of a firm affiliated with the EAD and chairman of the Community Advisory Board of the United States Employment Service. According to his plan, every working male between the ages of sixteen and sixty would receive a work card bearing his signature and photograph. In addition, those working in essential industries would receive a war service card; "Women working in essential industries are also entitled to this card if they wish it," read the EAD General Manager's report. If anyone stopped on the street by the police could not produce a work card, the ordinance provided a penalty of a $100 fine or thirty days in jail, or both. By this means, employers could compel men to find work.

A second part of the EAD-sponsored ordinance required a worker to surrender his work card when he quit an employer; this automatically made him a "criminal" subject to police arrest or harassment. Finally, the work card system reinforced vigilance and cooperation among personnel departments. Managers had the responsibility of reporting absent workers so that, in the words of the EAD, "a man cannot get a job, secure a card, leave at once and be immune from arrest." Thus, with the law and police unequivocally on their side, employers could counteract workers' bargaining power in the labor market and induce most male workers to "accept some form of employment when offered."[38]

Although the War Loafing Ordinance would only bear down on workers and not employers, leaders of the Detroit Federation of Labor (DFL) offered no objections when they were assured that labor would have one representative on the three-person executive committee in charge of administering the law. The employers and public would name the other two. The DFL saw the ordinance as a wartime public necessity. Provided the law was not wholly administered by the Employers' Association, the DFL believed it would only cause discomfort for "loafers," not hard-working and patriotic union men. George Krogstad, a business agent for the Patternmakers' Union and a labor representative on the Community War Labor Board, exemplified the patriotic attitude of craft labor in Detroit at this time. Appealing to skilled workers, Krogstad implored them to labor unstintingly in the production of war materials. He asked this as a sign of their "appreciation of the government's good will" in granting unions representation on the Community War Labor Board.[39]

The War Loafing Ordinance never went into effect because the war ended in mid-November. The cessation of hostilities, however, did not mean that the labor market crisis was over. "Labor conditions are very acute," reported the president of the Detroit Steel Tubes Company in the summer of 1919, "rates [of labor turnover] are very high, and operating a manufacturing business during these times is anything but a recreation." For more than two years after the Armistice, Detroit employers suffered labor and material shortages and a series of "extremely annoying" strikes. With the cancellation of war contracts, employment levels among Detroit factories began to fall in November 1918. Employment increased from mid-February to late October 1919, fell again slightly, and reached record levels in the late winter and spring of 1920. During these months, while the city's building trades unions expanded and consolidated their base in the construction industry (where they remained throughout the 1920s), the Automobile Workers Union waxed strong in the trimming and painting departments of Fisher Body, Packard, Studebaker, American Auto Trimming and Painting, Hudson, and at a dozen or more other companies, reaching a membership of over 18,000 by 1920. Strikes by the Auto Workers Union and Machinists over wages, the eight-hour day, and union recognition hit such auto industry suppliers as the Wadsworth, Detroit Timken-Axle, and Aluminum Castings companies. But the main automobile plants themselves were seldom directly attacked in the more than 100 strikes occurring in Detroit from 1919 to 1921. Most members of the Detroit AWU worked in the score of plants of the Fisher Body Company where, as a former AWU officer recalled, "we had what we call a Conference Committee [which settled grievances] that would meet once a month with Lawrence Fisher, Fred Fisher, and the other Fisher boys and the superintendent of Fisher Body." But with the loss of an untimely strike at Fisher Body in early 1921, the AWU's power in Detroit disintegrated and with it the collapse of a union presence in the local auto industry until the 1930s.[40]

The 1921 strike at Fisher Body occurred in the midst of the quick and devastating depression of 1920–1921; everywhere employers reestablished their domination in American industry. In Detroit, the spread of part-time employment, wage cuts, and work speed-up accompanied demoralizing rates of joblessness. A sample of statistics taken from the EAD's *Labor Barometer* indicates the extent of unemployment. Twenty-one firms—ten automobile companies and eleven suppliers of parts, bodies, and rubber tires—surveyed by the EAD on March 31, 1920, had a total of 162,700 industrial employees. Ford's plants in Highland Park and Dearborn had 64,000, the Dodge Brothers Company employed 22,300 at its plant in Hamtramck, Fisher Body had a force of 11,250, and there were 2,800 at Kelsey Wheel. By February 1, 1921, total employment fell to 44,970, a drop of 81 percent for the surveyed companies. Ford employed only 8,540, Dodge

1,650, Fisher Body 3,200, and Kelsey Wheel 310. Companies like Briggs Manufacturing and C. R. Wilson Body Company closed down altogether. By comparison, employees of Lincoln Motors, Studebaker, and Cadillac appeared fortunate; these companies lost 34, 43, and 45 percent of their workforces, respectively.[41]

In the 1920s, the labor market servicing Detroit's auto industry shifted significantly in favor of the employers. On the supply side, the depression of the early 1920s ushered in an era of chronic surplus in the labor market, despite the imposition of restrictive immigration quotas in 1921 and 1924. Migration from western Europe, Canada, Mexico, and depressed mining and agricultural regions within the United States provided sources for a new labor supply more fluctuating and mobile than before World War I. On the demand side, the industry's great rushes and chronic lulls deepened in the 1920s.

Beginning in 1923, automobile manufacturers had to reckon with a saturated product marketplace. In response, companies—most notably General Motors under President Alfred P. Sloan, Jr.—played to the fickle element in consumer habits, attempting to stimulate automobile buying through aggressive advertising, installment plan purchases, and frequent model changes. The overall result was a highly unstable industry. One study of seventy-eight automobile establishments, excluding auto accessory plants, found a continuous decline in the chance of a worker obtaining steady, full-time employment over the period from 1923 to 1928. Instability of employment was greater in auto than in the iron and steel and the men's clothing industries. The unpredictable sales end of the automobile business, along with seasonal and periodic shutdowns required to retool for new models, created among manufacturers a built-in demand for a migratory labor force consisting mainly of young, single men.[42]

## Rise of the "Suitcase Brigade"

With organized labor in retreat and a plentiful supply of hungry workers at hand, Detroit employers laid the foundations for a fifth and terribly simplistic labor market strategy—economic control based on market forces. Backed by a well-stocked labor market, Detroit employers understood that they could obtain all the labor they required merely with the lure of a high hourly wage. Coinciding with the scrapping of Ford's Sociological Department in 1921, employers ceased to disguise themselves as welfare capitalists, pretending they desired unending employee devotion. For the captains of industry, the high wage alone sufficed so long as it attracted enough workers to Detroit's factories. Researcher Myron Watkins described characteristics of the new labor market strategy:

> The men have been attracted to the [automobile] industry and held there by high pay, and their hearts are not in their work. . . . Except for a few "old timers," there is absolutely no loyalty to the establishment or organization in which these men daily labor for their living. They are continually on the alert for "better pay," and a difference of five cents per hour in favor of a new job will lead them to "throw up" an old job without delay. . . . Constancy in employment relations is no longer a virtue—at least not a common one.[43]

Before the war reformers of all types urged employers to develop social and moral bonds with their employees beyond the cash nexus. The direct payoff to employers was supposed to be less labor trouble, improved workforce morale, and lower labor turnover. In the 1920s, however, the open shop—which, according to Watkins's interviews with employment officials, "really means the closed non-union shop" —and a surplus of labor took care of those problems. Also in the 1920s, labor turnover was less of a concern to employers because it occurred within a labor market securely under management control, and the industrial regime itself mandated high levels of labor mobility. In addition, the tremendous rationalization of production in the auto industry during the postwar decade meant further simplification of jobs, thus enabling managers to quickly and cheaply train workers with little or no prior experience in industrial work. The composition of EAD Labor Bureau referrals provides a rough indication of this dilution process. In 1915 the bureau sent out nearly 20,000 men to member firms. Of these, two-thirds were highly skilled tradesmen, a mere 5 percent laborers and handymen, and the remainder defined as semiskilled. In 1928, the EAD sent out 62,000 workers, of which 20 percent were highly skilled, another 20 percent unskilled, and the remaining 60 percent somewhere in between.[44]

Given all these material preconditions—labor surplus, major technological changes, a migratory labor force, and a labor market structured and dominated by the unstable labor demand of large automobile corporations—employers turned irregularity of employment into a virtue. A happy meeting of interests occurred between Detroit's employers and the "suitcase brigade," that large group of young and unmarried sod-busters who migrated to the motor city from small midwestern and southern towns and farms. Migrants arrived in Detroit expecting to make top dollar, not learn a trade. According to Robert Dunn, a contemporary student of the auto industry, the migratory worker "is quite likely to regard his job as a temporary expedient and to be dreaming about leaving the 'auto game' and opening a garage or a filling station of his own." To these young men, automobile work was a transition to other goals in life. For the migrants who bore the brunt of seasonal and cyclical unemployment, the irregularity of employment in Detroit was less a disaster than a fundamental fact of life.[45]

In the 1920s, employers paid few of the social costs of these irregular employment patterns. This became obvious in 1926–1927 when, during the changeover to the Model A, the Ford Motor Company dumped thousands of workers onto the meager public and private charity systems in the Detroit area. Ford, like other employers, considered the labor market as simply a place to procure labor through the offer of wages and a place to dump workers when they were no longer required. "The whole situation," wrote Paul U. Kellogg, a keen observer of the Detroit automobile business, "the lure of the pay, the pressure for jobs, tended to create the picture of labor as a foot-loose commodity, welling in like a tide." Labor was something to be used and discarded. "Is it not to be wondered at," Kellogg asked, "that under such circumstances many an industrial executive comes to regard the employment reservoir as something to tap today and empty into tomorrow, without thought of its human entourage?"[46]

But there were dangers for employers inherent in the casual method of employment. Migrant labor had its practical limitations. Managers incessantly praised the antiunion, conservative tendencies of white Southerners who migrated in large numbers to Detroit after the war. Resident and experienced automobile workers, reported researcher William Chalmers, ridiculed the southern-born rate-busters who failed to understand that management would quickly reduce piece rates if workers actually met output standards. Many managers believed that southern migrants, for all their antiunionism and unstinting performance on the shop floor, had poor commitment to their employers, and companies could not count on migrants to stay when their farms beckoned them home in the spring. And eventually they, too, learned the "auto game" and began to restrict production.[47]

More seriously, the casual, high-wage, labor market strategy spread to the treatment of privileged and settled workers who had established permanent residences in Detroit. These workers, such as tool and die makers, had indispensable skills that protected their places in the automotive economy. As family men, they fit employers' image of the steady and dependable employee, and typically they owned a house, a radio, and an automobile. They participated in what had become a surrogate for welfare capitalism: the mass consumer culture of the 1920s. But this meant that they also had stake in a high annual income and in steady employment—increasingly uncommon during the decade given erratic production seasons and long periods of "down time" during model changes. Massive layoffs such as those at Ford reached into the ranks of the skilled working class, planting seeds of doubt and anxiety. Charles Walker captured the mood and sentiment among these workers in the late 1920s: "By late 1929, the family men were worried. Not in a panic, but thinking hard. They still had their homes, they still had the car, but their savings were gone. The expanding vacations [i.e., layoffs and down time] gave them an increasing sense of insecurity." Worker-residents, who probably agreed with their employers about the virtues of family, savings, and education, eventually saw everything collapse in the Great Depression. After 1933 it was precisely these long-term workers, the auto industry's aristocrats, who formed the vanguard of the industrial union movement which finally toppled open-shop absolutism in Detroit.[48]

## NOTES

An earlier draft of this paper was presented at the Social Science History Association's Annual Meeting in Toronto on October 28, 1984. The author wishes to thank John Bukowczyk, Christopher Johnson, Nelson Lichtenstein, Steve Meyer, and Robert Zieger for their help in preparation of this essay.

1. Studies which focus on labor-management struggles at the point of production include Harry Braverman, *Labor and Monopoly Capital: The Degradation of Work in the Twentieth Century* (New York: Monthly Review Press, 1974); Andrew L. Friedman, *Industry and Labor: Class Struggle at Work and Monopoly Capitalism* (London: Macmillan, 1977); David Montgomery, *Workers' Control in America: Studies in the History of Work,*

*Technology, and Labor Struggles* (New York: Cambridge University Press, 1979); Charles F. Sabel, *Work and Politics: The Division of Labor in Industry* (New York: Cambridge University Press, 1982); and Stephen Meyer III, *The Five Dollar Day: Labor Management and Social Control in the Ford Motor Company, 1908–1921* (Albany: State University of New York Press, 1981). The recent labor market literature is best represented by Sanford M. Jacoby, *Employing Bureaucracy: Managers, Unions, and the Transformation of Work in American Industry, 1900–1945* (New York: Columbia University Press, 1985); Robert Max Jackson, *The Formation of Craft Labor Markets* (Orlando, Fl.: Academic Press, 1984); and R. Loveridge and A. L. Mok, *Theories of Labor Market Segmentation: A Critique* (The Hague: Martinus Nijhoff, 1979). Several works manage to unite the shop floor and labor market in a single analytical framework. See Richard Edwards, *Contested Terrain: The Transformation of the Workplace in the Twentieth Century* (New York: Basic Books, 1979); David M. Gordon, Richard Edwards, and Michael Reich, *Segmented Work, Divided Workers: The Historical Transformation of Labor in the United States* (New York: Cambridge University Press, 1982); and a fine article by Charles F. Sabel and David Stark, "Planning, Politics and Shop-Floor Power: Hidden Forms of Bargaining in Soviet-Imposed State Socialist Societies," *Politics and Society* 11 (1982): 439–76.

2. U.S., Department of Commerce and Labor, Bureau of the Census, *Manufacturers, 1905*, pt. 2, States and Territories, 510, 520; U.S., Department of Commerce, Bureau of the Census, *Thirteenth Census of the United States: 1910*, vol. 10, *Reports for Principle Industries*, 955; Employers' Association of Detroit (hereafter, EAD), *Labor Barometer*, February 23, 1920; EAD *Labor Barometer*, September 18 and October 23, 1928; U.S., Department of Commerce, Bureau of the Census, *Fifteenth Census of the United States: 1929*, vol. 3, 258.

3. F. W. Hilbert, "Trade-Union Agreements in the Iron Molders' Union," in Jacob H. Hollander and George E. Barnett, eds., *Studies in American Trade Unionism* (New York: Henry Holt, 1912), 243. Besides Hilbert, other examinations of late-nineteenth-century union-employer accommodation through trade agreements include Bruno Ramirez, *When Workers Fight: The Politics of Industrial Relations in the Progressive Era, 1898–1916* (Westport, Conn.: Greenwood Press, 1978), 17–84; Jackson, *Formation of Craft Labor Markets*, chs. 9–13; Montgomery, *Workers' Control in America*, 49–54; Lloyd Ulman, *The Rise of the National Trade Union: The Development and Significance of Its Structure, Governing Institutions, and Economic Policies* (Cambridge, Mass.: Harvard University Press, 1955); and Philip S. Foner, *History of the Labor Movement in the United States* (New York: International Publishers, 1964), vol. 3, 28–31.

4. The discussion of labor markets too often is limited to internal labor markets created by employers for purposes of controlling workers by such indirect means as bureaucratic employment rules. See, for instance, Richard Edward's discussion of "bureaucratic control" in *Contested Terrain*, ch. 8. Unfortunately this neglects other institutions, such as trade unions, which

incorporate and sometimes impose a rationalized labor market upon an entire industry. For an example from the 1930s see Lawrence M. Kahn, "Unions and Internal Labor Markets: The Case of the San Francisco Longshoremen," *Labor History* 21 (Summer 1980): 369–91.

5. Arthur Rohan interview with Jack W. Skeels, August 14, 1961, transcript, 3, in Archives of Labor and Urban Affairs, Wayne State University, Detroit, Michigan (hereafter, ALHUA).

6. Ulman, *Rise of National Trade Union*, chs. 3–5; and Eric H. Monkkonen, ed., *Walking to Work: Tramps in America, 1790–1935* (Lincoln, Neb.: University of Nebraska Press, 1984).

7. Montgomery, *Workers' Control*, 54–57; Hilbert, "Trade-Union Agreements in the Iron Molders' Union," 234–37; Foner, *History of the Labor Movement*, vol. 3, 26–28; U.S., Department of Commerce, Bureau of the Census, *Historical Statistics of the United States, 1789–1945*, 72–73. The emergence of union business agents as custodians of local labor markets has been documented mainly for the typographical and building trades. For an example, see Mark Erlich, "Peter J. McGuire's Trade Unionism: Socialism of a Trades Union Kind," *Labor History* 24 (Spring 1983): 181–84.

8. Michigan, Bureau of Labor and Industrial Statistics, *19th* and *20th Annual Report* (Lansing, 1902, 1904), 35–55, 168; U.S., Department of Commerce and Labor, Bureau of the Census, *Twelfth Census of the United States, 1900: Occupations*, 544-48; John J. Whirl, EAD Annual Meeting, February 9, 1904; U.S., Department of the Interior, *Twelfth Census of the United States, 1900: Manufacturers*, vol. 2, 426–30; U.S., Department of Commerce, Bureau of the Census, *Thirteenth Census of the United States: 1910*, vol. 10, *Reports for Principle Industries*, 955.

9. Olivier Zunz, *The Changing Face of Inequality: Urbanization, Industrial Development, and Immigrants in Detroit, 1880–1920* (Chicago: University of Chicago Press, 1982), 99; Hilbert, "Trade-Union Agreements in the Iron Molders' Union," 234.

10. Henry M. Leland, Reading Room File, Burton Historical Collection, Detroit Public Library (hereafter, BHC); Chester M. Culver, *Reminiscences*, July 21, 1953, Ford Archives, Henry Ford Museum, Dearborn, Michigan; EAD Minute Book, December 13, 1902; EAD Annual Meeting, February 22, 1910. On the rise of belligerent antiunion employers' associations, see F. W. Hilbert, "Employers' Associations in the United States," in Hollander and Barnett, eds., *Studies in American Trade Unionism*, 183–217; Clarence Bonnett, *Employers' Associations in the United States: A Study of Typical Associations* (New York: Macmillan, 1922) and *History of Employers' Associations in the United States* (New York: Vantage Press, 1956); Foner, *History of the Labor Movement*, vol. 3, 32–60; Ramirez, *When Workers Fight*, 93–97; Jackson, *Formation of Craft Labor Markets*, chs. 10, 12; Montgomery, *Workers' Control*, 57–63.

11. Ulman, *Rise of National Trade Union*, 524–25.

12. Culver, *Reminiscences*; John J. Whirl, *Address to Wholesalers' Association*, ca. 1908. Dan Clawson analyzes output restriction for this period

in *Bureaucracy and the Labor Process: The Transformation of U.S. Industry, 1860–1920* (New York: Monthly Review Press, 1980), 149–55, 171-79.

13. On the rise of management, see Clawson, *Bureaucracy*, chs. 3–5, and Daniel Nelson, *Managers and Workers: Origins of the New Factory System in the United States, 1880–1920* (Madison: University of Wisconsin Press, 1975), chs. 3–4.

14. Basic sources on the EAD Labor Bureau are Culver, *Reminiscences*; EAD Annual Meetings, 1904–16, and EAD Executive Board Meetings, Minutes, June 14, 1916 to January 24, 1918; William Ellison Chalmers, "Labor in the Automobile Industry: A Study of Personnel Policies, Workers' Attitudes, and Attempts at Unionism (Ph.D. diss., University of Wisconsin, Madison, 1932), 187–94; and two essays written in the late 1930s for the Works Projects Administration by Blanche Bernstein, "Hiring Practices in the Automobile Industry" and "The Labor Market in the Automobile Industry," in Boxes 1 and 2, William E. Chalmers Collection, ALHUA.

15. Joseph W. Bryce, "On the Job Line," *The Square Deal* 15 (November 1914): 304–6; EAD Meeting, December 13, 1902; John J. Whirl, EAD Annual Meeting, February 17, 1907; E. T. Gilbert, EAD Annual Meeting, February 21, 1905.

16. EAD Annual Meeting, 1904, 1906, 1909, and 1912; Heathfield is quoted in an unidentified newspaper clipping, ca. 1904, in EAD Scrapbook #2, BHC. In his *Reminiscences*, Culver maintained that the EAD never kept a blacklist, that is, a list circulating among employers saying, "Don't hire these men." Rather, the EAD had what Culver called a "central personnel records file."

17. *Detroit News*, July 19, 1907; *Detroit News*, April 1, 1911.

18. Culver, *Reminiscences*.

19. Culver, *Reminiscences*; C. B. Gordy, "Craftsmen Needed," *American Machinist* (November 6, 1935): 823. Ford Motor Company quit the Employers' Association in July 1917, after it was discovered that Julius Bock, an ambitious and enterprising EAD employee, had sold some of the white cards to workers, guaranteeing the workers an entry at Ford and himself a tidy profit. See Culver, *Reminiscences*.

20. On the Studebaker strike, see John J. Whirl, EAD Annual Meeting, February 17, 1914; Jack Russell, "The Coming of the Line: The Ford Highland Park Plant, 1900–1914," *Radical America* 12 (May–June 1978): 40–42; Steve Babson, *Working Detroit: The Making of a Union Town* (Detroit: Wayne State University Press, 1986), 32–33; and Foner, *History of the Labor Movement*, vol. 4, ch. 16.

21. John J. Whirl, EAD Annual Meeting, February 20, 1912; Jack Russell, "The Coming of the Line: Rationalization and Labor at the Ford Highland Park Plant, 1910 to 1920," (typescript), 29–40.

22. John Higham, *Strangers in the Land: Patterns of American Nativism, 1860–1925* (New York: Atheneum, 1963), ch. 7; *Historical Statistics of the United States*, 33; Zunz, *Changing Face of Inequality*, 106; U.S., Department of Commerce, Bureau of the Census, *Fourteenth Census of the United States: 1920*, vol. 4, *Occupations*, 1101–4; Russell, "Coming of the Line," 61.

23. Sumner Slichter, *The Turnover of Factory Labor* (New York: D. Appleton, 1919); Meyer, *Five Dollar Day*, 83–85; U.S., Department of Labor, Bureau of Labor Statistics, *Proceedings of the Employment Managers' Conference,* April 2–3, 1917, Bulletin no. 227, 32; Ronald W. Schatz, *The Electrical Workers: A History of Labor at General Electric and Westinghouse, 1923–1960* (Urbana, Ill.: University of Illinois Press, 1983), 17; George W. Grant, EAD Executive Board Meeting, December 7, 1916.

24. Statements from anonymous employers in Detroit Board of Education, *Annual Report*, 1914–1915, 164–66; Stuart W. Utley, "Reports on Conditions, July 1, 1916 to June 30, 1917," Box 353, Truman H. Newberry Papers, BHC.

25. U.S., Department of Labor, Bureau of Labor Statistics, *Proceedings of the Employment Managers' Conference,* April 2–3, 1917, Bulletin no. 227, 29–47.

26. "A Partial List of Employers with Some Forms of Welfare Work," *Monthly Labor Review* (February 1917): 320–21; Meyer, *Five Dollar Day,* chs. 5–6. Stuart D. Brandes inventories an extensive range of welfare programs in *American Welfare Capitalism, 1880–1940* (Chicago: University of Chicago Press, 1976).

27. The literature on Americanization includes Edward George Hartman, *The Movement to Americanize the Immigrant* (New York: Columbia University Press, 1948); Higham, *Strangers in the Land,* 234–63; Gerd Korman, *Industrialization, Immigrants, and Americanizers: The View from Milwaukee* (Madison: Wisconsin State Historical Society, 1967). On Americanization at Ford, see Meyer, *Five Dollar Day,* ch. 7.

28. *Americanizing a City: The Campaign for the Detroit Night Schools* (New York, December 15, 1915), 11, BHC.

29. Americanization Committee of Detroit, Minutes, January 17, 1916, Bentley Library, University of Michigan, Ann Arbor.

30. For the proceedings of employment manager conferences see the reports of the U.S. Department of Labor, Bureau of Labor Statistics, for 1916 (Bulletin no. 196), 1917 (Bulletin no. 227), and 1918 (Bulletin no. 247).

31. EAD Executive Board Minutes, October 1917; February 1918; April 1918.

32. EAD Manager's Report, March 1918; EAD Executive Board Minutes, May 16, 1918.

33. EAD Manager's Report, June 1917; June–October 1918.

34. EAD Executive Board Minutes, August 9 and September 6, 1917; EAD Manager's Report, April 1918.

35. EAD Executive Board Minutes, September 21, 1917; Jack W. Skeels, "Early Carriage and Auto Unions: The Impact of Industrialization and Rival Unionism," *Industrial and Labor Relations Review* 17 (1963–1964): 577–80.

36. Meyer, *Five Dollar Day,* 174–86; Joan M. Jensen, *The Price of Vigilance* (Chicago: Rand McNally, 1968).

37. *Detroit Labor News,* May 24, 1918.

38. EAD Executive Board Minutes, May 2, 1918; EAD Manager's Report,

June–October 1918; *The Detroiter* [publication of the Detroit Board of Commerce], October 29, 1918, 2.

39. *Detroit Labor News*, October 11, 1918. Eventually, the DFL came around to oppose the War Loafing Ordinance on the grounds that Detroit's mayor did not consult with them in naming the labor representative to the administrative committee. *Detroit Labor News*, October 25, 1918.

40. Allen A. Templeton to Truman H. Newberry, August 15, 1919, Box 351, Truman H. Newberry Papers, BHC; Chester M. Culver, *Annual Report of the General Manager of the* EAD, ca. early 1920; Myron Watkins, "The Labor Situation in Detroit," *Journal of Political Economy* (December 1920): 843; *Monthly Labor Review* (June 1920): 165, and (May 1922): 184; Lester Johnson interview with William Sullivan, June 3, 1959, transcript, 18–19, ALHUA; Skeels, "Early Carriage," 581–82. Estimates of the greatest strength of the AWU in Detroit in 1919–1920 vary considerably. Watkin's figure of 18,000 is the only contemporary estimate by an independent investigator. Skeels, "Early Carriage," 579, and Meyer, *Five Dollar Day*, suggest 40,000. In his oral history (18), Arthur Rohan, a former AWU organizer, gave 30,000–35,000, which Roger Keeran also uses in *The Communist Party and the Auto Workers' Unions* (New York: Indiana University Press, 1980), 34. However, the organizer of the Detroit Labor Forum of 1919–1921, Reverend I. Paul Taylor (interview, November 2, 1960, 12), put the number at 10,000, noting that the Detroit Police Commissioner placed it as low as 7,000.

41. EAD, *Labor Barometer*, March 31, 1920, and February 1, 1921.

42. "Instability of Employment in the Automobile Industry," *Monthly Labor Review* (February 1929): 214–19. For Detroit in the 1920s, see Chalmers, "Labor in the Automobile Industry"; Bernstein, "Hiring Practices" and "The Labor Market"; Robert Dunn, *Labor and Automobiles* (New York: International Publishers, 1929); Keeran, *Communist Party*, ch. 2; and Babson, *Working Detroit*, 48–50.

43. Meyer, *Five Dollar Day*, 197–200; Allan Nevins and Frank E. Hill, *Ford: Expansion and Challenge, 1915–1933* (New York: Charles Scribner's Sons, 1957), chs. 6, 13; Watkins, "Labor Situation," 850–51. William Chalmers, "Labor in the Automobile Industry," 92–98, who did his doctoral research in Detroit in the late 1920s, testified to the general abandonment of welfare programs by automobile manufacturers. Detroit, however, may have been an exception to trends in the rest of American industry. In "Rise and Decline of Welfare Capitalism," David Brody sees the deepening of welfare capitalism throughout the 1920s, and only the 1929 depression put an end to the "paternalist course of American industrial relations"; see Brody, *Workers in Industrial America: Essays on the 20th Century Struggle* (New York: Oxford University Press, 1980), 48–81. But in *American Welfare Capitalism*, Stuart Brandes argues that welfare capitalism was dying out before the depression.

44. Watkins, "Labor Situation," 849; "Effect of Technological Change upon Occupations in the Motor-Vehicle Industry," *Monthly Labor Review* (February 1932): 248–52; "Digest of Material on Technological Changes, Produc-

tivity of Labor, and Labor Displacement," *Monthly Labor Review* (November 1932): 1032–33; EAD Annual Meeting, April 27, 1915; Chester Culver, *Annual Report of the General Manager of the* EAD *(for the Year 1928)*.

45. Dunn, *Labor and Automobiles*, 33. Michael J. Piore examines the economic strategy of migrants in *Birds of Passage: Migrant Labor and Industrial Societies* (New York: Cambridge University Press, 1979), ch. 3.

46. Paul U. Kellogg, "When Mass Production Stalls," *The Survey* (March 1, 1928): 686, 723.

47. Chalmers, "Labor in the Automobile Industry," 126–28, 180–81. See also Stanley B. Mathewson, *Restriction of Output among Unorganized Workers* (New York: Viking Press, 1931).

48. Charles R. Walker, "Down and Out in Detroit," *Forum* (September 1931): 129–36; Stuart Ewen, *Captains of Consciousness: Advertising and the Social Roots of the Consumer Culture* (New York: McGraw Hill, 1976). The critical role of skilled metal workers in the formation of industrial unions in the auto industry is examined by Steve Babson, "Pointing the Way: The Role of British and Irish Skilled Tradesmen in the Rise of the UAW," *Detroit in Perspective* 7 (Spring 1983): 75–96.

# 4

# The Persistence of Fordism: Workers and Technology in the American Automobile Industry, 1900–1960

STEPHEN MEYER

Technology and its influence on work and work processes have increasingly attracted the attention of labor and social historians. In recent years, two conflicting views have emerged about the nature and character of modern production technologies and their influence on work and work processes. In one view, labeled the "deskilling" thesis, Harry Braverman, David Noble, and Harley Shaiken maintain that new production technologies undermine workers' skills and enable management to control more effectively the work process. In the other view, sometimes termed the "craft revival" or "skill recomposition" thesis, Charles Sabel, Michael Piore, Jonathan Zeitlin, and Paul Adler argue that modern forms of economic organization and production may well lead to increased levels of skill and greater worker involvement in the production process.[1]

In his seminal work, *Labor and Monopoly Capital*, Harry Braverman, offered the first thorough formulation of the "deskilling thesis." Braverman maintained that twentieth-century management practice has generated a system of production that has transformed industrial and office work and led to "the degradation of work" in modern industrial societies. Braverman emphasized the contradiction between the increased application of technology which seemingly demanded "the greater exercise of intelligence and mental effort in general" and "a mounting dissatisfaction with the conditions of industrial and office labor." The thrust of Braverman's thesis has been that modern forms of work organization and production technology have steadily

73

reduced the skill necessary to do the jobs of modern factory and office workers. For Braverman, the managerial and technical innovations of the Ford Motor Company served as an important example of the "degradation of work." Although far-reaching in the way it posed questions about work and work processes, this thesis has lately received considerable criticism due to its schematic and often deterministic treatment of the problem of work in industrial society.[2]

In *The Second Industrial Divide*, Charles Sabel and Michael Piore have offered a widely noted revisionist view. They contend mass production was hardly inevitable; it was but one of two alternative production paradigms. Mass production methods, which emerged in the late nineteenth-century's "first industrial divide" and which achieved dominance to serve the emerging mass market, historically superceded a more flexible production system resting on general-purpose machines and craft skills. In an analysis of fragmented and specialized product markets and recent trends in production technology, they maintain that a "second industrial divide" built around "flexible specialization" remains a viable alternative to modern mass production. "Flexible specialization," they argue, "is a strategy of permanent innovation: accommodation to ceaseless change rather than an effort to control it." This alternative paradigm rests on flexible machines, skilled workers, and a public policy that favors innovation and discourages union efforts to maintain a sharp division between the interests of workers and managers. Piore and Sable see "a revival of craft production forms that were emarginated at the first industrial divide." And, they argue that as a viable production strategy, mass production, or Fordism, has come to an historic end.[3]

But are Piore and Sabel correct in their assertion that Fordism has been superceded in the second half of the twentieth century? Clearly, their provocative "craft revival" thesis has major implications for contemporary social policy and labor organization, and it is thus important to see if Fordism was in fact the inflexible production system portrayed in their work and in the works of other industrial relations specialists. For if it was not, if Fordism was in fact a system continuously evolving to accommodate new markets, new machines, and new workers, then we can see that Fordism is less the product of a particular set of production technologies or market forces and more a function of managerial drive to strengthen and extend its control of the work environment in capitalist society.

To examine this problem, this essay traces the social history of machine tool design and technical innovation in the American automobile industry from the 1900s through the 1950s, evaluating just how much has changed since the inauguration of this novel production system. The evidence suggests that a process of continual change has characterized the Fordist system but that managerial efforts to extend its control of machines and men has eliminated worker skills and displaced labor in the work process. To accomplish these tasks, a new breed of automotive engineers designed machinery and organized production to transfer skill more effectively from workman to machine. The result was the degradation, speedup, and elimination of labor, a chronic process that has continued in periods of both technical innovation and stagnation.

In his somewhat rambling, retrospective assessment of his many years at General Motors, Alfred P. Sloan offered an analysis of the relationship of the market to different stages in the growth of the American automobile industry.

> To set the scene, let me divide the history of the automobile, from a commercial standpoint, into three periods. There was the period before 1908, which with its expensive cars was entirely that of the *class* market; then the period from 1908 to the mid-twenties, which was dominantly the *mass* market, ruled by Ford and his concept of basic transportation at a low dollar price; and after that, the period of the mass market served by better cars, or what might be thought of as the *mass-class* market, with increasing diversity. This last I think I may identify as the General Motors concept.

Sloan's three stages of the automobile market corresponded to the different phases in the history of the technology of automobile production and in the history of work for automobile workers. These included phases where production relied on general-purpose machines, special-purpose machines, and semispecial-purpose machines. And after 1945, a fourth phase of automated machines must also be added to these three.[4]

Each phase of machine tool development required a different mix of worker skills and reflected a new market strategy. First, the new automobile industry started with the existing general-purpose machine tools that relied on the diverse and discrete skills of metal craftsmen to produce small numbers of automobiles for the luxury market. Second, around 1910, the Ford mass production revolution

introduced highly specialized single-purpose machine tools which
used semiskilled and unskilled workers to mass-produce automobiles for the common man. Third, when Alfred Sloan introduced the
concepts of style and a full product line with the production of a car
for "every purse and purpose" in the 1920s, the machine tool industry
responded with a new type of machine, the semispecial production
machine. A significant technical innovation, these new machines
were flexible high-volume production machines readily adaptable to
changes in the design of machined automobile parts. After a faltering
start in the late 1920s, automated machines, which contained limited elements of flexibility to adapt to style and market changes and
reduced the need for costly, unionized workers, finally appeared in
the automobile industry in the 1950s. In each phase, the new designs
of machine tools both permitted and facilitated fundamental changes
in the character of production methods and work processes.

## Craft Automobile Production

Automobile production, for what Sloan labeled the class market,
began in the mid-1890s and lasted until around 1908. In this phase,
production required skilled machinists who used general-purpose
machines to produce a wide range of different automobile components. During this period, craft methods of production prevailed in
the small shops and plants that manufactured limited numbers of expensive automobiles for wealthy customers. Skilled workmen, individually or in teams, machined the rough castings and then fitted and
assembled finished parts into components and the complete automobile. To be sure, some specialization existed in these small automobile enterprises, but even specialized workers tended to retain a considerable range of skills for their individual machine tool or assembly
operations.[5]

For skilled machinists, knowledge of the processes and problems
of production was a source of power at the workplace. And, compared with today, their knowledge was formidable. Fred J. Miller, a
prominent technical journalist in the 1890s, suggested that the proper
machinist had "the very highest grade of skill." In his mind, the
skilled machinist's work required patience, conscientiousness, inge-
nuity, and "the application of brains and discriminating skill." As
the aristocrat of the shop, the all-around machinist knew some me-

chanical drawing and mathematics, how to operate different classes of machine tools, and how to perform fitting, filing, and assembly operations at the bench. Of course, not all workmen actually reached this elevated ideal of craftsmanship, but it established the standard and set the tone for the whole machinist's trade.[6]

With Frederick W. Taylor, early automobile industry engineers and managers found such skilled workers an obstacle to their plans for a more systematic organization of production. W. K. Swigert, a production manager with the Stutz Motor Car Company, recalled automobile production methods in the early 1900s:

> In the old days, the workman was an all-round mechanic, very probably a journeyman who wandered from one place to another and who had to be skilled as an operator of a lathe, a milling-machine, a drilling-machine, a planing-machine, and all other machines, and as a bench hand, if he were to get a job, as no grinding machines, internal or external, were in use.

These workers did not have the accuracy or precision of the more modern machine tools. "The human element," Swigert continued, "entered very largely into all machine shop work, and, although the men were skilled mechanics, it was inevitable that much of the work was not exact." Regretting "the ever uncertain human element," men like Swigert looked to the production methods as a technical solution to their social problems.[7]

By the end of the nineteenth century, the division of labor and improvements in machine tool technology had already begun to alter and transform the machinists' skills. In his analysis of the "metamorphosis of the machinist's craft," Harold M. Groves, an economist, delineated two forces that undermined the traditional mix of skill —"the specialization of the machinist" and "the dilution of the machinist's skill." In the first instance, specialized machinists replaced the "all-around skilled mechanic" in the machine shop. Although they retained considerable skills, the new turners, millers, or fitters required less knowledge and experience, for they substituted "special skill for general [skill]." In the second instance, the specialization of machines diluted the skills of machinists. For example, Groves noted: "Lathes capable of only a few operations were substituted for the universal lathe. The new lathe operator found his task simplified. The circumference of his required skill and knowledge shrank a few degrees more."[8]

## Emergence of Fordism

The emergence of Fordism signaled the transition from Sloan's first phase of class production to his second phase of mass production. Sometimes labeled the "Second Industrial Revolution," Fordism was an expansion of production principles and methods already well established. Concerned with costs, efficiency, and productivity, the nineteenth-century "American System of Manufacture" had emphasized high-volume production, the use of specialized machinery, and the employment of less skilled workers. The Ford production strategy applied these principles with a vengeance to a complicated consumer durable good—the automobile. In fact, the automobile industry's second phase corresponded to Ford's decision to produce his "motorcar for the great multitude." With the introduction of the Model T Ford in 1908, Ford and his engineers inaugurated a production strategy that used semiskilled and unskilled workers to operate highly specialized single-purpose machines.[9]

F. K. Hendrickson, an engineer and designer with the Reed-Prentice Company, detailed the relationship between machine design and worker skills. He reported that the automobile industry "began to exert a great deal of pressure on machine-tool manufacture and design" between 1910 and 1913. The new industry, he reported, required sturdy machines to bear the strains of high-volume production: greater precision for use by less skilled workers, more power for more extreme loads, easier manipulation of the speed and feed mechanisms to avoid operator delay at faster production rates, more central gravity feed for lubrication, and numerous safety devices. These design changes made the machines usable by unskilled workers at high rates and volumes of production.

The new semiskilled and unskilled workers, who came from American or European rural backgrounds, often had neither the shop experience nor formal training that modern production required. Because these workers were very rough on unfamiliar machines, machines were built stronger with simplified operator controls. With apprenticeship training in eclipse, engineers designed the skill into machines for close tolerances. And, since these immigrants had never acquired the work habits so necessary for the care and maintenance of the costly new machines, critical maintenance operations such as lubrication were automatic. Hendrickson was quite specific about the reasons for these changes. In the design of his firm's automatic lathes, the idea behind single speeds and single feeds "was to eliminate the judgment of the operator and to predetermine the day's output." The changing social composition of the workforce, he noted, "comprise many who never saw a machine tool prior to their employment, and it is this class of help that made it necessary to safeguard every moving part of a machine to prevent them from getting injured." In the young and growing automobile industry, the design, construction, and operation of machine tools presumed the operation by and the control of unskilled workers.[10]

Such machines, the key to the Fordist production strategy, thoroughly transformed production methods and work processes. Based on the concept of a standardized Model T, they created a highly centralized production system, initially at Highland Park and later at River Rouge, for the "mass" production of an inexpensive means of transportation. From 1908 through 1914, Ford engineers developed the essentials of Fordism: the extensive use of single-purpose machine tools, the "progressive" production and assembly of automobile parts and components, and the relatively high pay that accompanied the arduous work regime. As a consequence, automobile work was radically and thoroughly transformed. Except for tool room workers, maintenance workers, and set-up men, few vestiges of the traditional craft skills remained in the new automobile production jobs. For the majority, their work rapidly acquired the repetitive, routinized, and monotonous features of modern factory life.[11]

Conceived for the mass market, the Model T's standard design meshed well with then current changes in machine tool technology. Since success in such a market assured an increasingly higher volume of production, Ford managers were able to replace the standard general-purpose machine tools, which used the varied skills of machinists, with single-purpose ones, which rarely required any skills from machine operators. Two methods achieved this objective: first, they adapted the general-purpose machines for specialized production through the extensive use of jigs and fixtures; and, second, they either built or purchased single-purpose machines for high-volume machine work. Some were simple machines for the performance of only one operation on a part; others, such as indexing machines, were complex mechanisms which combined several operations. In both instances, the machines removed skills from production work on the shop floor. The more complex machines also reduced labor input. In either case, the result was the elimination of skilled workers from direct production in the automobile shops.[12]

To be sure, not all workers in large automobile plants saw a substantial reduction of the skills required for their work. With the proliferation of specially designed and specially adapted single-purpose machines, the tool room became an important refuge for the highly skilled machinist in the automobile industry. And, the new machine tools called for new kinds of skilled workers on the shop floor. Since most new production workers did not have the skills necessary to maintain and adjust the new machines, large numbers of other skilled workers were necessary to do this work. These included millwrights who located the new machines in the shops, maintenance workers who repaired broken machines, and set-up men who adjusted the machines. Moreover, the larger number of foremen and subforemen, who maintained shop discipline and shop production quotas, also had to know and understand the operation of the complex machines in their shops.[13]

In his investigation of the new automobile factories, Charles Reitell, an economist who investigated worker skills in the automobile industry, reported that such skilled workers constituted about 5 to 10 percent of the workforce in the early 1920s. He found "skill or long experience at the top and brawn at the bottom both greatly lessened. A lessening which has meant the transfer of skill from the trained workers into intricate and complex machines; and on the other side the brute force of physical labor transferred into the powerful and gigantic lifting, carrying, and conveying machines." The automobile shops and plants saw a dramatic increase in the proportion of unskilled "machine tenders" and "assemblers," who now constituted about 66 percent of the auto industry's workforce. These were the production workers, that is, the semiskilled and the unskilled workers, who became the dominant figures in American automobile plants.[14]

Although their numbers and proportion increased, production worker skills became purely manual activities. At machines, they swiftly and dexterously attached and removed castings; at assembly operations, they routinely repeated the same operation over and over again. In a 1916 study of Cleveland, R. R. Lutz compared automobile work to that in other metal working shops, noting the extremely specialized work in the new automobile shops and factories. Its causes, he believed, were "the simplification of work through the improvement of machine tools" and "the introduction of new methods of shop organization." Due to the general use of "automatic and semi-automatic machines," Lutz reported, "the head work in the shop is limited to that involved in carrying out simple instructions." In assembly operations, Lutz continued, "again specialization is carried out to the nth degree." Although he acknowledged that some jobs, such as transmission or motor assembly, required a "comparatively high degree of skill, " the remainder, Lutz concluded, "rapidly grades off to occupations that can be learned in a day or two of the type described by an assembler who, when asked what he did, replied that he 'assembled nut No. 5.' "[15]

Much as they might marvel at the efficiency of the new production methods, contemporary observers were also struck by the dehumanization implicit in early Fordism. "Nothing was made by hand, measured by the eye, or fitted by 'trial and error,'" noted Myron Watkins, a political economist who took several Detroit factory jobs in 1920. "The accuracy of the operation depends upon the machine; the man is the mere tender." And in a similar critique that would be repeated again and again over the next sixty years, Reitell declared, "Automatic machines put padlocks on self expression. The work of the modern-machine tender leaves nothing tangible at the end of the day's work to which he can point with pride and say 'I did that—it is the result of my own skill and my own effort.' "[16]

## Sloanism as Flexible Fordism

A critique of classic Fordism also came from within the industry in these years, although it would be put forward on grounds quite different from that of the humanistically inclined observers. By the early 1920s, automotive engineers had recognized the limitations of the single-purpose machine tool. They were expensive and inflexible, and in a competitive and mature market, automobile firms following the lead of General Motors, sought a production strategy that could accommodate relatively more frequent changes in style and a proliferation of product models.

Unlike Ford, which produced a single and essentially unchanging model from 1908 to 1927, General Motors engineers established a manufacturing enterprise based upon variation and change. Under the leadership of its celebrated president, Alfred Sloan, GM developed a mass production strategy flexible enough to accommodate the annual model change and decentralized enough to produce a full line of automobiles for "every purse and purpose." Flexible machine tools and flexible systems of mass production would be essential to implement this program. In other words, a production strategy based upon the idea of "flexible specialization" appeared much earlier than scholars like Piore and Sable have supposed.[17]

Even before the emergence of the full Sloanist marketing strategy, engineers, especially in the smaller firms, had begun to question the utility of Fordist machine design. In 1921, for example, A. J. Baker, a Willys-Overland research engineer, argued that, although the specialized machines met the requirements of high-volume production, they "faced the ever-present danger that a change of design may render the machine of no value whatever." Because they were designed to produce only one piece, "Such machines have no value when divorced from the original purpose for which they were designed." To resolve this problem, Baker called for a new middle range machine that used the unskilled labor of the single-purpose machines and contained some of the flexibility of the general-purpose ones. In effect, a basic Fordist idea, the single-purpose machine operated by unskilled labor, was blended with the idea of production flexibility.

Such machines, Baker maintained, would meet "the special needs of the automobile industry." Some machine-tool builders, he added, "have produced machine tools in which the feeds and speeds cannot be changed at the will of the operator but can be transformed at the will of the executive by the transposition of gears. These machines permit adjustments, but only by the set-up man." For the manufacturer, these new machines were adaptable and flexible. But, for the machine operators, they were "only single-piece machines . . . and they can be regarded as a perpetual asset even though the model, or the detail of a model, were discarded and another took its place."[18]

Frederick R. Heitkamp, an engineer with the Cincinnati Milling Machine Company, provided a name for these new machine tools in 1927—semispecial machines. At the time, he noted "a wide development in the use of semi-special machines." These machines were hybrids of the standard, general-purpose machines and the special, single-purpose machines; they were especially suited to the new requirements of automobile production. These new machines had a standard base, easy for the tool builders to manufacture, and then they were either built "entirely new from the table up" or required "only special heads or special spindle carriers," which matched the needs for changes in style for the automobile industry. They also had special fixtures to hold the piece of work to the machine. When a part changed, rather than scrap the machine, engineers and tool room workers altered its superstructure to perform the new work.[19]

In his description of one milling machine, Heitkamp detailed its operation: "The taking of all four cuts simultaneously, together with an automatic dog-controlled table feed and rapid-loading fixture, make possible better production with a single piece on the table of the machine. . . ." In other words, the semispecial machine both adapted to changes in design and functioned in the manner of a specialized machine. Heitkamp also listed several advantages of the semispecial machine: the reduced costs due to standard construction, the ability to change designs without scrapping the machine, and the capacity to build the new machines more quickly.[20]

Despite the development of the semispecial machine tool to suit the needs of a more flexible Sloanist form of mass production, the automobile production worker, that is, the worker who produced automobile parts in the sequentially arranged machine shop, did not see any improvement in the character of his work. The Sloanist flexible production system retained the Fordist features of routinized work and work processes; it remained monotonous, repetitive, and machine-paced. To be sure, the flexible, semispecial machine did move more skilled people into the automobile plant, for these new machines did require sophisticated skills for their design and construction and for their rearrangement, set-up, and adjustment. Theoretically trained engineers and manually sophisticated tool makers worked in the machine shops and tool rooms to design and construct the new machine tools. Moreover, additional skilled workers moved onto the automobile machine shop floor to rearrange, set-up, and adjust these flexible machines. Nonetheless, the transfer of skill drastically diluted the productive skills of the overwhelming majority of automobile production workers. As the new machine tool technology diffused through automobile plants and factories in the late 1920s and 1930s, the skilled proportion of the workforce never amounted to more than 10 to 15 percent of the total.[21]

## Depression and Wartime

On the eve of the Great Depression, American automobile production technology had reached a high level of sophistication. For example, the Milwaukee A. O. Smith Corporation completely automated the production of automobile frames in the early 1920s. Since the automobile frame was a relatively simple product, the latest mechanical, hydraulic, and electrical devices controlled the production machinery. In effect, the A. O. Smith plant was one huge and complex production machine. "At the time it was introduced," Edward Wieck, a Russell Sage Foundation research associate reported in 1939, "it was rated as capable of making all the automobile frames needed in the United States with the employment of only two hundred men." In the early 1920s, the automated plant had arrived.[22]

In another example, the 1929 National Machine Tool Builders' Exposition featured an automatic feeding device for an automatic machine tool. The device demonstrated how far the mechanical sophistication of production technology had progressed. *American Machinist* reported: "No operator is now required for this machine. A long runway holds a store of work and a two-arm work-feeding mechanism picks up one part at a time and brings it into position between two tool-holding slides, one of which carried turning tools, and the other grooving, facing, and forming tools, where it is held between centers." After the machine performs its work, "a second arm automatically moves up and discharges the piece on a runway carrying it away from the machine, while the first arm moves in a new part for machining." In the late 1920s, the robotics revolution had also arrived.[23]

But for the Great Depression, automated production would have spread quite rapidly through the major firms of the American automobile industry. However, mass unemployment in the 1930s had made all forms of labor relatively inexpensive compared to the high cost of the new production methods. To be sure, the problems of very large capital costs and relative inflexibility to changes in product design would have also limited the diffusion of new production methods. Nonetheless, the new mechanical, electrical, and hydraulic technical complex could be adapted to a wide range of industrial requirements. In fact, the decade of the 1920s had brought extensive mechanization to the American automobile industry, but the depression decade saw few innovations or changes.

In 1939, Edward Wieck interviewed numerous automotive production managers and technical experts in Detroit. His notes indicated
that many automotive managers and engineers emphasized a phase
of extensive technical innovations in the 1920s and a virtual absence
of significant innovations in the 1930s. Joseph Geschelin, an automotive journalist, reported:

> From 1920 to 1929, there was a tremendous increase in mechanization
> in the industry. The depression hit them all hard—there was almost a
> complete stoppage in machine tool buying—almost to a zero point. From
> 1930 to 1935 tool buying practically stood still—[there was] marked
> change in 1936 which is still continuing. Many plants have much of the
> same machinery they had 12 and 15 years ago.

Similarly, L. W. Haskell, a Dodge production manager reported: "The
big increase in mechanization was made after the war—say 1920
to 1929." During the Great Depression, automobile manufacturers
shifted away from the large and fixed capital costs of technology
toward the inexpensive and more flexible costs of labor. Put simply,
it was cheaper to hire men than to build machines.[24]

The next major change came with the rise of the United Automobile Workers of America in the late 1930s and its consolidation
in the automobile plants in the early 1940s. Because UAW successes
in the areas of wages, seniority, and work rules made unionized
labor expensive, automation reemerged as a genuine possibility in
the post–World War II era. While the historical roots of integrated and
automated machine production reached back to the 1920s, the more
immediate origins resided in the early 1940s. Like so much of American technical development, the automated machining line was the
product of "military entrepreneurship." At the Rockford Arsenal in
Illinois, the United States Army Ordnance Department conceived of
an automatic plant for the production of artillery shells in 1941. Government funds inspired what Erik Olberg, an industrial journalist,
labeled "[b]old and ingenious ideas that would hardly have received
a hearing in peacetime days. . . ."[25]

Conceived in the midst of the 1941 "defense" crisis, the Rockford Arsenal's automated production system mirrored the social and
economic concerns of the time. Military and management planners
realized several possible wartime labor problems: the high wages
for recently unionized mass production workers; the CIO militancy
of relatively unskilled production workers in the controversial defense strikes at Allis-Chalmers, North American Aviation, and Vultee

Aviation; and the prospect of severe wartime labor shortages. Consequently, Olberg noted, the Army Ordnance Department envisioned a production system where "practically all manufacturing operations would be performed by women, and hence, to facilitate the operations, the controls were largely through pushbuttons." In his description of the Rockford Arsenal, John Diebold reported that the loading devices and the machine operations "are monitored by girls who preside over large consoles of signal lights and switches." Despite later claims that automation would upgrade the skill of workers, the initial design conception seemed to involve the elimination of large numbers of costly male workers and their replacement with fewer inexpensive female workers.[26]

Essentially, the Ordnance Department created a mass production system for women workers. Since the unprocessed stock for the artillery shells weighed as much as 125 pounds, the Rockford plant featured innovative mechanical devices for handling the work. These machines moved stock from machine to machine without direct human intervention. Olberg explained:

> To avoid the manual handling of shells, two fundamental types of equipment were provided—first, a complete conveyor system for transferring the heavy projectiles from operation to operation; and, second, a machine, on the success of which hung the entire handling process—a mechanical robot that would pick the shell (or other part) from the conveyor, load it into the machine, and upon the completion of the machining cycle, remove it from the machine, and transfer the machined part to an outgoing conveyor.

For the most part, the conveyors and the "robots" were a continuation of technological trends, already well established in the late 1920s.[27]

## Postwar Automation

After World War II, the UAW had become firmly entrenched in the principal firms of the automobile industry. From the manufacturers' perspective, significant labor problems plagued the industry of industries. During the largest strike wave in American history, unionized automobile workers were again on the march. They forcefully challenged management rights to set the pace of production, make work rules unilaterally, transfer workers, establish car prices, and regain wages lost from wartime inflation. Led by the imaginative Walter

Reuther, the UAW again took on the formidable General Motors Corporation in 1945. "To most close observers," Leonard Westrate noted in *Automotive Industries*, "the present struggle is much more fundamental and significant than the strikes over collective bargaining in 1937." The basic issue was "giving labor a measure of control over wages, prices, and profits." And, Westrate concluded that General Motors "is fighting the battle for all American industry and the free enterprise system."[28]

In the end, General Motors officials drew the line on the question of management rights, but they made some concessions on wages and benefits. At the same time, automobile managers and engineers began to consider replacing workers with machines and further investing in more modern production equipment and plant facilities. The experiments at the Rockford automatic factory provided the model for future production methods in the automobile industry; the new production technology promised both technical control over the workforce and economic relief from the high union wages. When automobile manufacturers sought to replace workers with machines, they picked up where machine-tool builders left off on the eve of the Great Depression.

In 1946, shortly after the bitter strike, the General Motors Corporation introduced the first successful automated transfer line in an American automobile factory in its Buick engine plant. Joseph Geschelin, an automotive journalist, described the Buick transfer line as "one of the first major changes in manufacturing technique to be found in the industry—the transfer process line for the machining of cylinder blocks." After the war Buick managers decided to use reconversion tax breaks to start from scratch and modernize production facilities. Their objectives included increased productivity, lowered costs, and improved quality. The result was a "unitized transfer line" that contained transfer and standard machines, connected with rollways and conveyors. The transfer machines, which included Ingersoll, NATCO, and Greenlee products, were multistationed machines with individual tools that performed from six to nineteen separate operations on the cylinder blocks. Once placed in a transfer machine, a piece moved from tool to tool until it finished its sequence of operations.[29]

Although the Buick cylinder-block line reduced the human labor required for engine production, it did not eliminate it. Production workers still moved the work from one transfer machine to another. Geschelin reported: "each of the machines in the line is a self-contained and automatic unit connected to the next operation by a short length of gravity roller conveyor. This enables the operator to examine the work before he loads it onto the next automatic fixture station." The General Motors automated system required production workers to load the machines and inspect the finished work. Over the next several years, automotive engineers refined the technical processes to reduce the need for human labor.[30]

In the early 1950s, the Ford Cleveland plant demonstrated how far automated systems could go in automobile production shops. Located in the suburb of Brook Park, this new production complex became the symbol for automated manufacture throughout the world. Technical journals, academic studies, and the popular press featured the Ford Cleveland plant as the near realization of a long-standing dream—the workless factory. In a press release describing the new plant, Ford officials announced it as "today's nearest approach to a fully automated factory in the automobile industry." In their description of the new production system, they noted: "Giant arms and fingers of steel, directed by electric nerve-centers without human guidance, pick up, turn over and shift from one automatic cutting machine to another such large pieces as 180-pound engine blocks." Officials proclaimed that, like Henry Ford's original assembly lines, "the Cleveland plant is another milestone." It was, they believed, as significant as the original Ford revolution.[31]

The Brook Park facility was the result of an extensive and expensive Ford automation program. From 1946 until the mid-1950s, D. J. Davis, Ford vice president of manufacturing, reported that his firm had "invested almost $2 billion in new facilities and plant expansion. . . ." Approximately 25 percent of this amount went beyond the replacement and upgrading of equipment and toward new automation equipment. In fact, Ford officials had established an automation department in 1947, which first worked on stamping and then moved on to engine machining operations. "All of Ford's new plant layouts in recent years," Davis said, "have been based upon the use of in-line or transfer machines and mechanical handling devices between them wherever our studies have shown that their use is justified." The principal justification was the lower cost of the mechanical handling devices in comparison with the cost of labor. In other words,

Ford automation meant the mechanized movement of parts from one transfer machine to another and the elimination of workers from productive operations.[32]

Conceived in the late 1940s and constructed between 1951 and 1954, the Ford Brook Park facility consisted of three separate buildings—Engine Plant No. 1 (completed in 1951), the Foundry (1952), and Engine Plant No. 2 (1952). Each plant was designed to employ about 3,000 workers; each constituted an integrated production complex for the manufacture of Ford, and later Mercury, engines. In 1952, Ford officials described the original engine plant and foundry to the National Labor Relations Board:

> The Cleveland foundry and engine plants are the Employer's newest major manufacturing unit, and represent the beginning of a new era in the application of advanced mass production techniques. The extremely high degree to which automation and other forms of mechanization have been incorporated makes this establishment approach the category described in popular parlance as "Push-button plants."

The two additional Ford plants, they reported, "will constitute a highly integrated production operation, with complete interdependence in both scheduling and production."[33]

The Ford Cleveland plant, which so raised the specter of automation in the 1950s, was a realization of the technical possibilities first presented in the 1920s and later in the Rockford Arsenal. Until the Cleveland plant, automobile workers were essential to productive operations in the automotive machine shops. Even in the most modern plants, they were required to move the castings from machine to machine. Since operators continued to handle the work, they also managed to control productive operations. "Despite metalworking's progress in building and using the high-speed machine and the transfer machine," Rupert Le Grand, associate editor of *American Machinist*, wrote, "operators still generally handle loading, cycle starting, and unloading. The operator paces output." In the Brook Park plant, Le Grand continued, Ford engineers overcame "the failure to realize the true potential of modern machine tools and metal-removal rates." In other words, modern machine tools could cut metal faster than workers could load and unload the machines. Moreover, the use of automation produced "[i]mportant gains . . . in respect to the number of pieces that can be produced hourly and in savings of direct labor." Ford official Davis claimed that automation achieved 80 percent efficiency, whereas without automation "you would be lucky to get 65 percent efficiency in that line. . . ."[34]

The mechanization of handling materials was the secret of the Ford success in automation. If the earlier Rockford equipment stressed conveyors and "robots," the Ford automated production line used conveyors and "automation devices" for materials handling. In fact, Del Harder, the Ford official who coined the term "automation," used the term to refer to these transfer devices. "In the postwar boom," Rupert Le Grand reported, "Ford had to conserve jobs where human skill is needed, and it had to get more pieces through existing machines in a shift." Their method was the substitution of mechanical loaders for people. These loaders, or automation devices, eliminated worker intervention between machines on the huge transfer lines. Ford vice-president D. S. Harder complained of the human limitations in machine loading: "The speed of some of these machines is beyond the ability of man to supply it [sic] with materials and to remove finished products fast enough." In other words, people simply could not work as fast or as continuously as the Ford automation devices.[35]

At the Cleveland engine plant, the reduction in production costs was genuinely phenomenal. For the most part, the reduced costs came from the displacement of semiskilled machine operators and the increased speed of operations. In the automated Ford plant, sociologist Bernard Karsh noted: "one man runs a transfer machine performing more than 500 machine operations, whereas conventional methods required thirty-five to seventy men. Formerly 400 workers took forty minutes to turn out one engine block; now, under automated methods, forty-eight workers complete a block in less than half that time." Others described similar reductions in the required workforce for production operations. Karsh also described the altered social composition of the factory workforce: "There is left, on the one hand, the unskilled worker, the broom pusher, whose job may be too menial to automate and, on the other, the highly skilled worker who designs, constructs, repairs and programs the machine." Large numbers of semiskilled or unskilled machine operators disappeared from the Ford automated production lines. Ultimately, an important, and by the 1950s, well-paid, middle layer of the shop social structure disappeared from automated plants and factories.[36]

Among themselves, automobile manufacturers were quite honest about the displacement of workers in their automated plants. For example, E. J. Tangerman, the executive editor of *American Machinist*, interviewed a number of auto executives for a special issue of his trade journal. "Automation," one Big Three manager told Tangerman, "is any operation that removes a man from production." But upon reflection about the UAW, this executive added: "But don't pin my name on that. We have a labor problem to think of." To be sure, the displaced workers did not necessarily disappear from the automobile plants. Ford vice-president Davis told a congressional committee that only 6 percent of the total Ford factory jobs were automated and that expanded production permitted displaced workers to move to other jobs. Over time, however, the automation and mechanization of other operations resulted in a gradual erosion of production jobs in the automobile industry.[37]

## Workers and Automation

For the most part, the automation technology moved quite rapidly through the highly competitive automobile industry. Through the late 1940s and early 1950s, most automobile manufacturers, large and small, experimented with automatic transfer lines in their plants. To remain competitive, even the smaller financially insecure firms invested considerable amounts of capital in automation programs. Old, yet still familiar names—Willys-Overland, Studebaker, Packard, Hudson, Nash, Kaiser-Frazer—embarked on extensive and expensive campaigns to mechanize and automate their productive operations. Most likely, the economic shakeout, which resulted in mergers and bankruptcies in the 1950s and 1960s, was a consequence of heavy capital investments in the new industrial technologies. E. J. Tangerman noted that only Ford paid for its automation program out of its own earnings. General Motors went $300 million into debt. Chrysler borrowed $250 million, while the newly reorganized Studebaker-Packard and American Motors corporations each borrowed about $70 million. Furthermore, the pace of industrial innovation also quickened in the early 1950s. Not only automobiles but also other mass production industries began extensive campaigns to improve and modernize production methods. This faster rate of technological change on the shop floor accelerated fears and anxieties about the social impact of automation.[38]

While automation displaced production workers, it also increased the need for skilled workers to maintain the sophisticated production machines. In Ford Engine Plant No. 1, one analyst reported that skilled maintenance workers constituted 21 percent of the workforce, a significant increase over the conventional 5 to 10 percent. Although automation meant more skilled workers on the shop floor, it also transformed the character of skilled work. In older automotive machine shops, skilled maintenance workers in automobile plants were traditionally far removed from direct production operations, worked within strictly defined craft boundaries, and ι ad considerable autonomy in and control over their work routines.[39]

However, the new automated production systems attached skilled workers more directly to production work on the shop floor. The new situation of skilled workers, Ford officials related, constituted "a significant change in the relationship between production and maintenance employees. It has brought them closer together to the extent that they now merely play different positions on the same team." In other words, skilled workers became skilled *production* workers.[40]

But unlike the nineteenth-century craftsman, the new skilled worker had little control over the work process. Management fears of mechanical breakdowns, which could halt an interconnected sequence of operations, put added production pressures on the skilled workers who maintained the automated production systems. "Under such a system," Ford officials concluded, "it becomes essential that maintenance functions be synchronized with production so that such mechanical interruptions may be held to an absolute minimum." In automated plants, skilled work became an amalgam of production work and craft work.[41]

Furthermore, automated production systems eroded craft boundaries because they needed new combinations of worker skills. For example, the Ford Brook Park contract with the UAW called for two new job classifications—automation equipment operator and automation machine setter. The two new classifications required some combined knowledge of the machinist's, electrician's, and pipefitter's trades. According to the contract, the operators "will make normal tool adjustments and changes and will assist the Machine Setter on major changes." The operator received about 6 percent less than the setter. In other words, the automation machine setter was a slightly more skilled and higher paid classification. Frequently, union grievances broke out over the delineation of the boundaries between these two new job classifications or between one of them and the skilled trades. Often, when the company needed only one person to operate a machine on overtime, it gave preference to the machine setters since they could handle major mechanical breakdowns. Similarly, to maintain production on the automated machines when machines broke down, machine setters, or sometimes shop supervisors, performed the work of skilled tradesmen before the appropriate craftsman arrived; this created friction within the bargaining unit.[42]

In short, the longstanding Fordist principle of setting production quotas and standards according to the capacities of the machines continued to prevail. Because the machines worked faster than the workmen, workers had to keep up with the pace of the machine and keep the machine going even if it meant "overworking" the maintenance worker.

## Conclusion

In conclusion, Fordism was a complex social and economic strategy for mass production that continued to dominate the American automobile industry through the 1950s. Although its details have changed through the century, Fordism remained a managerial strategy for the control of workers and the reduction of labor costs. The classic Fordist paradigm existed for less than the decade after the mid-1910s; a more flexible Sloanist variation quickly superceded it in the mid-1920s. Sloanism was flexible Fordism—a production strategy that used adaptable semispecial machines for a modified and more flexible system of mass production. At the same time, Fordist social premises about work and workers prevailed in the design and construction of the new Sloanist production machines. For the most part, the people who worked at these machines faced the tedium of frequently repetitive but always machine-paced work, the dilution or elimination of skill in their work, and the reduction of the need for their labor.

Furthermore, as automated production became a reality in the 1950s, the design of machines continued along Fordist premises, especially if costly unionized workers might be displaced in the process. To be sure, the new automation systems sometimes rearranged the skills of some workers who became much more important on the shop floor. However, Fordist premises about the control of work processes and the reduction of costs still suffused and saturated management attitudes toward the installation of new technical systems. Of course, a 1950s automation hysteria gave way to the more sanguine promises of an enlarged economy in the 1960s and 1970s. Along with industrial expansion, the restructured American economy found places for those workers displaced by the technical erosion of possible jobs. As foreign competition threatened the American national and world automobile markets and as the size of the economic pie shrank, employment possibilities in the automobile industry eroded. Additionally, the automobile firms possessed short historical memories. Ford, which courted economic disaster with the inflexible mass production in the late 1920s, repeated the process in the mid-1950s with its large capital investments in relatively inflexible automated production systems. Because the firm forgot the advantages of Sloanist semispecialized production systems, the progress of automation stalled until more flexible, computer-controlled machines emerged. Possibly, the expanded use of computers and robots may indeed initiate a round of technical innovation as significant as the original Fordist one and its Sloanist and automated modifications of the 1920s and the 1950s.

Nonetheless, the automobile production workers will bear the weight of the American past, its technical history and its social traditions. For them, "labor-saving" machines have not eased their plight, but rather they have diluted skills, intensified work, and eliminated possible jobs. Despite current analyses which proclaim the possible "end of Fordism," the basic thrust of automotive technical innovation has been "the degradation of labor" in the twentieth century. And, unless the basic premises about production, machines, and workers substantially change, this most likely will continue well into the twenty-first century. In the end, people were, are, and will remain the most flexible element in the production process.

## NOTES

1. Harry Braverman, *Labor and Monopoly Capital: The Degradation of Work in the Twentieth Century* (New York: Monthly Review Books, 1974); David Noble, "Social Choice in Machine Design: The Case of Automatically Controlled Machine Tools, and a Challenge for Labor," *Politics and Society* 8 (1978): 313–47; David Noble, *The Forces of Production: A Social History of Industrial Automation* (New York: Knopf, 1984); Harley Shaiken, *Work*

*Transformed: Automation and Labor in the Computer Age* (New York: Holt, Rinehart and Winston, 1984); Michael J. Piore and Charles F. Sabel, *The Second Industrial Divide: Possibilities for Prosperity* (New York: Basic Books, 1984); Charles F. Sabel and Jonathan Zeitlin, "Historical Alternatives to Mass Production: Politics, Markets and Technology in Nineteenth-Century Industrialization," *Past and Present* 108 (August 1985): 133–76: David Gartman, *Auto Slavery: The Labor Process in the American Automobile Industry* (New Brunswick: Rutgers University Press, 1986); and Paul Adler, "Technology and Us," *Socialist Review* 85 (January–February 1986): 67–96.

2. Braverman, *Labor and Monopoly Capital*, 3–4.

3. Piore and Sabel, *The Second Industrial Divide*, 17; Charles F. Sabel, *Work and Politics: The Division of Labor in Industry* (New York: Cambridge University Press, 1982), 194.

4. Alfred P. Sloan, Jr., *My Years with General Motors* (Garden City, N.Y.: Doubleday, 1973), 172.

5. W. K. Swigert, "Modern Automobile-Production Methods," *Journal of the Society of Automotive Engineers* 21 (October 1927): 286–88, and Guy Hubbard, "Metal-Working Plants," *Mechanical Engineering* 52 (April 1930): 404–14.

6. Fred J. Miller, "The Machinist," *Scribner's Magazine* 14 (September 1893): 316, 318–19, 321; Fred H. Colvin, *Sixty Years with Men and Machines: An Autobiography* (New York: McGraw Hill, 1947), 41–46; "Glossary" in the United States Bureau of the Census, *Special Reports: Employees and Wages* (Washington, D.C.: Government Printing Office, 1903), 1168; R. R. Lutz, *The Metal Trades* (Philadelphia: The Survey Committee of the Cleveland Foundation, 1916), 14; and Noble, "Social Choice and Machine Design," 324–25.

7. Swigert, "Modern Automobile Production Methods," 287.

8. Harold M. Groves, "The Machinist in Industry: A Study of the History and Economics of His Craft" (Ph.D. diss., University of Wisconsin, Madison, 1927), 77–78.

9. S. Meyer III, *The Five Dollar Day: Labor Management and Social Control in the Ford Motor Company, 1908–1921* (Albany: State University of New York Press, 1981), 9–15; and David Hounshell, *From the American System to Mass Production 1800–1932: The Development of Manufacturing Technology in the United States* (Baltimore: Johns Hopkins University Press, 1984), 217–61.

10. F. K. Hendrickson, "The Influence of the Automobile on the Machine-Tool Industry in General," *Mechanical Engineering* 43 (August 1921): 529–30.

11. Meyer, *The Five Dollar Day*, 16–36, 37–65; Hounshell, *From the American System to Mass Production*, 217–61; Allan Nevins and Frank E. Hill, *Ford: The Times, the Man, the Company* (New York: Charles Scribner's Sons, 1954), 387–414; and Horace L. Arnold and Fay L. Faurote, *Ford Methods and the Ford Shops* (New York: Engineering Magazine, 1915).

12. Meyer, *The Five Dollar Day*, 24–29 and Hounshell, *From the American System to Mass Production*, 230–34.

13. Arnold and Faurote, *Ford Methods and the Ford Shops*, 41, 307–8; Lutz, *Metal Trades*, 14; and Sterling Bunnel, "Jigs and Fixtures as Substitutes for Skill," *Iron Age* 93 (March 5, 1914): 611.

14. Charles Reitell, "Machinery and Its Effect upon the Workers in the Automobile Industry," *Annals of the American Academy of Political and Social Science* 116 (November 1924): 39–40.

15. Lutz, *Metal Trades*, 22–23, 82, 83–84, and 84–85.

16. Myron Watkins, "The Labor Situation in Detroit," *Journal of Political Economy* 28 (December 1920): 846–47, 848; Reitell, "Machinery and Its Effect upon the Worker in the Automobile Industry," 41.

17. On Sloanism, see Ralph C. Epstein, *The Automobile Industry: Its Economic and Commercial Development* (Chicago: A. W. Shaw, 1928), 60–61, 102–5; James J. Flink, *The Car Culture* (Cambridge, Mass.: MIT Press, 1975), 171–75; Emma Rothschild, *Paradise Lost: The Decline of the Auto-Industrial Age* (New York: Vintage, 1974), 35–40; Sloan, *My Years with General Motors*, 171–93; and Hounshell, *From the American System to Mass Production*, 263–301.

18. A. J. Baker, "Selection of Machine Tools," *Transactions of the Society of Automotive Engineers* 17 (1922): 689, 688. See also Swigert, "Modern Automobile Production Methods," 288; and O. C. Kavle, "Fitting the Machine Tool to the Job," *Journal of the Society of Automotive Engineers* 19 (October 1926): 399–408.

19. Baker, "Selection of Machine Tools," 689. See also Swigert, "Modern Automobile Production Methods," 288, and Kavle, "Fitting the Machine Tool to the Job," 399–408.

20. Frederick B. Heitkamp, "More Semi-Special Tools," *Iron Age* 119 (April 14, 1927): 1074, 1072.

21. John Barnard, "The General Motors Tool and Diemakers' Strike of 1939," *Labor History* 27 (Spring 1986): 165–87. On the needed skills for the automobile industry, see H. A. Frommelt, "A Comprehensive Apprenticeship Program for the Automobile Industry," *Journal of the Society of Automotive Engineers* 20 (April 1927): 443–45, 446; and Norman G. Shidle, "Automotive Factory Labor Cost Cut 10 to 50% in Last Two Years," *Automotive Industries* 53 (September 10, 1925): 402–3.

22. A. O. Smith Corporation, "A. O. Smith Automatic Frame Factory—Fact Sheet," mimeo; "The Automatic Factory," *Fortune* 34 (November 1946): 160; A. W. Redlin, "Handling Materials in an Automatic Frame Plant," *Transactions of the American Society of Mechanical Engineers* 52 (1930): 101–5; and Edward A. Wieck, "Production Standards in the Automobile Industry," Automobile Industry Production Standards, 1939–1949, in File 3, Box 10, Edward A. Wieck Collection, Archives of Labor History and Urban Affairs, Walter P. Reuther Library, Wayne State University, Detroit, Mich. (hereafter cited as ALHUA).

23. "Noteworthy Progress in Machine Tool Design to Be Featured at the Cleveland Show," *American Machinist* 71 (September 19, 1929): 472.

24. Notes for interviews with Joseph Geschelin, November 4, 1939, and

L. W. Haskell, November 6, 1939, in File Interviews, Detroit, October–November 1939, Box 10, Wieck Collection, ALHUA.

25. For an early example of military entrepreneurship in nineteenth-century American arsenals, see Merritt Roe Smith, "Military Entrepreneurship," in Otto Mayr and Robert C. Post, eds., *Yankee Enterprise: The Rise of the American System of Manufactures* (Washington: Smithsonian Institution Press, 1981), 63–102. For a more recent example for the post–World War II period, see Noble, *Forces of Production*, 195–211. On the Rockford Arsenal, see John I. Snyder, "Exhibit B. Rockford Ordnance Plant," in *Automation and Technological Change: Hearings before the Subcommittee on Economic Stabilization of the Joint Committee on the Economic Report* (Washington, D.C.: Government Printing Office, 1955), 369–71, and John Diebold, in *Automation*, 73–83. Also Erik Olberg, "The Automatic Manufacturing Plant—Mass Production Shop of the Future," *Machinery* 52 (February 1946): 253.

26. Olberg, "Automatic Manufacturing Plant," 254; and Diebold, in *Automation*, 78.

27. Olberg, "Automatic Manufacturing Plant," 254.

28. Leonard Westrate, "With Collective Bargaining Established Union's Next Step Is Management Control," *Automotive Industries* 93 (December 1, 1945): 17. For accounts of the postwar labor upsurge see, William Serrin, *The Company and the Union: The Civilized Relationship of the General Motors Corporation and the United Automobile Workers* (New York: Vintage, 1974); Nelson Lichtenstein, "Auto Worker Militancy and the Structure of Factory Life, 1937–1955," *Journal of American History* 67 (September 1980): 335–53; Howell Harris, *The Right to Manage: Industrial Relations Policies of American Business in the 1940s* (Madison: University of Wisconsin Press, 1982); John Barnard, *Walter Reuther and the Rise of the Auto Workers* (Boston: Little, Brown, 1983). For contemporary management accounts of the UAW threat, see "Union's Usurpation of Management and the Threat to the War Effort," *Automotive Industries* 92 (April 1, 1945): 17–19, 56, 58; and Leonard Westrate, "Let's Have Some Responsibility on the Union's Side," *Automotive Industries* 94 (January 1, 1946): 17 and 96.

29. Ford had experimented with transfer machines in the 1930s. In 1932, it developed a two-station in-line transfer machine; in 1936, it used a seven-station Baird transfer machine to manufacture the drive train. However, these experiments did not immediately lead to widespread innovation in the Ford plant. William Abernathy, "Case 12/Extensive Integration of Engine Plants Using Transfer Lines" in *Productivity Dilemma: Roadblock to Innovation in the Automobile Industry* (Baltimore: Johns Hopkins University Press, 1978), 204–5. Joseph Geschelin, "Buick Cylinder Blocks Now Machined on First Unitized Transfer Line," *Automotive and Aviation Industries* 96 (February 1, 1947): 20–27, 62; and Joseph Geschelin, "Independent Units Protect Automatic Transfer Lines," *Automotive and Aviation Industries* 97 (October 1, 1947): 30–32.

30. Geschelin, "Buick Cylinder Blocks," 21.

31. The Ford Brook Park plant was prominently featured in James R.

Bright, *Automation and Management* (Boston: Harvard University Press, 1958). See also, for example, Michael Harrington, "The Advance of Automation," *Commonweal* 62 (May 20, 1955): 175–78; and Bernard Karsh, "Automation's Brave New World . . .," *Nation* 185 (October 5, 1957): 212–13. Ford officials quoted in Ford News Bureau, Press Release, March 30, 1952, in File 5, Box 97, Walter Reuther Collection, ALHUA.

32. "D. J. Davis Testimony," in *Automation and Technological Change*, 53, 61. On the Ford automation department, see also Rupert Le Grand, "Ford Handles by Automation," *American Machinist* 92 (October 21, 1948): 108.

33. Ford Motor Company File, Cleveland Corporate Files, Cleveland Public Library, Cleveland, Ohio. Ford Motor Company Brief, April 7, 1952, Case No. 8-RC-1519, et al., National Labor Relations Board, 5 and 6, in File Ford Local 1250, Box 5, UAW Region 2 Papers, ALHUA.

34. Rupert Le Grand, "How Ford Automates Production Lines," *American Machinist* 96 (March 17, 1952): 135, and "D. J. Davis Testimony," in *Automation and Technological Change*, 62.

35. Le Grand, "How Ford Automates Production Lines," 136–38; D. S. Harder, "Automation—Key to the Future," August 27, 1954, Address before Quad-City Conference on Automation, Davenport, Iowa; and Joseph Geschelin, "Engine Plant Operation by Automation," *Automotive Industries* 106 (May 1, 1952): 36. See also Joseph Geschelin, "Ford's New Foundry Combines Automation and Worker Comfort," *Automotive Industries* 105 (December 15, 1951): 42–44; Geschelin, "Many Automatic Machines in Ford's New Engine Plant," *Automotive Industries* 107 (July 1, 1952): 44–49, 90; and Geschelin, "Specialized Machine Tools for Lincoln Engine Production," *Automotive Industries* 107 (July 15, 1952): 44–49.

36. Bernard Karsh, "Automation's Brave New World," 210, 212. See also, Harrington, "The Advance of Automation," 176; and Ben B. Seligman to Victor G. Reuther, Memorandum, April 17, 1957, in File 23, Box 54, UAW Washington Office Papers, ALHUA.

37. E. J. Tangerman, "Why $1.1-Billion Was Spent on Retooling . . . and How," *American Machinist* 98 (November 8, 1954): 118; and "D. J. Davis Testimony," 61, 62–63.

38. Tangerman, "Why $1.1-Billion Was Spent on Retooling," 118. For the smaller firms, see Joseph Geschelin, "Studebakers's Modern Equipment for V-8 Engine Production," *Automotive Industries* 103 (December 15, 1950): 34–36, 103–4; and Geschelin, "Some Outstanding Operations at Studebaker V-8 Engine Plant," *Automotive Industries* 104 (February 1, 1951): 46–48, 100; Geschelin, "Willys-Overland's Latest Equipment for Car Production," *Automotive Industries* 106 (March 1, 1952): 38–40, 58; and Geschelin, "Special Equipment Cuts Machining Time," *Automotive Industries* 102 (January 1, 1950): 52, 78.

39. Hyman Lumer, "Automation," n.d. [c. 1956], 6, in File 11, Box 14, Nat Ganley Papers, ALHUA.

40. Ford Motor Company Brief, April 7, 1952, Case No. 8-RC-1519, et. al.,

National Labor Relations Board, 11, in File Ford Local 1250, Box 5, UAW Region 2 Papers, ALHUA.

41. Ibid.

42. "Automation Agreement," March 2, 1953, *Local Agreements between Local 1250 UAW and Ford Motor Co.*, revised 6/1/56, 16–17, UAW Small Contracts Collection, ALHUA. On worker grievances, see Grievance Review Board Discussions for cases 65 and 66, December 10, 1953, and January 6, 1954, and Union Brief to Umpire for cases 65 and 66, n.d., in File Ed Schultz, Board of Review and Appeal Cases, Local 1250, Box 5, UAW Region 2 Papers, ALHUA.

# 5

# "Matters of Mutual Interest": The Unionization Process at Dodge Main, 1933–1939

## STEVE JEFFERYS

A 1946 incident on Dodge Main's final assembly line underlines what was special about industrial relations at Chrysler.[1] Shop steward Jim Stern and his fellow second shift workers in the headlamp section were looking for any excuse to stop working and get to the ball game. Then a foreman asked Jim to cover another man's job, fitting the left headlamp as well as the right, an extra task he had occasionally done before. This became the required excuse: it would be dangerous to leap across the track. "Let's go!," Jim shouted to the twenty headlamp workers, and they took off for Briggs stadium. When he returned to work the following day the foreman commented to Jim: "Don't do that. They really come down hard on me when you do that." That was all. No discipline, just a plea from the foreman to stop causing him problems.

This incident was not an unusual part of shop floor life. In fact, it illustrates three features of Chrysler's industrial relations, at least until the late 1950s: management tolerated sectional strikes, viewed as a legitimate method of redress by many workers; collective bargaining on work loads was still located at shop floor level; and foremen and shop stewards were the primary shop floor bargainers. By contrast, the industry pacesetter General Motors never formally recognized shop stewards, and in the aftermath of the 1945–1946 strike it felt confident enough of its shop floor managerial authority to discipline several local officers for implementing the UAW's International Executive Board call for a two-hour protest stoppage against the Taft-

Hartley Act. Just a few miles away, local officers, plant committee members, and stewards in Chrysler's Detroit plants who also shut down production in the UAW-called protest not only were not disciplined, but they were also confident enough to threaten solidarity action if the dismissals imposed by GM were not withdrawn.[2]

Why was shop floor unionism more strongly based in Chrysler than in GM plants? This chapter focuses on the unionization of Chrysler Corporation, and especially upon the giant Dodge Main plant in Hamtramck, which employed roughly half of Chrysler's 60,000 workforce in the 1930s. Our story unravels the complex interaction of economic, social, and political forces in which managerial behavior is given a prominence often ignored by American labor historians. The argument here suggests that Chrysler managers were unable to come to terms with the social conflict of the 1930s and failed to make effective use of their growing economic power.[3] Management acted in ways which undermined its shop floor authority and legitimized shop floor bargaining. A minority of workers, radicalized by the clash between the workers' rights rhetoric of the New Deal and the dashed expectations of their own depression era experience, used these bargaining opportunities. At first tentatively, and then more decisively, they established a strong shop floor tradition where sectional bargaining and industrial action were legitimate and routine. At GM, by contrast, the radicalized minority was faced with a management that acted more carefully to avoid acts that might serve to institutionalize collective bargaining at the point of production. Finally, the greater legitimacy extended by management to shop floor bargaining in Chrysler during the years from 1933 to 1939 meant that workers' organization in its plants was also better able to withstand the bureaucratic, centralizing pressures of the post-1940 industrial relations system than were GM locals.

The argument is developed first by outlining Chrysler's financially successful navigation of the depression and its pattern of labor relations in the early 1930s. Then the years from 1933 to 1936 are considered, when under the influence of Section 7(a) of the National Industrial Recovery Act, Walter Chrysler met the threat of AFL unionism with a company-sponsored series of works councils. Under the influence of "Radio Priest" Charles E. Coughlin, these councils transformed themselves into the independent Automotive Industrial Workers' Association in 1935. Finally, the period from 1936 to 1939

saw unionists inflict two significant defeats on Chrysler management at the same time as they eliminated the influence of the Homer
Martin faction inside the International UAW. These victories for a
militant brand of unionism embedded a steward organization and
sectional collective bargaining in Chrysler plants as traditions built
in daily struggle. These were not work rules imposed from above;
instead, these specific agreements and procedures for mediating the
frontier between workers and management were fixed and constantly
renewed in conflict situations. It would take another twenty years
before Chrysler succeeded in uprooting them.

## Chrysler in the Depression

In May 1928 Walter Chrysler purchased the ailing Dodge Brothers
Company and its key thirty-acre Hamtramck plant, Dodge Main. This
was a well-timed and well-executed take-over. Overnight it created a
company that could produce a quarter of a million cars each year. The
new Chrysler Corporation was America's third largest automaker,
and with car sales increasing by 57 percent between 1927 and 1929,
the Dodge purchase allowed Chrysler to double its output and generate substantial profits to cushion it through the early 1930s. Chrysler
increased its market share as the depression wiped out many of its
smaller competitors; then it continued to expand its share from 1935
to 1941 (see Table 5.1).

By 1936 Chrysler's market share overtook that of Ford, making it
number two behind GM—a position it would hold until 1950 when a
long UAW strike allowed Ford to regain the second spot. The postwar
view of Chrysler, as a company that has been constitutionally a junior
partner to Ford, should not be read back into the 1930s. Then, the
two former GM managers who headed the company, Walter Chrysler,
and after 1935, K. T. Keller, proved expert at mobilizing productive
resources at the right market moment.

Chrysler's economic and financial success, especially after 1933,
gave its employees a self-confidence and job security still absent from
the industry as a whole. The 1933–1937 auto recovery created a particularly high demand for all types of labor in its plants. Between
1931 and 1941, sales of the leading Chrysler car, the Plymouth, rose
on average 25 percent each year. Sales of the two cars assembled at
Dodge Main, the Desoto and Dodge models, grew by an average of 21

**Table 5.1.** Chrysler Production,[a] Market Share and Profitability,[b] 1925–1945

| Five year average | Passenger car production (in hundred thousands) | Car market share (in percentages) | Return on sales, car and noncar (in percentages) |
|---|---|---|---|
| 1925–1929 | 316 | 10.03 | 11.16 |
| 1930–1934 | 292 | 15.51 | 0.34 |
| 1935–1939 | 724 | 23.14 | 8.36 |
| 1940–1941 | 907 | 24.24 | 7.95 |
| 1942–1945 | | | 6.13 |

[a]Based on new passenger car registrations from 1925–1934.
[b]Before tax operating margin as a percentage of net sales.

Sources: Chrysler Corporation, *Financial and General Fact Book*, June 1973; *Wards Automotive Year Book*, 1969, 79.

percent a year. By comparison, GM's leading car, the Chevrolet, saw sales rise by an average of just 8 percent a year and Ford's Model A and its successor, the V-8, had an annual average rise of only 4 percent.[4] Dodge Main regained its full complement of 30,000 workers in 1934, two years earlier than most other plants in the industry.

In part, Chrysler was the victim of its own success. It became ripe for unionization earlier than GM and Ford because the consistently high demand for its products stabilized Chrysler's semiskilled labor force and gave its workers enhanced bargaining potential. And, equally strengthened by this economic success, Chrysler's top management became more convinced of its own managerial structure, its marketing strategy, and its paternally authoritarian labor control system. The group around Walter Chrysler exuded such self-confidence that it did not consider drawing up contingency plans to deal with the changing national political situation and the possibility that its employees might demand recognition of a union presence.

Walter Chrysler's industrial relations policy was unexceptional in the late 1920s and early 1930s. It mixed antiunionism and parsimonious "welfarism." A "Good Cheer Fund" paid for company picnics and a legal advice bureau; after 1928, when he inherited the Dodge Brothers' marginally better provisions, Chrysler added a group life insurance package, free dances for employees, and a welfare department that might give a worker a small loan.[5] Although restriction of output among these unorganized workers clearly took place on occasion,[6] the experience of most auto production workers in the late 1920s was of unrestrained managerial authority. One Dodge Main worker reported in 1927: "In Department 66 only the bosses and their friends are working. The other workers are sent home."[7] And as the proportion of workers who were "separated" by their employer when they were laid off rose from 70 percent in 1930 to 99 percent in 1932, even the 10 to 15 percent of skilled workers who had previously been able to count upon being rehired became disaffected.[8] So, too, did declassed white-collar workers. John W. Anderson, a University of Wisconsin graduate, was hired as a metal finisher at Dodge Main on December 2, 1932.

> To hold my job I had to work continuously from 12 to 14 hours a day, seven days a week from the day I was hired until 7 p.m. on Christmas Eve. . . . On December 24 the foreman told me, "You're being laid off until further notice. We'll call you when we need you." During those 23 days I worked almost 300 hours and at 52 cents per hour I earned about $150. There was no premium pay for overtime or working Saturday or Sunday, yet we metal finishers were among the highest paid in the industry.[9]

During the worst years of the depression, the seasonal employment pattern dictated by annual changes meant that even in a survivor company like Chrysler, near-full employment might last just four or five months.

Total job insecurity was a fact of life as companies adjusted their labor force up or down according to last week's sales figures. But this insecurity was compounded by the political consequences of placing the control of the adjustment process in the hands of front-line supervision. Often foremen had the personal authority to recruit family or friends or workers from similar ethnic backgrounds.[10] If this internal labor market was insufficient, the foremen would pass on the word that the company was hiring and then queues would start to form outside Dodge Main's employment office at 3 a.m., five hours before it opened. Those lucky enough to get inside might have to wait until 9 p.m. to be told whether they were hired or not.[11]

In December 1933, a report on the Dodge Main drop forge department highlighted the two key areas of uncertainty for the workers: anxiety about employment and about pay. The peak employment in the department had been 250 manual workers; it was then 230, and in the "slow season" it varied between 75 and 130. Pay was equally volatile: hourly rates ranged from 54 cents to 96 cents, and, including the bonus, actual earnings varied from 65 cents to $1.85, while the hours worked each week also varied between 30 and 35.[12] Workers fortunate enough to get jobs found this still did not guarantee steady wages. John Zaremba recalled bitterly the way the piecework system operated at Dodge Main: "The bonus was a farce at all times. We never knew what we were going to receive as pay, whether it was going to be 50 cents, 61 cents, or 76 cents. . . . The amount of the bonus was a 'secret.' Everybody would work and work and work. It seemed the more we worked, the less bonus we got."[13] These uncertainties were compounded by the politics of the labor control system. The power to decide whether an individual was laid off or recalled, what rate and bonus a worker was paid, and his or her working hours, all lay with the foreman or general foreman.

Resentment about the arbitrary exercise of managerial authority over employment and pay was reinforced by the foreman's power of instant dismissal over a range of petty indignities. In the Dodge Main heat treatment department "it was a cardinal sin to speak during working hours to your fellow workers."[14] Gertrude Nalezty started in Dodge Main's first floor wire room in 1934: "Before the union you had to work fast. The supervisors were on your back all the time. Once the whistle blew you could say 'Good morning' or 'Good afternoon,' but that was that. You couldn't talk to one another while you worked."[15] The grievances were considerable; thus, as Chrysler hired workers for longer periods and then tended to rehire them again for the next year's models, from 1933 through 1937, it was quite likely that the most articulate of its employees would start to investigate ways to reduce the arbitrariness and insecurity of their situation. But what transformed this potential into a reality? Who were these articulate employees? Why was their collective response to create an enduring shop steward structure?

## From Works Council to Union

President Franklin D. Roosevelt's election victory in November 1932 proved a critical development which legitimized the hopes of many workers that they might attain the same citizenship rights within the factory as within civil society. The Democratic share of the Detroit vote went up by over half: from 37 percent in 1928 to 59 percent.

The impact of the massive migration from rural areas in the 1920s and the coming of political age of the second generation of "new" pre-1914 immigrants had made itself felt. They now expected results. So, too, did the key layers of young activists who emerged in the auto industry in the mid-1930s: the white collar workers declassed by the depression into menial, repetitive manual jobs, and those workers whose previous skilled jobs or European origins had already given them a taste of unionism.

At Dodge Main the link between the expectations raised by the New Deal and the new spirit on the shop floor was forged by the organizational skills and perspectives of these last elements. These future UAW leaders included college graduates Richard Frankensteen and John Zaremba; Harry Ross, whose father had wanted him to go to college; former businessman Leon Pody, who had been ruined in the depression; and Irish immigrant Pat Quinn.[16] What made men like these play a key role in unionizing Dodge Main was not any particular job or skill: Zaremba worked in the heat treatment department, Ross on the cushion line, and Frankensteen in the large trim department. None of these key figures in Dodge Main's first mass union had served apprenticeships as skilled workers. What they shared was not a sense of being deskilled but personal frustration, organizational talent, and a responsiveness to the personal and political indignities management was forcing on them and other young workers.[17]

The Briggs strike of March 1933 was the first sign that auto workers could be mobilized,[18] and when Roosevelt signed the National Industrial Recovery Act (NIRA) in June, many more rights-conscious workers saw this as legitimizing collective activity. A forty-eight–hour strike of dingmen (highly skilled metal repairmen) at Dodge Main was followed in September by the inaugural meeting of an AFL federal local. Nineteen Dodge workers attended a Sunday afternoon meeting where the AFL auto organizer, John Panzner, extended a Federal Labor Union charter and organized the election of officers. Jack L. Andrews, elected vice president, wrote the names of those present on a blackboard so they could get to know each other.[19] Andrews was also a company spy employed for Chrysler by Corporations Auxiliary. Chrysler's hostility to these early organizing moves was made clear eight days later when the five workers from the fifth floor trim department cushion line who attended the meeting were all fired. Harry Ross recalled his foreman coming up to him and his partner on the cushions, a man who had worked twenty years at Dodge Main, asking: "What have you two guys been doing? I have just got orders to fire both of you." Zaremba survived; he had told the meeting a fictitious name.[20]

Nonetheless, the impetus to union membership engendered by the NIRA's Section 7(a) did force the business community to give a more serious consideration to labor policy. U.S. management's principal ideological objection to unions in this period was antipathy to the idea of "outsiders" participating through collective bargaining in a company's internal decision-making process. The National Association of Manufacturers distributed a notice for its members to post in their factories telling workers it was not the NIRA's intention that "employees should pay money into any organization."[21] Instead most major employers responded to the NIRA by launching their own company union works council schemes.[22] This development was indirectly backed by Roosevelt in March 1934 when he imposed a settlement of a threatened AFL auto strike with a formula that "favors no particular union or particular form of employee organization or representation."[23] But if the trend to company unions was widespread, the degree of managerial forethought involved, as well as the form and content of the various schemes, differed significantly from company to company. For example, the principal architect of Chrysler's works council scheme was Walter Chrysler, acting on personal intuition, but the GM plan emerged from a July 1933 meeting of divisional managers and reflected its commitment to management-by-policy.

The Chrysler scheme offered workers considerable participation in decision making. Walter Chrysler put his personal imprint on the plan launched in October 1933: "As a former shop-worker I have long looked forward to the time when the Employees and the Management of the Chrysler Corporation would sit down around a table to discuss and decide matters of mutual interest to all of us."[24] The plan purported to give workers "an equal voice with the Management in deciding jointly all matters affecting wages and working conditions." On the Dodge Main Joint Council decisions were to be taken by two-thirds majority vote at monthly meetings held between fifty-three elected workers and fifty-three appointed supervisors and staff.[25] A secret referendum on the plan showed 95 percent of the workforce in favor. The first employee representative elections were held early in 1934.[26]

GM had been a member of the post–World War I big business Special Conference Committee that generally favored the works council form of employee representation.[27] But before 1933 it had only implemented a pale imitation in its Flint Mutual Association. When Section 7(a) forced labor relations to the center of policy making, GM's divisional managers met immediately to discuss its implications, and they drafted a works council scheme involving a maximum of six or seven representatives that GM then imposed without an employee vote.[28] The following year GM's policy statement on labor-management relations made it clear that its endorsement of works councils did "not imply the assumption by the employee of a voice in those affairs of management which management, by its very nature, must ultimately decide upon its own responsibility."[29] The door was firmly closed against workers' expectations of significant concessions. Although many GM workers who played important roles in the early UAW gained their first experience of facing management on the works councils, the GM company unions did not themselves develop into genuine bargaining forums.[30]

However, Chrysler's company union scheme was very important in shaping the subsequent growth of collective bargaining and unionism. The Joint Council helped to identify and then bring together a sizable element of the Dodge Main plant's more articulate workers. Meetings of the fifty-three elected workers' representatives gave the different areas of the highly concentrated plant a unity they might otherwise have had considerable difficulty establishing. And in what was to serve as a model for the rights of shop stewards, the scheme also gave the representatives time off their work if they felt it necessary for "the normal discharge" of their duties.[31] It also allowed them to meet independently, separate from the management's Joint Council members. At such a meeting the first major step to a full union organization of the plant was taken.

The move to organize a plant-based union at Dodge Main followed nearly eighteen months of frustration for the workers' representatives on the Joint Council. District 23 employee representative Zaremba recalled bitterly that "it was nauseating for us to listen to the company recite about holes to be repaired in the floors and windows to be repaired in the departments."[32] Frankensteen had worked at Dodge Main from 1926 to 1928 while attending night school and, unable to get a job after graduating from the University of Dayton, found himself back in the trim department in 1933. Elected District 7 employee representative in 1934, he later remembered: "As for the Works Council, we bargained for clean windows and floors without grease, and many things that were important but meaningless in take-home pay. When it came to dollars and cents, when it came to economics, we were powerless."[33]

Chrysler's response to the aspirations of its more articulate workers was a blank refusal. Dodge Main general manager and Chrysler vice-president for manufacturing W. J. O'Neill told the representatives in May 1935: "I don't want you fellows to think because you don't get a 15 percent increase, and 65 cent rate, that this isn't Collective Bargaining."[34] But that was exactly what they did think—particularly when two months later management sacked the chairman of the employee representatives' committee for making "a slur on the President of the Chrysler Corporation" by asserting that the company's plea of hard times was a sham because "there were hidden profits."[35] Instead of being a forum for management-labor togetherness, the Chrysler works councils fostered antimanagement resentment among those most actively involved. Even when several staff representatives used the cover of the secret ballot to vote with the manual workers for a 10 percent rise in earnings, thereby winning the coveted two-thirds majority, O'Neill summarily rejected it.[36] The works councils legitimized the articulation of collective *demands*, but Chrysler management continued to deny the right to collective *bargaining*.

In Detroit during 1934 and early 1935, one man symbolized the struggle for the social justice denied to Dodge Main's employee representatives: Father Charles E. Coughlin. Canadian-born and educated, Coughlin had been broadcasting sermons on Detroit radio since 1926. By the early 1930s "the radio priest" reached as many as forty million Americans with his blend of social justice and anticommunism. He was known as a strong Roosevelt supporter who told his listeners: "The New Deal is Christ's Deal." By mid-1934, however, Roosevelt had begun to distance himself from the unpredictable and demagogic priest. Coughlin responded by forming the National Union for Social Justice; its aim was "to organize for social united action which will be founded on god-given social truths." In Dodge Main Coughlin's audience included thousands of native-born Catholics like Frankensteen, semiskilled English-speaking Polish immigrants, and even many native Protestant Americans attracted by both his denun-

ciation of the auto companies and his fulsome anticommunism.[37] It
was quite natural that in the winter of 1934–1935 a number of Dodge
Main employee representatives sought Coughlin's advice. Soon regular Friday night meetings were being held at Coughlin's home, and
Coughlin, who opposed the "racketeers and gangsters" of the AFL,
encouraged Dodge Main workers to use the Joint Council to form an
"independent" union based on the principles of his own National
Union. In April 1935 these employee representatives met on their
own, on company time, inside Dodge Main and decided to issue dues
cards for the Automobile Industrial Workers' Association (AIWA). Its
objects were:

> To promote the interests of those engaged in the automotive and allied
> industries by improving working conditions, by fostering better coopera-
> tion between employers and employees, and by promoting and fostering
> legislation tending to better the welfare and interests of the said em-
> ployees.[38]

Coughlin's AIWA was free of communist contamination: it offered a
legitimate, "respectable" form of unionism under the flag of social
justice; and it was only a step away from Chrysler's own Joint Council.

The new association appealed both to skilled native Americans
who felt Chrysler was depriving them of any basic control over their
lives and to second-generation Polish immigrants, the largest ethnic
group of Dodge Main workers, who were attracted by Coughlin's
Catholic reformism. A July AIWA rally attracted 30,000 to Detroit's
Belle Isle to hear Coughlin and Frankensteen; and by the end of 1935
its membership in Chrysler plants was about 10,000. In contrast, total
UAW membership in GM plants at the time was only a few hundred.
The Coughlin credentials were a key to its success. But so were its
low dues and clear industrial orientation: members paid 25 cents a
month instead of the $1.00 the AFL demanded. Anyone could join,
and everyone in the same department would be in the same local. Excluded, however, were the one to two thousand black workers whom
Chrysler employed in the foundry and in cleaning jobs.

Because of the AIWA's strength members of the rump AFL federal
local, like Harry Ross and John Zaremba, paid dues to both unions,[39]
and early in 1936, their presence inside the AIWA leadership, combined with Coughlin's growing ambition, paved the way for a merger

between the AIWA and the new UAW. Coughlin urged amalgamation at the April 1936 South Bend UAW convention,[40] and—although a sizable 35 percent voted "no" in a union referendum[41]—all the AIWA Dodge locals met together with the tiny UAW Local 3[42] in August 1936 "to form one big union of the entire plant."[43] The AIWA members were approximately one-third of the UAW's total national membership at this time and provided the new expanded union with a higher union density and greater continuity of tradition than existed elsewhere— some six months *before* winning recognition.

At the time of the AIWA-UAW merger the president of Chrysler Corporation was K. T. Keller, although Walter Chrysler was still active in the wings as board chairman until 1938. Like Chrysler, Keller was a former GM manager who shared a strong antipathy to union organization. He was determined to move quickly to contain the new union. Foremen throughout Dodge Main were given special forms on which to list workers they believed should not be recalled on the 1937 models, and on August 26, 1936, 3,000 workers were sent letters saying they would not be called back. Among them were dozens of key AIWA-UAW activists who were beginning to function as de facto shop stewards. Harry Ross, Local 3's recording secretary, was fired for the second time. Keller had, however, underestimated the widespread support existing for the AIWA-UAW in the plant. A month later, when the other production workers were recalled, Local 3 mounted a leafletting campaign on the theme, "What security have you? None unless you act NOW," and then followed it up with a series of afterwork departmental meetings to take strike votes: by October 12 eight important departments had voted to strike with just eleven workers opposed.

Management faced a dilemma. At a time when Chrysler could sell every car Dodge Main built, was it worth risking immediate profits to defeat a union that nationally still had under 50,000 members? Keller decided not. On October 16, 1936, he announced the recall of all 1933 seniority workers, including those previously "separated." In the following three weeks the company recalled all 1935 men as well and— three years ahead of GM—agreed to pay time and a half for overtime.[44] Without appreciating the significance of his actions, Keller had legitimized shop floor unionism at Dodge Main. Workers who had previously supported management and supervisors who had always ruled without any fear of workplace resistance were told that the union was now a force with which management would bargain. Foremen had to live with workers they had fired as troublemakers just ten weeks before.

This important union victory preceded President Roosevelt's 1936 landslide reelection by only a few weeks and helped contribute directly to the rapid shift in prounion consciousness that occurred in the winter of 1936–1937.[45] Roosevelt's reelection and the election of prolabor governors like Frank Murphy in Michigan, however, did more than encourage workers in the belief that their demands for citizen's rights inside the plants were justified: it also represented a sharpening ideological crisis for management. The electoral confirmation that massive support existed for the New Deal strengthened those elements in the business community arguing for some form of pluralistic industrial relations system, and it meant that for at least several months management would be unable to rely upon the state apparatus to police labor on its behalf. Against this political background of labor strength and managerial weakness UAW activists seized the opportunity to move decisively against GM and Chrysler.

## 1937 Sit-down

At General Motors the minority involved in the sit-down was very small. At the center of the strike in Flint less than 10 percent of the city's 47,000 GM workforce were in the UAW in December 1936 when the sit-downs began.[46] The numbers occupying the Chevrolet No. 1 plant varied from "over one thousand on some days . . . to a low of 90 on one occasion," and the Michigan National Guard reported 450 workers inside the No. 2 plant on January 5, falling to 17 on January 26, 1937.[47] In the second wave of GM sit-downs that occurred briefly in Detroit, GM's plant guards ensured no one could join or rejoin the sit-down if he or she left. One account suggests only 208 workers sat inside at Cadillac, 49 at Fleetwood Fisher Body, and 96 at Guide Lamp.[48]

The four-week Chrysler strike began on March 8. At the time some 11,000 to 13,000 of the 67,000 Chrysler workers were already signed up in the UAW, and of these as many as 6,000 may have taken part in the sit-down strike itself.[49] Department 76, the body-in-white, claimed the "best record for any group in Dodge Main" for participation in the sit-down. "Over one-third of its total membership sat in voluntarily," reported the *Dodge Main Strike Bulletin*.[50] But even this was a distinct minority. In Chrysler plants, as at GM, the sit-down tactic was used because it let a minority exercise greater strike power than if it had left the plant. The *Dodge Main Strike Bulletin* explained: "If they [the workers] went outside, some *scab* might come in and take their jobs. That is why we are staying in: *to protect our jobs.*"[51]

When recognition was finally conceded by Chrysler's management, the former AIWA shop floor activists understood Chrysler's capitulation to the UAW as a legitimization of their own efforts. At Chrysler union recognition was seen as an achievement struggled for by a large number of workers; this sharply contrasted to the situation in GM plants, where both the number of union members prior to the sit-downs and the level of involvement were much lower. The relatively high density of union members in Chrysler plants by the winter of 1936–1937 also meant that the minority who participated in the Chrysler sit-down was relatively more independent of the UAW international than was the movement of the dedicated few against GM.

A critical examination of the number of workers involved in the GM and Chrysler 1937 sit-down strikes helps establish two points: first, the contrast in the penetration of auto unionism in the two companies; and second, the prevailing weakness of shop floor unionism at what is often celebrated as its greatest moment. By pointing to different degrees of union *weakness* in the 1930s, this perspective helps demystify the dichotomous post–sit-down situation: at GM the institutional recognition of the UAW was accompanied by the strengthening of managerial authority on the shop floor; at Chrysler workers continued to powerfully contest management prerogatives until their resistance was finally overcome during a major recession in the late 1950s. The reality bears little resemblance to the oversimplified contrast of a militant pre–World War II period and a postwar "labor truce."[52]

Indeed, most sit-down strike participants did not see their actions as radical; and, of course, the majority of workers who passively supported the active minority did not either. Above all, they demanded abolition of the piecework system and institution of a "fair" seniority system. Most members of the business community viewed such union goals as an outrageous infringement of managerial absolutism, but, as a core of progressive managers close to the New

Deal pointed out, they did not challenge the substance of managerial control. They were simply demands that foremen act in a "fair,"
nonarbitrary way to provide greater job and pay security. In a sharp
contrast to the situation in the British auto industry in the 1950s
and 1960s when union density increased as management succumbed
to demands for greater shop floor bargaining opportunities between
workers and foremen over layoffs and higher piecework rates, in
the United States there was little pressure from workers to manipu-
late either piecework rates or the short-run labor market in their
favor. Both the sit-down tactic and the subsequent union effort to rationalize seniority and layoff policies arose from the weakness of the
worker's position in industrial America rather than from confidence
in labor's market power.

The chief reason for the remarkable participation of Chrysler
workers in the sit-down strike and for their two-decade hold on shop
floor power lay with the steward system they had erected even before
the sit-down strike. In December 1936 Local 3 agreed to hold departmental meetings throughout the plant to "elect their Chief Steward,
stewards and captains. Each elected man to be given a 30-day trial,
if not competent then he should be removed."[53] In January 1937 the
Chrysler local started regular joint meetings of chief stewards (black
buttons) and sectional stewards (blue or white buttons). By March
there were 180 chief stewards and probably around 500 sectional
stewards in the plant. The steward system was firmly in place, and
in the last Joint Council election in February 1937 even nonunion-
ists voted overwhelmingly for the employee representative-steward
structure: UAW stewards won forty-seven of the fifty-three districts.[54]
When a phone call told John Zaremba inside Dodge Main that the sit-
down was on, all he had to do was to signal his blue button stewards:

> "Shut it down!" From my department it snicked around. . . . It crossed
> the docks again. People were waiting for a signal there too. "Shut her
> down!" And this is just how it happened. Within five minutes after the
> signal was given from the outside, there was not one piece of machinery
> moving.[55]

These Dodge Main stewards played a key role in the strike: they
stopped the plant, and then they ran the sit-down. The chief stewards became the Dodge Strike Committee and immediately took the
decision to bar the superintendents, foremen, and office staff and,
after two weeks, to throw out the security guards.[56] They also led

the opposition to UAW president Homer Martin's insistence that they agree to the court injunctions Chrysler secured against the sit-down.[57] When, after several votes, they finally left the plant, the stewards continued to organize extremely vigorous picketing and interrogate workers suspected of spying for Corporations Auxiliary; meanwhile, a flying squad operated outside the UAW-Chrysler negotiations in Lansing. These activities infuriated Martin who, on April 4, wound up all the Dodge strike committees. This, he claimed, was because they were "Communists" and "third degree methods were being employed in questioning suspected people." He also argued that the Lansing pickets "have by their actions delayed the satisfactory settlement of the present strike."[58] Both John L. Lewis, who led negotiations with Walter Chrysler, and Martin wished to settle as soon as Chrysler conceded the same terms as GM had a month earlier. But, since Dodge Main's Local 3 had already achieved de facto recognition, the Coughlinite activists there agreed with the communists within the UAW who argued that the union advantage should immediately be pressed further.

The communist smear was particularly inappropriate at Dodge Main. Not only were the activists there so many as to significantly reduce the influence of the customary handful of Communist party members, but the continuing right-wing and Catholic influence in Local 3 led to the strike committee's voting to ban communist literature from being passed out either inside or in front of the plant.[59] One of the few prominent Communist party members was the chairman of the Outside Strike Committee, A. J. Alden, and he received fewer than 1,000 votes in the May 1937 Local 3 election for president. Dodge Main's powerful shop floor union tradition owed less to the influence of the organized left than to its Coughlinite origins. The sit-down was legitimate in the eyes of most Dodge Main workers; as the strike bulletin asserted:

> The men in the factory seem to be real Americans, good citizens, some property owners. They want to have real collective bargaining which rightfully belongs to them and guaranteed by the U.S. Government. They want to have fair play with the management; they have Democracy within their Union. They want Democracy within the automobile industry as well as Democracy within the whole country.[60]

Shop floor life was being viewed through the prism of the New Deal. While the demand for "fair play" might seem threatening and com-

munistic to the business community, and while independent organization might appear communistic to UAW President Martin, Dodge
Main's workers viewed both as their natural rights.

Although the UAW was recognized by both GM and Chrysler after the
sit-down strikes of early 1937, the greater participation by Chrysler
workers and the 1934–1936 legitimization of works council/AIWA departmental representatives laid the basis for small but significant
differences in the strike settlements. Both GM and Chrysler insisted
that the word "steward" not appear in the written agreement. In
GM plants only small "shop committees" were recognized; but in
Chrysler plants all *existing* "district committeemen"—described in
the UAW version of the agreement as "chief shop stewards"—were
recognized for bargaining purposes alongside new GM-style "plant
committees." This effectively legitimized the existing steward structure, including its network of "regular stewards" who were still encouraged to "pass out grievance slips to those who desire them." In
practice Chrysler had erected a dual bargaining system in which both
the plant committee *and* the chief stewards were given authority to
bargain with foremen and general foremen.[61] The power balance between chief stewards and plant committeemen was still unclear but
would be determined in two stages: first, during the UAW factional
struggles of 1937–1939, when the issue was resolved in favor of the
shop stewards and sectional bargaining; second, at Chrysler itself
during the tumultuous "control" strike of 1939.

## Factionalism and Control

A factional struggle among the small number of UAW staff workers
and their supporters had broken out even before the ink was dry on
the GM and Chrysler contracts. The complex story of the 1937–1939
UAW faction fight has been told largely by top UAW and CIO officials.[62]
But from the viewpoint of the Dodge Main workers the defeat of UAW
president Homer Martin in 1938 and 1939 was much more than an internal bureaucratic fight for the spoils of office. It reinforced the influence of those within the union arguing for more shop floor bargaining
power and the right to take sectional strike action. This defeat was
particularly traumatic for the Martin forces at Dodge Main, whose
Coughlinite origins had made the plant Detroit's principal right-wing
stronghold before the faction fight erupted.

Dodge Main had several Communist and Socialist party activ-

ists, but at the onset of the 1937–1939 factional struggle their influence was small compared to the majority of organizing activists,
who were either center or right-leaning Democrats led by Richard
Frankensteen. Backed by the former AIWA vice president R. J. Thomas
(of the Chrysler Jefferson Avenue plant), Frankensteen fully supported Martin's summer 1937 purge of the radical UAW staffers.
When the national-level Progressive and Unity caucuses were established shortly thereafter, representing the Martin-Frankensteen and
Mortimer-Reuther groups respectively, local faction organizations appeared at Dodge Main as well. The Progressive caucus argued for
"responsible" unionism on the shop floor: "We will fight mercilessly
against any person responsible for using this [strike] weapon irre-
sponsibly or without authorization."[63] In contrast, the left-wing Unity
caucus stood for "enlarged powers for the shop stewards," including
"powers to decide on shop problems."[64]

This difference was crucial at Dodge Main. In theory, the strike authorization power rested in the hands of the Progressive-controlled
plant committee and Local 3 executive board, but in reality the chief
or blue button stewards, who negotiated directly with the foremen,
determined the union's industrial action policy. In July 1937 the
Dodge Main executive board warned workers not to attend "unofficial" meetings, a move aimed against the Unity caucus, and in May
1938 it called for the exclusion of blue button stewards from stewards' meetings.[65] The Unity caucus retaliated in verse:

> Hitler hides his face in shame
> His methods are so clean
> When compared to the tactics of
> The monster MARTIN-STEEN . . .[66]

And Dodge Main workers retaliated at the ballot box. In the 1938
local elections Martin supporters Frank Reid and Ed McCann kept
the positions of president and vice-president in Progressive hands,
but their slate lost six other seats on the twenty-four–person local
executive board.[67] When Frankensteen himself finally threw his lot in
with the Unity caucus in 1938 the already thin ranks of Dodge right-
wingers split: only five Local 3 executive board members voted to
support UAW president Homer Martin's suspension of Frankensteen;
by twelve votes to eleven the executive board rebuked Martin for this
action.[68]

On issues other than personal support for Frankensteen, the symbol of AIWA independence, the Progressives still held a majority, at least until R. J. Thomas also broke with Martin early in 1939, precipitating Martin's attempt to build an anti-CIO UAW. Yet Frankensteen's personal defection from the old AIWA-Progressive Local 3 leadership hit the right-wingers hard. His move appeared to endorse the view that Martin and the remaining Coughlinite Local 3 leaders were breaking with the already-legitimized Dodge Main pattern of shop floor bargaining backed by sectional militancy.

In November and December 1938, when the national factional struggle was reaching its height, the small Progressive executive board majority tried to restrict the power of the Dodge Main chief stewards. It ruled that "when a Chief Steward has completed his business with the Plant Committee members, he should immediately leave the plant committee room."[69] And later it gave the plant committee the veto of all industrial action by threatening disciplinary action against "any steward of Local No. 3 who causes or sanctions any interruption in production without first receiving permission from his officers of his Unit and the Plant Committee." Stewards could only initiate action with the written permission of "at least a majority of signatures of Plant Committee members."[70] This attack on steward organization proved disastrous: it lost the local Progressive leaders their activist backing at the very moment Martin precipitated a split in the UAW by suspending fifteen members of the International Executive Board. Martin's supporters in Local 3 then attempted to rig the big meeting that debated the issue by bribing black workers to vote for Martin; when this failed they tried to wreck the meeting.[71] The initiative passed to Dodge Main's Unity caucus, which put armed guards in the Local 3 hall and backed Local 3 Financial Secretary Harry Ross when he refused to countersign checks for the outstanding dues McCann tried to send Martin.[72]

The Progressives were routed in the elections for delegates to the Cleveland UAW-CIO convention in March 1939. Of twenty delegates the only Progressive elected was the Local 3 president, Frank Reid. And in the elections for new local officers that followed, the joint left-center "CIO slate," headed by Pat Quinn, swept the board. Not only were the Progressives who did not defect to Homer Martin's UAW-AFL totally discredited, but also their appeal to the local tradition, claiming their candidates as "active members of the old AIWA" and "proven Union Builders," fell on deaf ears. Even their anticommunist propaganda against the left-center slate failed to dent support for the slogan that "the CIO is Americanism."[73] When the National Labor Board election was held in September just 837 Dodge votes went to the Martin rump while 17,654 workers voted UAW-CIO.[74] The defeat of the UAW's most strident anticommunist, antisocialist, and procentralization elements was highly significant for Dodge Main. By reinforcing the local's militant, decentralized bargaining tradition, it provoked management to stage an unsuccessful challenge to the new system.

To forestall another UAW president from emulating Homer Martin's effort to centralize union powers, the International UAW-CIO convention in March 1939 had voted through a highly democratic constitution. Six months later, Local 3 followed with a new local constitution that explicitly confirmed the primacy of the chief steward over the plant committee: "The Plant Bargaining Committee shall not invade the jurisdiction of a Chief Steward, except at his or her invitation, or at the discretion of the Executive Board."[75] But it did not merely strengthen the departmental steward's status; the constitution also strengthened the control of ordinary members over their representatives. The constitution ruled that the departmental steward "cannot settle a grievance unless it meets with the approval of a majority of the union men affected" and called for the appointment or election of "at least one deputy steward for a group of 20 or less."[76] Thus, the outcome of the struggle at Dodge Main strengthened union structure and steward power among rank-and-file workers.

Chrysler Management was clearly horrified by this development. It was ill-prepared to live with the new local officers and the strengthened steward system. On the false assumption that the 1938–1939 sales trough would continue, Keller determined to confront the local in an attempt to regain the power to unilaterally determine production standards on the 1940 models. Like GM, Chrysler had refused to extend its agreement with the UAW-CIO for more than a month at a time after March 1939 on the grounds that it did not know which UAW it was really dealing with. Then in September 1939, when a massive pro-CIO vote by Chrysler workers ruled this argument out, management simply announced its refusal to renew the contract. Instead, company executives introduced a major production speedup at Dodge Main and other plants.

The confrontation began when Dodge foremen were instructed to refuse to bargain with the stewards: workers had to accept new standards or go home. After two weeks in which Chrysler closed whole departments for days on end and fired 105 workers, largely chief or blue button stewards, the UAW-CIO International Executive Board agreed to allow a Chrysler-wide strike vote over the Dodge Main speed-up. Frankensteen and Thomas, the new UAW president, saw Chrysler's challenge at Dodge Main as a threat to their own political base in the UAW and did what they could to ensure a total stoppage. At Dodge Main the vote was 13,571 to 1,324; and at Chrysler plants employing the other half of the workforce large majorities also voted to strike. The strike began on October 18 and lasted forty-five days. Unlike most subsequent disputes the issue of managerial authority was openly acknowledged by both sides to be at the center of the struggle. The top two union demands were: "a general wage increase with a bonus for afternoon and night shift workers," and "joint fixing of production standards by the corporation and the union."[77] In response Dodge Main's general manager, Herman Weckler, replied: "Production schedules are the management's function. You may as well know now that we do not intend to give your union control of production."[78]

By the end of November Chrysler was getting desperate. To Chrysler's surprise, GM and Ford were selling cars extremely rapidly as the 1940 model year turned into the start of the 1940–1941 car market boom. Keller decided something had to be done, and he authorized an attempt to break the strike by using Martin's UAW-AFL rump to mobilize a back-to-work movement among some of the 1,700 black workers employed at Dodge Main. The UAW had made virtually no headway in recruiting black members at this time; this was not surprising since it welcomed blacks as members in the foundry or as plant laborers, but it supported management's refusal to allow blacks to work in white production areas.

Some fighting took place between pickets and a number of black workers trying to enter the plant to collect paychecks still owed to them, and three days later a 1,000-strong police escort accompanied 181 blacks and 6 whites through a mass picket of over 5,000 that included local black leaders sympathetic to the UAW-CIO. The following day the number of strikebreakers rose to 430, but this was nowhere near the numbers necessary to mobilize a back-to-work movement among the white workers. While these events were unfolding on the streets, Keller came under massive criticism from fellow employers and from Detroit and national political figures for increasing racial tension.[79] With no end in sight and GM and Ford selling all the cars they could make, Keller decided to cut his losses. On the following day, November 29, 1939, Chrysler signed a contract with the UAW that formally recognized the union's steward system and institutionalized sectional collective bargaining.

The new contract legitimized job bargaining in workers' eyes as a *struggled-for* advance. Chrysler gave chief and assistant chief stewards super seniority, the right to move about their areas at will, and the right to leave work to confer with other chief stewards or the plant committee. The contract language was more ambiguous on production standards, but its declaration that standards should be established "on the basis of fairness and equity" according to "the reasonable working capacities of normal operators" opened wide the window of bargaining opportunity. This meant the acceptance of on-the-job bargaining, confirmed by a clause which gave foremen power to "adjust the matter" if workers (or their blue button stewards) complained the rate was too fast. If agreement were not reached at that point, the chief steward and departmental general foreman or superintendent would argue the case; if there were still disagreement, only then would the matter proceed to the formal grievance procedure.[80] Discretion was formally placed in the hands of lower level management. This group, without any training in labor relations, was subject to strong informal pressure from rank-and-file workers and now had to operate without the support of the "no strike" protection provided in the first two contracts. Little wonder, then, that the new plant newspaper born out of the strike, the *Dodge Main News*, crowed: "The workers are now allowed a say in the setting of production rates, one of the main issues in the dispute. Sole bargaining rights are granted, squeezing out the rump and other company unions. Seniority is retained no matter how long the worker is laid off. The no strike clause is eliminated."[81] Ten months later newly hired Ed Liska reported of the body-in-white department: "The foremen were very nervous about giving orders to the workers."[82] The frontier of control had shifted decisively in favor of rank-and-file workers.

## Conclusion

Restraints over Chrysler management's authority to determine labor costs—wage rates, shift payments, arbitrary allocation of hours of work—and important aspects of the labor process—speed, allocation of work, discipline—were considerable by 1940–1941. The frontier of control was defined by a vigorous shop floor union infrastructure that had, since 1933, built a system of "rights" that workers cherished and management accepted. Technology, production, marketing, and casual labor market conditions faced by GM and Chrysler before World War II were all roughly similar. But the differences in union organization and workplace labor relations between Chrysler and GM were already huge. GM's immense size had imposed on its management the multidivisional form that encouraged a wider input into labor relations policymaking than was the case at Chrysler, dominated by a large single plant. Highly reactive day-to-day decision making at Dodge Main became the next day's "policy" for the whole corporation. The interaction of Chrysler's successful, autocratic top management with a workers' political awareness fueled by the New Deal and initially organized by a Catholic priest created the dynamic for change. The outcome was a sectional bargaining tradition viewed by both management and workers as legitimate.

This tradition survived until the late 1950s. During World War II Dodge Local 3 withstood three Chrysler attempts to restore management authority. When it ran down civilian auto production in 1941, management attempted to reassert its control over the labor movement;[83] in 1943 it tried to take advantage of the cumbersome procedures of the War Labor Board to delay grievance handling and enforce new production standards,[84] and in 1945 it used a new time study technique to standardize how much "non-production time" each worker could take.[85] But each of these attempts failed; thus, when Chrysler resumed large-scale auto production in 1946 its prewar shop floor bargaining tradition was restored almost intact. In GM, by contrast, the union's defeat in the long 1945–1946 strike effectively removed any gains made by shop floor organization during the war years.

Strike statistics for the two companies in the postwar period reveal the extent to which shop floor control was still openly contested in Chrysler but suppressed at GM. From 1945 to 1959, the frequency of strikes not authorized by the UAW at Chrysler plants averaged 22.3 per year for every 10,000 hourly workers.[86] These were years in which the steward system remained the principal forum for collective bargaining in Chrysler plants. Over the same period at GM, where the steward system had never been strong and had not reappeared after the war, unauthorized strike frequency ran at just 1.1 strikes per year.[87]

It took the permanent loss of its ranking as America's second biggest automaker, the onset of declining profitability from the mid-1950s, and the retirement of K. T. Keller, the last of the corporation's key figures from the 1920s, to create the possibility of a major change in Chrysler's labor relations practice. The erosion of local democracy within the UAW from the late 1940s and the antilabor political climate of the Eisenhower period helped. But the catastrophic impact of the 1958 recession on the labor market—as deep as the one between 1979 and 1982—gave management the space and the confidence to pursue the new policy. Then Chrysler management was able to wrest control back into its hands and virtually eliminate section strikes and bargaining from its plants. That offensive began when management introduced new work standards on the 1957 models, claiming: "These standards are comparable to those of the same jobs at Ford and GM."[88]

The International UAW also found the easier production standards existing in Chrysler plants something of an embarrassment and, according to one Chrysler vice president, turned a blind eye to the offensive.[89] In 1958 the International responded to the deep recession in the auto industry by advising its locals to keep working without a contract, and Chrysler seized this opportunity to tear up the remaining custom and practice agreements that still restrained its right to manage. Ultimately, the Dodge Main workforce was provoked into a plantwide strike in December 1958. Despite the fact that eight other Chrysler locals were queuing up for strike authorization, the International let Dodge Main fight alone and then saw its defeat generalized throughout the corporation. The memorandum on production standards that ended the strike was a total management victory; it replaced the 1939 qualities of "fairness and equality" with the unchallengeable scientific truth of "time study." And it reduced workers' personal relief times down from anything between thirty to ninety minutes a shift to a standard twenty-four minutes.[90] After 1958 effective bargaining on work discipline was removed from the shop floor and restricted to encounters between middle and higher level plant managers, including professional labor relations personnel, and the International representatives and full-time local officers and members of the plant committee.

The emergence of unionism at Chrysler in the 1930s thus suggests a general argument about workers' collective organization. A dialectical process is at work shaping the pattern of shop floor unionism, neither a mirror of international union organization nor the independent product of rank-and-file workers. The political climate of the time, including the independent aspirations, or lack thereof, of worker citizens, affects the organizational strength of workers in the labor market. But management actions are of equal importance. Its organization and initiative are clearly key factors interacting with these political and market forces to shape the specific form and traditions of shop floor unionism.

## NOTES

1. Incident recalled to me by Professor Jim Stern of the Industrial Relations Research Institute, University of Wisconsin, May 4, 1984.

2. John W. Anderson and Steve Jefferys, "Enlisted in the Suitcase Brigade: The Life of an Autoworker Who Stayed in the Shop" (unpublished manuscript, 1983), ch. 11.

3. This argument is developed at greater length in Steve Jefferys, *Management and Managed: Fifty Years of Crisis at Chrysler* (New York: Cambridge University Press, 1986).

4. Chrysler Corporation, *Financial and General Fact Book*, June 1973.

5. Robert W. Dunn, *Labor and Automobiles* (New York: International Publishers, 1928), 153.

6. Stanley B. Mathewson, *Restriction of Output among Unorganized Workers* (New York: Viking, 1931), 40, 45.

7. Dunn, *Labor and Automobiles*, 103.

8. Sidney Fine, *The Automobile under the Blue Eagle* (Ann Arbor: University of Michigan Press, 1963), 18–20.

9. Not to be confused with the communist leader of the MESA of the same name. Anderson and Jefferys, "Suitcase Brigade," ch. 3.

10. Anderson and Jefferys, "Suitcase Brigade," ch. 2; E. Greer, *Big Steel: Black Politics and Corporate Power in Gary, Indiana* (New York: Monthly Review Press, 1979), 89.

11. Harry Ross, oral history, 3, Archives of Labor History and Urban Affairs (ALHUA), Walter Reuther Library, Wayne State University, Detroit, Mich. (hereafter cited as ALHUA).

12. Report dated December 11, 1933, Harry Ross Collection, Box 3, ALHUA.

13. John Zaremba, oral history, 4, ALHUA.

14. Ibid.

15. Interview by author with Gertrude Nalezty, August 10, 1982.

16. Frankensteen, Ross, Zaremba, oral histories, ALHUA; P. Friedlander,

*The Emergence of a UAW Local, 1936–1939: A Study in Class and Culture* (Pittsburgh: University of Pittsburgh Press, 1975), 121–22.

17. This develops Ron Schatz's finding, "Union Pioneers: The Founders of Local Unions at General Electric and Westinghouse, 1933–1937," *Journal of American History* 66 (1979): 586–602, that male union organizers at General Electric and Westinghouse in the 1930s "were members of an elite stratum of the industry's work force." But at Dodge Main (and at Fleetwood Fisher Body—see Anderson and Jefferys, "Suitcase Brigade," ch. 3), not skill but social origin constituted the entry ticket to the elite.

18. Roger Keeran, *The Communist Party and the Auto Workers' Union* (Bloomington: Indiana University Press, 1980), 77–95.

19. Local 18277 Minute Book, September 24, 1933, in Frank Marquart Collection, Box 3, ALHUA.

20. Ross, oral history, 7–12, ALHUA; Zaremba, oral history, 5, ALHUA.

21. William McPherson, *Labor Relations in the Automobile Industry* (Washington, D.C.: Brookings Institute, 1940), 13–14.

22. Irving Bernstein, *Turbulent Years: A History of the American Worker, 1933–1941* (Boston: Houghton Mifflin, 1969), 39–40, cites a contemporary Bureau of Labor Statistics survey of 593 company unions of which 378 were established during the NIRA period.

23. Ibid., 184–85.

24. Letter in Zaremba Collection, Box 6, ALHUA.

25. *Employee Representation in the Plants of Chrysler Motors*, Zaremba Collection, Box 6, ALHUA.

26. Zaremba Collection, Box 1, ALHUA.

27. Robert Ozanne, *A Century of Labor-Management Relations at McCormick and International Harvester* (Madison: University of Wisconsin, 1967), 156.

28. Fine, *Automobile under the Blue Eagle*, 155.

29. Quoted in ibid., 288.

30. Individuals active on GM workers councils and later active in the UAW have been identified at Fleetwood Local 15 and at Norwood Local 674; Anderson and Jefferys, "Suitcase Brigade," ch. 6; John G. Kruchko, *The Birth of a Union Local: The History of UAW Local 674, Norwood, Ohio, 1933–1940* (Ithaca: Cornell University School of Industrial and Labor Relations, 1972), 16.

31. *Policy for Works Council and Employee Representatives Meetings*, 1934 document, Zaremba Collection, Box 6, ALHUA.

32. Zaremba, oral history, 8, ALHUA.

33. Frankensteen, oral history, 5, ALHUA.

34. Dodge Main Works Council minutes, May 2, 1935, in Frank Marquart Collection, Box 3, ALHUA.

35. Ibid., July 3, 1935.

36. Ibid., July 11, 1935.

37. Alan Brinkley, *Voices of Protest: Huey Long, Father Coughlin, and the Great Depression* (New York: Alfred A. Knopf, 1982), 83–102. Brinkley

argues that Coughlin's support came disproportionately from the ranks of skilled workers. But neither does he produce evidence for this, nor does this argument rest easily with the character of "Coughlin's Union," the AIWA, which was clearly an *industrial* union whose strength in 1935 was that, unlike the AFL, it primarily recruited semi- and unskilled workers.

38. Minutes of Employee Representatives Meeting, April 9, 1935, in Zaremba Collection, Box 1, ALHUA.

39. Ross was reinstated by the Automotive Labor Board in 1934. By early 1936 the UAW Local 3 born from the AFL Federal Local only had about fifty members left.

40. Irving Howe and B. J. Widick, *The UAW and Walter Reuther* (New York: Da Capo Press, 1973), 13; table in Marquart Collection, Box 3, ALHUA.

41. Friedlander, *Emergence of a UAW Local*, 116. In the spring of 1936 Coughlin believed he could take over the UAW; but within four months, after he decided to run his own election candidate against Roosevelt for president and after the UAW affiliated with the newly-formed CIO, he began denouncing both the CIO and the UAW.

42. The federal labor local became UAW Local 3 after the August 1935 meeting of auto industry federal locals when the UAW was presented a charter by the AFL, but it was also told it could neither choose its own president nor retain all the industrial members it recruited.

43. Leaflet in Ross Collection, Box 3, ALHUA.

44. Works Council minutes, October 16, November 11, 1936, in Zaremba Collection, Box 1, ALHUA; Anderson and Jefferys, "Suitcase Brigade," ch. 6.

45. Bernstein, *Turbulent Years*, 553.

46. Bert Cochran, *Labor and Communism: The Conflict that Shaped American Unions* (Princeton: Princeton University Press, 1977), 118.

47. Sidney Fine, *Sit-down: The GM Strike of 1936–1937* (Ann Arbor: University of Michigan Press, 1969), 142–44. The reliability of these figures as measures of plant participation is, however, in doubt since the UAW was calling laid-off GM workers throughout Flint into the plants to show support and access was not consistently blocked.

48. Ibid., 251. Even these more reliable figures are based on special counts that can still slightly exaggerate participation: at Fleetwood, a small plant employing about 1,200 on the day shift, forty-nine voted to sit-down, and some of them left the plant within hours. Anderson and Jefferys, "Suitcase Brigade," ch. 6.

49. Membership figures derived from totals voting in 1936 and 1937 Local 3 elections for president: 5,739 and 9,517. Dodge Main employed roughly half Chrysler's workforce in this period; *Dodge Main Strike Bulletin*, March 18, 1937.

50. Ibid., March 12, 1937.

51. Ibid., March 11, 1937.

52. See the crude periodization in David Gordon, Richard Edwards, and Michael Reich, *Segmented Work, Divided Workers: The Historical Transfor-*

*mation of Labor in the United States* (New York: Cambridge University Press, 1982), 177.

53. Local 3 Business Meeting minutes, December 27, 1936, in Dodge Local 3 Collection, Box 3, ALHUA.

54. Zaremba, oral history, 28, ALHUA; Nalezty interview; Stewards' Meetings minutes, January 25, April 5, 1937, in Dodge Local 3 Collection, Box 3, ALHUA. Local 3 Membership Meeting minutes, January 30, 1937, in Ross Collection, Box 3, ALHUA; Works Council minutes, February 9, 1937, in Marquart Collection, Box 1, ALHUA.

55. Zaremba Collection, Box 9, ALHUA; account written by Zaremba on flyleaf of the Henry Kraus autobiography, *The Many and the Few.*

56. Ibid., March 10, March 11, 1937; document in Zaremba Collection on security guards' activities, Box 9, ALHUA.

57. *Dodge Strike Bulletin,* March 17, 1937.

58. Dodge Main Stewards' Meeting minutes, April 5, 1937; *Dodge News,* April 7, 1937, in Dodge Local 3 Collection, Box 4, ALHUA.

59. Strike Executive Board minutes, March 23, 1937, in Zaremba Collection, Box 9, ALHUA.

60. *Dodge Main Strike Bulletin,* March 10, 1937.

61. Chrysler-UAW Agreement, April 14, 1937; Supplemental Agreement, April 6, 1937.

62. Bernstein, *Turbulent Years,* 555–69, presents a standard account.

63. Martin-Frankensteen, *Progressive Caucus for the Preservation of the UAW and the CIO.*

64. *Program of the Unity Caucus,* August 1937.

65. Local 3 Executive Board minutes, July 1, 1937; Local 3 Steward Body minutes, May 1, 1938; Zaremba Collection, Box 1, ALHUA.

66. Poem in Ross Collection, Box 2, ALHUA.

67. Election results in Marquart Collection, Box 3, ALHUA.

68. Keeran, *Communist Party and the Auto Workers' Union,* 196; Local 3 Executive Board minutes, June 16, 1938.

69. Executive Board minutes, November 10, 1938.

70. Ibid.

71. Executive Board minutes, February–March 1939.

72. Ross, oral history, 26, ALHUA.

73. Various leaflets in Marquart Collection, Box 3, and in Ross Collection, Box 3, ALHUA.

74. *United Auto Worker: Dodge Local 3 Edition,* October 4, 1939.

75. Local 3 Constitution, *United Auto Worker: Dodge Local 3 Edition,* October 10, 1939.

76. Ibid.

77. *United Auto Worker: Dodge Local 3 Edition,* October 18, 1939.

78. Ibid.

79. August Meier and Elliott Rudwick, *Black Detroit and the Rise of the UAW* (New York: Oxford University Press, 1979), 667–71.

80. UAW-Chrysler Contract, November 29, 1939.

81. *UAW-Dodge Main News*, December 6, 1939.

82. Interview by author with Ed Liska, August 11, 1982.

83. *Dodge Main News*, July 15, 1941.

84. *Dodge Main News*, June 1, June 15, 1943; Chrysler Corporation, *Beyond the Facts and the Records* (1943).

85. *Detroit News*, February 25, 1943.

86. Letter to author from Chrysler Corporation Industrial Relations Office, October 26, 1981.

87. Letter to author from General Motors Wage and International Labor Relations Administration, December 20, 1982.

88. Letter "To the Men and Women of Chrysler Corporation" from L. T. Colbert, September 5, 1956, in Dodge Local 3 Collection, ALHUA.

89. Frank W. Misch quoted in *UAW-Spotlight*, Special Chrysler Bulletin, March 1957.

90. UAW-Chrysler Contract, November 29, 1939, 14; UAW-Chrysler Memorandum, December 19, 1958, 1–3.

Workmen massed in neat rows at the Labor Bureau (here called the Employment Department) of the Employer's Association of Detroit, January 24, 1914.
Less than two weeks before, thousands of anxious workers had created a
near riot outside Ford's Highland Park factory when that firm began hiring
on the basis of its new "Five Dollar Day." Immediately thereafter, and until
1917, Ford agreed to accept employment applications only through the EAD.
(American Society of Employers, Detroit, Michigan)

Ford's River Rouge complex in the late 1930s. The dock and raw materials storage areas are in the foreground; the powerplant and foundry are at the upper left. The Rouge, employing 63,000 workers in seventeen separate facilities, was by far the largest and most integrated production complex in the nation after it was finished in the mid 1920s. (Archives of Labor History and Urban Affairs, Wayne State University)

The Dodge Main plant in Hamtramick in the late 1950s. Built just before the First World War, Dodge Main evolved into a production complex almost as integrated as the Rouge. Its multistoried configuration made it increasingly obsolete in the postwar era, and it was torn down in 1980. Drawing workers from the heavily Polish neighborhoods that surrounded it, the plant employed upwards of 40,000 at its peak in World War II. (ALHUA)

The body drop at Ford's River Rouge Assembly Plant in Dearborn, early 1930s. The Ford Motor Company's 1927 decision to retool for production of the Model A, seen above, represented an abandonment of classic Fordism as production strategy and consumption ethic. (ALHUA)

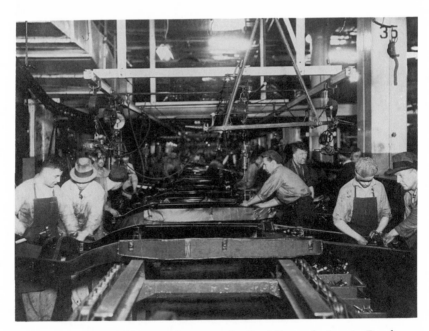

Ford workers assembling car frames at the Ford Rouge factory in Dearborn, 1932. Note the density of the workforce. Such production was easily mechanized; in fact the A. O. Smith Company in Milwaukee had "automated" frame assembly and welding as early as 1922. (ALHUA)

Women riveting a section of aircraft wing at the Ford Motor Company's Willow Run Bomber plant outside Yplislanti. A giant fixture holds the metal panels in place so that unskilled workers can perform the work. By 1943 more than 40 percent of all airframe workers were women. (ALHUA)

UAW members practice time and motion studies at a union sponsored summer school held at the FDR-CIO Camp in Port Huron, Michigan, 1946. Shop stewards and committeemen used such training to challenge management's postwar effort to tighten working conditions, but they found the grievance procedure relatively ineffective when it came to resolving production standards issues. (ALHUA)

Studebaker workers hand finishing automobile fenders in 1955. Labor intensive work such as this at the South Bend plant had given the firm a reputation for craftsmanship, but postwar managers were determined to reorganize the production process along more classically Fordist lines. (ALHUA)

The gear production shop of a Standard Motor Car, Ltd. factory in England in the mid 1950s. The strong shop steward system at Standard and other postwar British car firms was based in part upon the maintenance of a piece-rate production system that often divided the shop into bitterly competing groups of workers. (ALHUA)

A Cross Transfer-Matic machine for automatic machining operations on *V*-8 cylinder blocks. Automation equipment such as this was first deployed by Ford in the early 1950s at its new engine plant outside Cleveland. Although manpower requirements were drastically lowered, such "Detroit automation" of the early postwar era proved extremely expensive and inflexible. (ALHUA)

Workers at Murray Body, UAW Local 2, demonstrate for the return of jobs lost to automation in the mid 1950s. Murray was one of several independent supplier firms either closed down or merged into the Big Three after the Korean War. Their demise inaugurated an era of permanently high unemployment in Detroit. (ALHUA)

# 6

## Rosie the Riveter Revisited: Management's Postwar Purge of Women Automobile Workers

### RUTH MILKMAN

One of the most important questions facing historians of American women involves the defeminization of basic industry at the end of the Second World War. The economic mobilization for war dramatized the possibility of employing women in "men's jobs" on an unprecedented scale and seemed to throw into question the sexual division of paid labor as a whole. Yet, in the course of postwar reconversion, women were systematically purged from their wartime jobs, and the prewar sexual division of labor in manufacturing was effectively reconstructed. The automobile industry is a prominent case in point. At the peak of wartime employment, women workers comprised over one-fourth of the labor force in auto; by September 1945, a month after V-J Day, the female share of employment in the industry had dropped below 10 percent, where it would remain for many years to come.[1]

The question, of course, is why women were not retained in the postwar years, despite the success with which they were integrated into the production workforce of industries like auto during the war. This is ultimately a specific—and extreme—version of a more general problem, namely, why the sexual division of labor, as it has developed historically within and between industries, has been so resistant to change. Although this is by no means a new problem, in the period since the war it has become increasingly urgent. Despite the rapid growth of female labor force participation over the postwar decades and despite the fact that the resurgence of feminism has undermined the legitimacy of sex discrimination in the labor market, occupational segregation by sex and the wage inequality that accompanies it have remained largely intact.[2]

In recent years several studies have considered the critical moment in women's labor history immediately following the end of World War II. Most of them have focused on the auto industry, primarily on the failure of the United Auto Workers (UAW) to protect women's employment rights in the aftermath of the war. The scholarship of Sheila Tobias and Lisa Anderson, Lyn Goldfarb, and Nancy Gabin has demonstrated quite convincingly that, although women workers overwhelmingly wanted to stay in "men's jobs" in auto after the war, the UAW colluded in the purge of women from the industry. Despite an official union policy in support of women's seniority rights, the UAW did little to protect women's jobs, especially at the local level. And, in many instances, the union actively supported excluding women from postwar employment in the auto industry.[3]

Recent research has greatly deepened historians' understanding of the complex relationship between women and industrial unions in the 1940s. However, it does not adequately explain the exclusion of women from the postwar auto industry. And, because it focuses primarily on the role of the union, this body of scholarship is ultimately quite misleading. Although it is true that the UAW colluded with management and that effective union resistance to the policy of purging women from the postwar workforce might have altered the situation, to understand why the postwar sexual division of labor in auto took the form it did, one must look to *management* first and foremost. Indeed, the central question remains: Why was management so intent on excluding women from postwar employment in the first place? During the war, women auto workers won enormous praise for their performance from all sides. Why should employers have been so reluctant to retain them in the postwar? Given the historical "cheapness" of female labor, management's postwar policy seems especially paradoxical.

This essay analyzes the postwar shift in the sexual division of labor in the auto industry, giving center stage to the policy and practice of automotive management and placing the UAW's role in a broader perspective. Although I am most concerned with the 1940s directly, the first section begins with a discussion of the formation of the sexual division of labor in the prewar auto industry. This is crucial for the analysis of postwar developments, because the logic of the managerial policy which excluded women from automotive employment in the reconversion period in many respects recapitulates that which shaped the industry's sexual division of labor in the early twentieth century. Ever since the rise of Ford's mass production system and the introduction of the famous five-dollar day in 1914, auto had been a high-wage industry. Moreover, high wages have always been central to the Fordist system of control over labor. Under these circumstances, automotive management never had much incentive to substitute female for male labor, despite the relatively low wages of the former; thus, the vast majority of jobs in the industry were sex-typed as "men's work" from the outset. Females entered the industry in large numbers during World War II, and then only in the face of an extraordinary shortage of male labor. Moreover, the mobilization of female labor during the war emergency only temporarily disrupted the sexual division of labor in the industry. Indeed, for management, the exclusion of women workers from postwar employment in auto was a foregone conclusion.

But what about the seniority system institutionalized in UAW contracts in the years immediately preceding the war? The previously mentioned studies focus on the union's failure to protect women's seniority rights and presume the seniority system was the main determinant of whether women workers hired in wartime would be retained after the war. However, as I argue in the second section of this essay, seniority was actually of secondary importance in the immediate postwar period because the industry expanded very rapidly and turnover rates were extremely high. Even with the large influx of returning veterans, who held a special seniority status, large numbers of vacancies in the industry's workforce clearly could have been filled by women, had management cared to hire them. In sharp contrast to their policy toward women, automotive employers did hire large numbers of blacks in the postwar era, dramatically departing from prewar practice. Therefore, management's *hiring policies* were the critical determinant of the composition of the auto industry's postwar labor force. The UAW's failure to fight on behalf of women's postwar employment rights and the opposition to women's inclusion in the postwar labor force which this failure suggested were important insofar as they reinforced management's position. This is where studies of the UAW's role are relevant, but we must keep in mind that the union's ambivalent stance was only one reason management never seriously considered permanently institutionalizing the changes in hiring policy that the war had forced upon them.

## Fordism and the Sexual Division of Labor in Auto

The historic structure of the industry and the character of its labor process proved the most important reason female substitution was not an attractive option for automotive management in the immediate postwar period. The Fordist revolution, which organized mass production around the moving assembly line, laid the basis for automobile manufacturing to develop as a high-wage, capital-intensive industry; thus, employers had little incentive to substitute female labor for its more expensive male equivalent. Despite the fact that the obstacles to substitution were minimal in the early days—auto was a rapidly expanding and completely new industry with no tradition of union organization and no history of sex-stereotyped jobs—management showed negligible interest in employing women workers.

Because they have historically been performed by men, production jobs in the auto industry are frequently described as "heavy," completely reversing the actual line of causality. In fact, however, the need for workers capable of great physical exertion was eliminated early in the history of the industry, given mechanization and streamlined organization of production. Henry Ford wrote in 1922: "The rank and file of men come to us unskilled. They do not have to be able-bodied men. We have jobs that require great physical strength—although they are rapidly lessening; we have other jobs that require no strength whatsoever—jobs which, as far as strength is concerned, might be attended to by a child of three."[4] Similarly, in a 1924 essay on the auto industry Charles Reitell observed that

> quickly—overnight as it were—the machine, gigantic, complex and intricate, has removed the need of muscle and brawn. As Frederick W. Taylor put it, "The gorilla types are no more needed." Instead we have a greater demand for nervous and mental activities such as watchfulness, quick judgements, dexterity, guidance, ability and lastly a nervous endurance to carry through dull, monotonous, fatiguing rhythmic operations.[5]

These were precisely the characteristics of manufacturing jobs commonly thought to be most appropriate for women workers in the early part of the century, according to the prevailing stereotypes. So one might have expected management, ever eager to maximize profits, to have had an enormous incentive to utilize the ample supplies of "cheap labor" available in the female population in this period. However, this did not occur. Women remained a tiny minority of the auto manufacturing labor force throughout the pre–World War II period. They were employed mostly in parts plants and in the "cut-and-sew" (upholstery) departments of body plants. Although occasionally women were substituted for men, and at lower pay, management's apparent disinterest in any serious effort at large-scale feminization is far more striking.[6]

A crucial difference between the auto industry and those manufacturing industries employing large numbers of women at low wages in this period is that in auto, the supreme lever of control over the workforce was a *high*-wage policy, the magic of the Fordist revolution. Mechanization was carried forward to such a great extent that wages became a relatively small component of costs. "Machinery," said Henry Ford, "is the new Messiah."[7] The industry quickly gained a reputation for good pay after the famous 1914 announcement of the five-dollar day by the Ford Motor Company, then the largest firm in the industry. Ford had pioneered in the development of control over labor through the use of the moving assembly line, an innovation that spread rapidly throughout the industry along with the high wages it made possible.

Relative to other branches of manufacturing, pay rates were quite high in the auto industry after 1914. Even during the depression, when wage cuts were endemic throughout the economy, the weekly earnings of auto workers were 24 percent above the comparable average for all manufacturing.[8] Women auto workers earned substantially less than men, generally about two-thirds as much (on an hourly basis) in the prewar era.[9] Yet management did not seek to depress wage costs by substituting women for men in auto, even during the severe profitability crisis of the 1930s.

Most women employed in auto manufacturing were engaged in the production of auto parts. Unlike the rest of the auto industry, parts manufacturing had many characteristics of the secondary sector of the economy.[10] Machine pacing was used far less extensively, and piece rates—the standard form of wage payment in the heavily female "sweated" manufacturing industries of the day—remained the predominant form of wage payment as late as 1950. The auto parts industry was also relatively competitive, with some notorious sweat-shop operations like Briggs, where women's labor was used quite extensively and wage rates were reported to be as low as 4 cents per hour in the 1930s.[11] But this was atypical. In the major auto firms, the predominant policy was to pay high wages in exchange for sub-ordination to the machine-paced organization of production. In fact, thanks to the "new Messiah," even the five-dollar day was an econ-omy. The combination of dramatically lowered turnover rates and the extra production extracted by means of the speed-up meant Ford workers produced more per dollar of wages after the implementation of the five-dollar day than before. Ford himself justifiably called it "one of the finest cost-cutting moves we ever made."[12]

That classic comment captures the essence of management strategy at Ford, a model for the auto industry generally. There was no incen-tive to seek supplies of cheap female labor in this situation. On the contrary, Ford, and the other auto firms as well, were in a position to offer their predominantly male workforce pay rates approximating a "family wage," an ideal with great resonance in the early twentieth-century working-class community. In his 1924 autobiography, Ford explicitly embraced the concept:

> If only the man himself were concerned, the cost of his maintenance and the profit [sic] he ought to have would be a simple matter. But he is not just an individual. He is a citizen, contributing to the welfare of the nation. He is a householder. He is perhaps a father with children who must be reared to usefulness on what he is able to earn. . . . The man does the work in the shop, but his wife does the work in the home. The shop must pay them both. . . . Otherwise, we have the hideous prospect of little children and their mothers being forced out to work.[13]

Among other things, this supplied the rationale for excluding those few females who did work for Ford from the much-lauded five-dollar day. Ford himself told the U.S. Commission on Industrial Relations in 1916 that only one-tenth of the women in his employ received the $5.00 minimum.[14]

Once the auto industry's basic pattern of employment by sex had been established, with men in the vast majority of jobs and women concentrated in small parts production and in cut-and-sew opera-tions, the sexual division of labor proved extraordinarily stable. As is the case throughout the economy, once an auto production job came to be ideologically labeled male or female, the demand for labor to fill it tended to expand or contract as a sex-specific demand, barring major disruptions of labor supply or a basic restructuring of the labor process itself. In day-to-day managerial practice, the established system of sex labeling guided decisions as to whether to hire a male or female in each job opening. Thus, auto employers—and auto workers as well—came to view certain jobs as quintessentially male and others, a far more limited group, as suitable for women. Neither the 1921 recession, the Great Depression, nor the rise of industrial unionism significantly altered the sexual division of labor in auto; it remained unchanged throughout the prewar era.

Even during World War II, employers were initially quite resistant to the idea of hiring women for war jobs in auto plants. They did so only when military conscription had exhausted the supply of male labor in an era of rapidly increasing war production. The federal government intervened in 1942, setting male employment ceilings and giving the War Manpower Commission the power to enforce them.[15] The results were quite dramatic: the proportion of women employed in the auto industry swelled from only 5 percent just before Pearl Harbor to 25 percent two years later.[16]

Once it became clear that there was no alternative, managerial attitudes about the employment of women in production jobs also seemed to shift dramatically. As early as June 1942, George Romney, then head of the Automotive Council for War Production, reported to a meeting of automotive managers and government planners on wartime labor supply problems that "the consciousness of the capability of women is growing all through the [auto] industry." He recounted a conversation at another meeting of automotive employers, held a short time earlier, where the topic of women's employment had been discussed: "One of the fellows said, 'Where will we have any use for men? Why should there be any men?' One fellow said, 'At least one thing a man can still do better than a woman, and that is being a father.' That is where they wound up in their discussion."[17] During the war, numerous testimonials from management conceded that women's production record exceeded that of men on the same or similar jobs.[18] For example, women hired to do "men's jobs" at the four largest plants of the Ford Motor Company "job for job . . . outproduced the men in most cases," according to a 1943 report.[19]

Despite this general enthusiasm for the performance of women war workers, wage differentials between the sexes did not disappear during the war years—a consideration one might expect, given the glowing praise for the performance of women war workers, to have generated some management interest in retaining women permanently in the kinds of jobs they held during the war emergency. The UAW, to be sure, contested wage discrimination, rather successfully, in a series of "equal pay for equal work" cases before the War Labor Board. Although sex differentials in pay in the auto industry were narrowed considerably following these struggles, they were not fully eliminated. In August 1944, women's average straight-time hourly wage in Michigan's auto plants was 90 percent of the male average.[20]

Employers claimed extra costs associated with the employment of women, particularly in previously all-male plants. UAW President R. J. Thomas, questioned at a 1945 Senate hearing about auto industry employers' reluctance to hire women for postwar jobs, summarized the prevailing view:

> Managements have told us some of the reasons. First is that as you know on most jobs equal rates are paid for equal jobs today. . . . Management doesn't want to pay women equal rates with men. Not only that but in many of these plants additional facilities have to be put in, such as toilet facilities to take care of women. More space has to be taken to give an opportunity of changing clothes and more safety measures have to be instituted. I think it is pretty well recognized that it is an additional expense to a management to have women.[21]

This was an accurate report of the reasons auto managers themselves adduced for their reluctance to employ women; however, it seems unsatisfactory when considered alongside other economic factors. Despite equal pay provisions, women's wages were lower than men's in many instances, and few had "equal jobs," even during the war, as job segregation by sex persisted within the war economy.[22] As for the costs of maintaining special "facilities" for women, these were installed largely at government expense during the war; they could hardly have been a major financial consideration in any event. Surely sex differentials in pay would have outweighed any expense firms would incur in maintaining such facilities. Indeed, if only the obvious, direct economic costs and benefits to the auto corporations of female employment were taken into account, one might expect management to have consistently discriminated in favor of women and against men in postwar layoffs and rehiring. Particularly in view of the vigorous efforts of employers to increase labor productivity in the reconversion period, management should have preferred to retain women permanently in the "men's jobs" they had just demonstrated their capabilities to perform.[23]

However, in the aftermath of the war, just as in the early development of the industry, automotive employers ignored the opportunity to feminize the workforce. Indeed, in the massive layoffs immediately following the end of the war, women were thrown out of work at a rate nearly double that for men in the manufacturing sector as a whole. The disparity was even greater in auto and other "heavy" industries that had employed very few women in the prewar period. In the month following V-J Day, there was a precipitous drop in women's share of the automotive workforce, from 18 percent in August 1945 to 10 percent in September.[24] The dramatic wartime employment gains of women in the industry were thus rolled back even more rapidly than they had been made. As postwar hiring resumed, it became clear that auto would once again rely on an overwhelmingly male labor force. Wage levels remained high, even increasing during the postwar years. As in the prewar era, management's efforts to boost productivity focused on tightening control over labor, not on reducing pay levels.[25] Management continued to nourish the basic conviction, historically rooted in the logic of Fordism—as operative in the postwar situation as in the prewar—that women were simply not suitable for employment in automotive production jobs. Employers saw the successful performance of women war workers as, at best, a fortunate outcome of an experiment in which they had participated with great trepidation and only because there had been no alternative. Women had performed better than anyone had expected during the war, true enough, but now the emergency was over, and men's jobs were men's jobs once again.

## Seniority, the UAW, and Reconversion Hiring Policy

Studies of the impact of the postwar transition on women auto workers have focused primarily on the issue of women's seniority rights and the role of the UAW. Source materials available on this aspect of the problem are far more extensive than those regarding the role of management; perhaps this accounts for the detailed attention the seniority issue has received in the pioneering work of Tobias and Anderson, Goldfarb, and Gabin.

The starting point is the observation that women's departure from the automotive labor force, contrary to popular belief at the time, was not voluntary. In fact, the overwhelming majority of women working in the industry during the war intended not only to continue working after the war but to stay in the same type of work. Eighty-five percent of the women war workers responding to a 1944 UAW survey wanted to remain in the labor force after the war, and almost all of them preferred to continue doing factory work. Another survey conducted by the U.S. Women's Bureau at about the same time found that 78 percent of women workers in Detroit planned to continue working after the war and that 85 percent of the Motor City's female factory workers planned to remain in manufacturing. The same employment preferences persisted in the immediate aftermath of the war. In July 1946, the Detroit office of the U.S. Employment Service had nearly twice as many applications on file for semiskilled and unskilled manufacturing jobs from women as from returning male veterans, but the applicants for clerical and service work included a higher proportion of veterans than of women. When officials alerted automakers and other manufacturing employers to the availability of women for the factory jobs being spurned by men, the demand for workers in auto remained overwhelmingly male.[26]

This situation presented the UAW with a serious dilemma. After the war ended, the full employment economy, the crucial precondition for female incorporation into "men's jobs" in industry in the first place, could no longer be sustained. As a result, women war workers now directly competed for jobs with their male counterparts—a problem intensified by the influx of large numbers of returning veterans into the industrial labor force. Moreover, fear of a return to the high unemployment levels of the depression years after the war was widespread, especially among workers in durable goods industries like auto, always particularly sensitive to cyclical economic changes. This situation naturally produced considerable hostility toward women.

In the late 1930s, the fledgling UAW had fought long and hard for the establishment of seniority systems to distribute employment equitably in just such situations as this. During the war, it was already obvious that postwar demobilization would bring the first real test of the seniority principle. At the same time, the UAW's commitment to eliminate all forms of discrimination provided an opening for women union activists to work toward the equalization of seniority rights. They pursued this goal energetically and relatively successfully. By the end of the war, the UAW's official policy stance was that women should enjoy the same seniority rights as men. Locals were urged to eliminate separate women's seniority lists and other sex-discriminatory contract provisions, and many did so.[27]

However, in the absence of full employment, the principle of seniority, even if properly enforced, had mixed implications for women war workers. Because their employment gains were so recent, concentrated in the three-year period of war production, the "last hired, first fired" principle embedded in the seniority system meant women would be laid off in disproportionate numbers. Indeed, this is the basis for the argument *against* strict seniority systems advanced in recent years by advocates of affirmative action for women and other industrial minorities; however, this view did not enjoy much credibility in the 1940s. Female union activists concerned about women's postwar employment pressed not for preferential treatment for women, but simply for the enforcement of the limited seniority rights women war workers already had.[28]

But preferential treatment was widely advocated for one group of workers: returning veterans. Popular appreciation of the hardships of military service thoroughly legitimized the idea that veterans should not be further penalized for their absence from the labor market during the war, and UAW contracts granted seniority equal to the time spent in military service to veterans previously employed by an auto company as well as to those newly hired after their military discharge.[29] At the same time, the union, wary of the potential division between veterans and other workers, strongly opposed so-called super-seniority rights for veterans, which would have given them preferential status over virtually all other workers.[30] To this extent, the UAW's official policy unambiguously protected women's seniority rights, limited as they were.

Official union policies were one thing, but their enforcement was another matter altogether, as the recent feminist scholarship points out. There was tremendous ambivalence about women's rights to postwar jobs in industry on the part of both UAW leaders and the rank-and-file, despite the union's formal opposition to sex discrimination.

Internal battles over women's seniority rights raged within the UAW, and all too often the union's practice was inconsistent with its official policy. Separate women's seniority lists remained in effect at the war's end in some locals, although in many others women activists had succeeded in eliminating them during the war. There were other blatantly discriminatory arrangements as well. The national General Motors contract, for example, provided that women employed on "men's jobs" during the war would accumulate temporary seniority, applicable "for the duration only." [31]

In many plants, women did have equal seniority rights according to the contract, and the main problem was lack of enforcement. As postwar production resumed and hiring increased, many complained that women war workers were not being recalled according to seniority, in violation of contract provisions. The situation Ida Griggs of UAW Local 306 described to the union's 1946 convention is representative:

> In our plant, and I guess it is the same in most plants, we have women laid off with seniority . . . and every day they hire in new men off the street. They hire men there, they say, to do the heavy work. The women do light work. During the war they didn't care what kind of work we did, and still we have to work on hard jobs now, and some of the men with lesser seniority get the small jobs. [32]

Explicit job classification by sex was still prevalent at this time; thus, management had only to reclassify jobs in the course of postwar reconversion—from female to male, or from light to heavy—in order to justify not recalling women. Protective legislation, temporarily eased during the war, now became another mechanism by which jobs that women had performed quite adequately during the war, and wanted to keep, were reclassified as "men's jobs." [33]

Recent scholarship offers extensive documentation of the UAW's failure to challenge management in these practices, as well as many instances of explicit union collusion with management in purging women from the industry's labor force. We also know, thanks to this literature, that women workers themselves valiantly sought to defend their seniority rights, even in the face of united opposition from both management and their male coworkers. In the rare cases where their protests were effective and women were ultimately rehired, management proved unrelenting in its determination to oust them from the plants. Those who returned to work under these conditions were subjected to various forms of managerial harassment. "They'd hassle them by putting them on the broom—as it was called—janitorial [work]," recalled Mildred Jeffrey, the head of the UAW Women's Bureau at the time. "They'd hassle them by putting them on night shift or afternoon shift, or just putting them on one job after another. Say, 'do this,' and then in the same day, move them to two or three different jobs, giving them very hard jobs."[34]

It is indisputable that the seniority system was stacked against women, even where nominally nondiscriminatory, and that women war workers' seniority rights, limited as they were, were honored more in the breach than in the observance. However, the seniority system and the UAW's failure to protect women's limited job rights still do not *explain* the virtual absence of women in the postwar auto labor force because this line of argument ignores management's crucial role in shaping the postwar sexual division of labor. Far more important than the seniority system, properly enforced or not, in determining the composition of the future labor force in auto was *hiring policy*. Here, managerial control was virtually complete. So many new workers were hired in the industry after the war that the seniority lists were of marginal significance. Contrary to general expectations, the postwar years saw enormous expansion in the auto industry, after a relatively brief interlude of reconversion unemployment. The postwar boom was based on a vast consumer demand for automobiles, as a result of both the unavailability of cars during the war and the general prosperity of the period. By 1947, the number of production workers in the nation's auto factories already exceeded that at the peak of war employment.[35]

Postwar expansion in the auto industry was so massive that even the dramatic influx of veterans, with their preferential seniority treatment, left plenty of room for recalling women war workers with seniority and even hiring additional women workers. In addition to the rapid postwar expansion of employment in the industry, the emigration of large numbers of war workers (mostly male) from war production areas and the normally high attrition meant that the composition of the postwar labor force was shaped primarily by hiring policies.

The auto industry's employment of many veterans in the reconversion period is indisputable. Between December 1945 and July 1946, veterans constituted on the average 47 percent of all workers hired in the industry. By mid-1946 they made up fully 23 percent of the workforce in automobile factories.[36] But this high rate of veteran entry into the industry reflected employers' preference for young male workers, not seniority. "Employers in the auto industry prefer white males, between 20 and 25, weighing over 150 pounds and in good physical condition," the U.S. Women's Bureau reported in July 1946.[37] These were precisely the characteristics the military had sought in conscripting soldiers, and so it is hardly surprising that veterans were hired in large numbers. Andrew Court, a labor relations executive at General Motors at the time, recalled that the 1945–1946 strike against GM increased the representation of veterans in the firm's workforce:

> There was a lot of moaning and groaning about the strike, but really it was one of the best things that happened to our labor supply. We lost people we'd hired during the war who were not as desirable as the GI's. They went somewhere else and didn't come back after the strike, and it was settled when the GI's were coming back, so we had a fairly good supply of young, vigorous, fairly adequate men. A few years later they made a study, and General Motors got "all A's" for having hired so many GI's, and this was the reason.[38]

Most veterans who found postwar employment in the auto plants were young men who had not worked in the industry before; even when granted seniority credit for their time in the military, few had greater seniority status than the women whose wartime "service" had been in war jobs rather than in the armed forces. Only about 20 percent of all returning World War II veterans nationally were entitled to reemployment rights.[39] That those veterans without formal reemployment rights got a seniority bonus meant that employers' preference for them did affect the seniority system, but this was offset by other factors.

Women war workers had at least as much seniority as most of the veterans. Turnover rates among the latter were quite high, with quits alone averaging 5.4 percent monthly between December 1945 and July 1946.[40] Nonveterans, especially migrants, also left the industry in droves at this time. Between 100,000 and 150,000 people left Michigan between V-E Day and mid-September 1946 alone, many of them southerners returning home. Men predominated in this group.[41] Although the number of veterans with substantial seniority in the auto industry cannot be precisely determined, it can be estimated for the immediate postwar period at a maximum of 100,000.[42] But in the twenty months between V-J Day and April 1947 alone, total employment in auto rose by more than twice that figure—230,000.[43] The high rate of veterans' employment in the auto industry clearly reflected employers' hiring preferences, but it does not explain the exclusion of women from the postwar labor force.

Perhaps the most convincing way to demonstrate that women's low seniority standing was not the cause of their poor postwar representation among auto workers is to compare the impact of reconversion on women with that on black workers in the industry. Like women, black workers as a group had relatively low seniority standing at the conclusion of the war. They, too, had first entered the auto industry in large numbers during the war mobilization period. The proportion of blacks in Detroit's automotive plants rose from 5.5 percent in May 1942 to 15 percent by the spring of 1945. Black workers gained access to semiskilled auto jobs on a significant scale for the first time during the war years, in a process paralleling the expansion in the number of jobs open to women.[44]

The experiences of these two groups, so similar during the war, diverged sharply with reconversion to consumer automobile production. While women were ousted from their new positions in the industry at the end of the war, and in most cases not recalled, blacks were more fortunate. "Once the painful transition to peacetime was over," Meier and Rudwick conclude, "blacks found that they retained the foothold in semiskilled machine production and assembly-line work which they had won during the war."[45] Data on black employment in individual auto firms confirm this. The proportion of blacks in Chrysler's production workforce actually rose just after the war, from 15 percent in 1945 to 17 percent in 1946, in stark contrast to the "exodus" of women from the industry. By 1960, blacks were 26 percent of the labor force in Chrysler's Detroit plants and 23 percent of GM's production workforce in that city. Ford, the one auto manufacturer that had employed blacks in significant numbers before the war, also increased its black employment in the postwar years; by 1960 blacks comprised over 40 percent of the production workforce at the huge River Rouge plant.[46]

This divergence between the experience of women and blacks can only be understood in the context of management's hiring policies. The female proportion of the workforce might have been marginally greater in the postwar years if the UAW had more effectively defended women's seniority rights. But given the high turnover rates for all auto workers and the vast postwar expansion of the industry, even if the UAW had secured the reinstatement of every woman war worker, there would still have been a sharp decline in female representation in the industry's labor force, unless additional women were added as well. Only an insistence on sex-blind hiring policy—which the UAW had no means to enforce—could have substantially altered the situation.

But why was postwar hiring policy different for blacks vis-à-vis women? In the prewar period, management's lack of interest in hiring blacks—like women, a source of "cheap labor"—for auto production jobs had the same basis as its disinterest in feminization. Both were by-products of the industry's general program of labor discipline, to which high wages were central. And, again paralleling the case of women, racial stereotypes rationalized and legitimized racially exclusive hiring. Yet, by the late 1940s, at least in the North, race discrimination had already lost much of its former legitimacy. A large and vital civil rights movement enjoyed substantial UAW support, and management might have expected vigorous protests if it pursued racially discriminatory employment policies.[47]

When blacks were first hired in large numbers in Detroit's auto factories during the period of economic mobilization, there had been considerable opposition among white workers, most dramatically expressed in the numerous "hate strikes" which erupted in the plants and in the "race riot" of the summer of 1943.[48] But by the end of the war, there was no longer any legitimate basis for excluding blacks from postwar jobs in the Detroit auto industry. During the war, Detroit had become a major center of the civil rights movement. The Motor City had the largest branch of the National Association for the Advancement of Colored People (NAACP) of any city in the nation, with a membership of 20,000 by 1943. And the UAW had developed into a strong ally of the NAACP and other civil rights groups. Although discrimination persisted in the auto industry regarding promotion of blacks to the elite skilled trades, no one contested their claim to semiskilled jobs.[49]

The sharp regional variations in patterns of racial hiring within the auto industry suggest the critical importance of the legitimacy or illegitimacy of racial exclusion in shaping employment policies. The proportion of blacks in Detroit's auto plants rose quite dramatically in the 1940s and 1950s, reaching well over 25 percent of the production workforce by 1960, but in the United States as a whole the percentage of nonwhite workers in the auto industry grew much more modestly, from 4 percent in 1940 to only 9 percent in 1960. The national figures reflect the continuing practice of excluding blacks from employment in southern plants. As a manager at a GM plant in Atlanta told the *Wall Street Journal* in 1957, "When we moved into the South, we agreed to abide by local custom and not hire Negroes for production work. This is no time for social reforming and we're not about to try it."[50]

The situation of women auto workers was quite different from that of northern blacks. The incorporation of women into the industry provoked no riots or "hate strikes," precisely because female employment was explicitly understood as a temporary expedient "for the duration" of the war. There was no parallel expectation regarding black men, whose interests were aggressively defended by a growing interracial constituency of liberals, unionists, and civil rights supporters throughout the North. Although women war workers wanted to remain in the auto industry, their preferences seemed to have little social or political legitimacy. No significant feminist movement existed, nor did a popular consciousness of women's job rights emerge at this critical juncture when the sexual division of labor which would characterize the entire postwar period was crystallizing. Unlike race discrimination, which might have proven politically and socially costly, management could rely upon minimal resistance, either from women themselves or from the UAW, to purging women from the auto workforce in the war's aftermath.

Although there were some protests against postwar sex discrimination, these were both rare and generally unsuccessful.[51] At best, they secured postwar employment for small groups of women war workers with contractual seniority rights. Demanding that management also refrain from discriminating against women in hiring new workers, once the seniority lists were exhausted in the course of postwar expansion, was never "on the agenda." But this is precisely what would have been required for women to maintain their wartime gains in the industry.

Instead, the typical pattern was collusion between male workers and management in excluding women from postwar employment.

This was due to not only the general cultural setting but also the particular structural features of the auto industry. The response of male workers to the postwar transition was quite different in some other industries. In electrical manufacturing, for example, the same fear of unemployment which led to union collusion with management's violation of women auto workers' seniority rights produced strikingly opposite results. In the electrical case, it was impossible to think of excluding women from employment; the indu try had been one-third female even before the war. Instead, male w rkers responded to the wartime upheaval in the sexual division of labor (and the anticipated postwar upheaval as well) by fighting *against* sex discrimination and challenging the whole system of job segregation by sex in a struggle for equal pay for jobs of comparable worth. As in auto, the goal was to decrease the likelihood of permanent (i.e. postwar) female substitution. Because auto management had never seriously attempted to replace men with women, except, of course, during the war emergency, the UAW had little incentive to protest hiring policy; in electrical manufacturing, management's extensive use of female labor generated a radical challenge to sex discrimination in the form of a comparable worth demand. In this way, management policy not only shaped the sexual composition of the labor force in each industry but also profoundly influenced the character of labor struggles over women's position.[52]

If management ever seriously considered the permanent substitution of women for men in the postwar auto industry—and no evidence suggesting that has been uncovered—there would have been good reason to anticipate protest from male workers. Minimally, management could have anticipated a postwar fight for equal pay for equal work for women, if postwar hiring had not been exclusively male. More generally, in view of the tremendous fear of unemployment in the demobilization period, auto industry managers might reasonably have expected that any effort on their part to renege on the wartime assurances that women were in "men's jobs" only "for the duration" would have precipitated considerable resistance from men.[53] Thus, the UAW's role was not the only, or even the primary, cause of the postwar expulsion of women workers from the auto industry; but it did tend to reinforce the managerial logic of reconstructing the prewar sexual division of labor.

## Conclusion

The primary determinant of the postwar sexual division of labor in the auto industry was management's preference for male workers. Historically rooted in the logic of Fordism, as it shaped the industry's structure in the early twentieth century, the sexual division of auto production work became such a permanent characteristic of the industry that even the dramatic transformation of the war years had no lasting impact. The UAW's failure to challenge the sexual division of labor in the immediate aftermath of the war reinforced management's policy. Moreover, the failure was also very much a product of the policy, for the history of predominantly male employment in auto itself defined the possibilities for struggle over "woman's place" in the industry.

Except the brief interlude during World War II, women have always remained a small minority among auto production workers. Even in the 1970s, when the proportion of women in the industry's blue-collar workforce increased slightly, the changes were quite modest, particularly given the dramatic rise in female labor force participation in the economy as a whole. The effect of the women's movement of the late 1960s and 1970s on auto employment in some respects paralleled the impact of the civil rights movement in the 1940s; however, since there was no comparable expansion of employment in the 1970s, the scale of change was far smaller. Gains made through affirmative action have been significantly eroded since 1978, when women's employment peaked, as a result of the increased plant closings and layoffs.[54] In general, the continuity of the sexual division of labor in the auto industry is far more striking than the changes which have occurred. The reconstruction of the prewar situation in the aftermath of World War II is but the most extreme instance of that general continuity, rooted in the structural characteristics of the industry and its labor process.

### NOTES

1. U.S. Department of Labor, Bureau of Labor Statistics, *Women in Factories*, mimeo, August 1947, 7.

2. See U.S. Department of Labor, Bureau of Labor Statistics, Report 673,

The Female-Male Earnings Gap: A Review of Employment and Earnings Issues, September 1982.

3. Sheila Tobias and Lisa Anderson, "What Really Happened to Rosie the Riveter: Demobilization and the Female Labor Force, 1944–1947," MMS Modular Publications, Inc., Module 9 (1973), 1–36; Lyn Goldfarb, Separated and Unequal: Discrimination against Women Workers after World War II (The U.A.W., 1944–1954) (Washington, D.C.: The Union for Radical Political Economics, 1976); and Nancy Gabin, "Women Workers and the UAW in the Post–World War II Period: 1945–1954," Labor History 21, no. 1 (Winter 1979–1980): 5–30.

4. Henry Ford, in collaboration with Samuel Crowther, My Life and Work (Garden City, N.J.: Doubleday, 1923), 79.

5. Charles Reitell, "Machinery and Its Effects upon the Workers in the Automotive Industry," Annals of the American Academy of Political and Social Science 116 (1924): 43.

6. Examples of substitution are noted in Robert W. Dunn, Labor and Automobiles (New York: International Publishers, 1920), 73, 76; and in William H. McPherson, Labor Relations in the Automobile Industry (Washington, D.C.: Brookings Institute, 1940), 8–9.

7. Keith Sward, The Legend of Henry Ford (New York: Rinehart, 1948), 1.

8. Andrew T. Court, Men, Methods and Machines in Automobile Manufacturing (New York: Automobile Manufacturers Association, 1939), 9.

9. In 1925, women auto workers averaged 47 cents per hour, compared to 73 cents for men in the industry. Similarly, in April 1934, women averaged 52 cents an hour in auto factory jobs, compared to 73 cents for men. A third survey in September 1934 found average earnings of 54 cents for women and 75 cents for men. (All three sets of figures exclude auto-parts plants, where wages were substantially lower for workers of both sexes.) See U.S. Department of Labor, Bureau of Labor Statistics, Bulletin no. 438, Wages and Hours of Labor in the Motor Vehicle Industry: 1925 (1927), 2–3; and N. A. Tolles and M. W. La Fever, "Wages, Hours, Employment and Annual Earnings in the Motor-Vehicle Industry, 1934," Monthly Labor Review 42, no. 3 (March 1936): 527.

Despite these differentials, a U.S. Women's Bureau survey of Flint, Michigan, in 1925 found that the $20.10 per week women averaged in that city's auto industry (and this did include parts plants workers) was more than they were paid in any other type of work. See U.S. Women's Bureau, Bulletin no. 67, Women Workers in Flint, Michigan (1929), 19.

10. As I have argued elsewhere, dual labor market theory has many deficiencies in regard to its propositions about the sexual division of labor. But the distinction between primary and secondary economic locations does seem useful here. For a critique of the overall framework as applied to gender, see Ruth Milkman, Gender at Work: The Dynamics of Job Segregation by Sex during World War II (Urbana: University of Illinois Press, 1987), ch. 1.

11. "Automotive Parts: Wage Structure, March–April 1950," Monthly Labor

*Review* 72, no. 1 (January 1951): 37; Robert Blauner, *Alienation and Freedom* (Chicago: University of Chicago Press, 1964), 89–92; William McPherson, "Automobiles," in Harry A. Millis, ed., *How Collective Bargaining Works* (New York: Twentieth Century Fund, 1942), 611–12; Philip S. Foner, *Women and the American Labor Movement: From World War I to the Present* (New York: Free Press, 1980), 260, 270.

12. Sward, *Legend of Henry Ford*, 56.

13. Ford, *My Life and Work*, 128. See also Martha May, "The Historical Problem of the Family Wage: The Ford Motor Company and the Five Dollar Day," *Feminist Studies* 8, no. 2 (Summer 1982): 399–424.

14. U.S. Commission on Industrial Relations, *Industrial Relations*, vol. 8, Final Report and Testimony (1916), 7637.

15. "Meeting for Discussion of Labor Supply and Future Labor Requirements," June 26, 1942, Detroit, Michigan, 23–35 of transcript, in Folder: "241.11R Labor—Women—Recruiting Drive," Box 1016, Records of the War Production Board, RG 179, National Archives; interview with Edward Cushman, former head of the War Manpower Commission's Detroit office, Detroit, June 25, 1981. For a detailed discussion of the war years, see Milkman, *Gender at Work*, ch. 4.

16. U.S. Bureau of Labor Statistics, *Women in Factories*.

17. "Meeting for Discussion of Labor Supply," 30–31 of transcript.

18. National Industrial Conference Board, *Wartime Pay of Women in Industry*, NICB Studies in Personnel Policy, no. 58 (1943), 27.

19. "Women Outdoing Men, Ford Survey Reveals," *New York Daily News*, September 8, 1943.

20. "Women's Rates Advance," *UAW Research Report* 4, no. 9 (October–November 1944): 4. For discussion of the equal pay struggles, see Milkman, *Gender at Work*, ch. 5.

21. U.S. Senate Hearings before a Special Committee Investigating the National Defense Program, *Manpower Problems in Detroit*, 79th Congress, 1st Session, March 9–13, 1945, 13112–13.

22. See Milkman, *Gender at Work*.

23. Howell John Harris, *The Right to Manage: Industrial Relations Policies of American Business in the 1940s* (Madison: University of Wisconsin Press, 1982), 66–67, 91–93.

24. U.S. Bureau of Labor Statistics, *Women in Factories*. (The August figure of 18 percent was well below the wartime peak of 26 percent female.)

25. This is the main thesis of Harris, *The Right to Manage*.

26. U.S. Women's Bureau, Bulletin no. 209, *Women Workers in Ten War Production Areas and Their Postwar Employment Plans* (1946), 31, 42; "Women's Postwar Plans," *UAW Research Report* 4, no. 3 (March 1944): 3; Karen Anderson, *Wartime Women: Sex Roles, Family Relations and the Status of Women in World War II* (Westport, Conn.: Greenwood Press, 1981), 170–71.

27. "Policy on Women's Seniority Problems," *UAW-CIO Ammunition* 2,

no. 3 (March 1944): 13; "Women in Trade Unions during the War Period," p. 10 of draft report, in Box 1351, Records of the U.S. Women's Bureau, RG 86, National Archives.

28. For a representative statement, see the National Women's Trade Union League pamphlet, *Action Needed: Postwar Jobs for Women* (1944), 11–12. See also sources cited in note 3.

29. The UAW had a "Model Veterans' Seniority Clause," written into contracts with Chrysler, North American Aviation, and Mack Truck, among others, by 1946. See *UAW-CIO Ammunition* 4, no. 6 (April 1946): 23.

30. Robert P. Brecht, "Collective Bargaining and Re-employment of Veterans," *Annals of the American Academy of Political and Social Science* 227 (May 1943): 94–103; Joel Seidman, *American Labor from Defense to Reconversion* (Chicago: University of Chicago Press, 1953), 231–32.

31. For discussion, see sources cited in note 3.

32. *Proceedings of the 10th Convention of the United Automobile, Aircraft and Agricultural Implement Workers of America (UAW-CIO)*, March 23–31, 1946, 53.

33. For discussion, see sources cited in note 3.

34. Mildred Jeffrey, oral history, "The Twentieth-Century Trade Union Woman: Vehicle for Social Change—Oral History Project," 63–64 of transcript. For other examples of this sort of harassment, see William Oliver, "Report on Employees Laid Off from the Bomber Project, Highland Park Plant—(Johnson's Division)," February 9, 1945, in Folder: "William Oliver Reports," Box 16, UAW Ford Department Collection, Wayne State University Archives of Labor History and Urban Affairs (hereafter ALHUA); Jennie Lee Murphy and Minnie P. Sowell to Thomas J. Starling, April 13, 1946, in Folder: "Ford Dept., 1946–47," Box 23, Walter Reuther Collection, ALHUA. Many additional examples of this phenomenon could be cited.

35. U.S. Bureau of Labor Statistics, *Women in Factories*. Regarding the universal expectation of postwar depression, see Harris, *The Right to Manage*, 129.

36. The figure of 47 percent is the mean of the percentages for each of the eight months from December 1945 to July 1946; it does not reflect monthly variations in hiring rates. See "Veterans Return to the Nation's Factories," *Monthly Labor Review* 63, no. 6 (December 1946): 924–34.

37. "Recent Trends Affecting the Employment of Women in Automobile Manufacturing in Detroit," July 26, 1946, in Folder: "247 Michigan Dept. of Labor," Box 1290, Records of the U.S. Women's Bureau, RG 86, National Archives.

38. Interview with Andrew Court, Detroit, Michigan, June 25, 1981.

39. This is Alan Clive's estimate in his *State of War: Michigan in World War II* (Ann Arbor: University of Michigan Press, 1979), 216. David Ross also stresses the limited reemployment rights of veterans in *Preparing for Ulysses: Politics and Veterans during World War II* (New York: Columbia University Press, 1969), especially 157.

40. "Veterans Return to the Nation's Factories."

41. Olga S. Halsey, "Women Workers and Unemployment Insurance since V-J Day," *Social Security Bulletin* 9, no. 6 (June 1946): 4.

42. Unfortunately, detailed statistics on the long-term postwar employment situation of veterans are not available for individual industries. However, existing aggregate data are suggestive. A special survey of veterans by the U.S. Census Bureau conducted in October 1955 found that ten years after the end of World War II, 28.5 percent of all veterans were employed in manufacturing jobs; 60 percent of these veterans were under thirty-five years old in 1955. (The survey included both Korean War and World War II veterans, but the latter comprised 85 percent of the total of 21 million veterans in the United States in 1955.)

Of the six million veterans employed in manufacturing jobs in 1955, five million were World War II veterans. About two million of these were thirty-five years old or older in 1955. In 1947, the auto industry employed 5 percent of *all* manufacturing workers; if we assume that auto also employed 5 percent of the veterans in manufacturing, we can estimate that 100,000 veterans over age twenty-five worked in auto in 1945. This is surely a maximum figure, since veterans' turnover was high and auto firms were known to discriminate against older workers of both sexes. Also, Korean War veterans were probably disproportionately represented in the under–thirty-five age group in the 1955 census. For the figures on veterans, see *Readjustment Benefits: General Survey and Appraisal. A Report on Veterans' Benefits in the United States by the President's Commission on Veterans' Pensions* (House Committee Print No. 289, for the use of the House Committee on Veterans' Affairs, Staff Report No. IX, Part A, 84th Congress, 2d Session, September, 1956), 276. The 5 percent figure for auto employment is from the *1947 Census of Manufactures*, Vol. I, 70–77.

43. U.S. Bureau of Labor Statistics, *Women in Factories*.

44. Robert C. Weaver, *Negro Labor: A National Problem* (New York: Harcourt, Brace, and World, 1946), 285; August Meier and Elliott Rudwick, *Black Detroit and the Rise of the UAW* (New York: Oxford University Press, 1979), 213.

45. Meier and Rudwick, *Black Detroit*, 215.

46. The figures on Chrysler for 1945–1946 are from Weaver, *Negro Labor*, 289. All the 1960 figures are from UAW documents submitted at the *Hearings before the U.S. Commission on Civil Rights*, held in Detroit on December 14–15, 1960, 63–64.

47. See Meier and Rudwick, *Black Detroit*.

48. *Ibid.*; Weaver, *Negro Labor*.

49. The NAACP membership figure is from Meier and Rudwick, *Black Detroit*, 113. Their book is the best account of the development of the alliance between the UAW and Detroit black organizations in the 1940s. See also Karen Anderson, "Last Hired, First Fired: Black Women Workers during World War II," *Journal of American History* 69, no. 1 (June 1982): 86–87 especially, where she compares white male workers' attitudes toward women and blacks.

50. Both the employment figures and the quote are from Herbert R. Northrup, Richard L. Rowan, et al., *Negro Employment in Basic Industry* (Industrial Research Unit, Wharton School of Finance and Commerce, University of Pennsylvania, 1970), 65–75. The national employment figures are from the U.S. Census. Since they, unlike the figures for Detroit, include nonproduction as well as production workers, they overstate the difference between Detroit and the nation as a whole; the vast majority of nonproduction workers were white in this period. The quote is from the *Wall Street Journal*, October 24, 1957.

51. For an excellent analysis of some of these protests, see Nancy Gabin, " 'They Have Placed a Penalty on Womanhood': The Protest Actions of Women Auto Workers in Detroit-area UAW Locals, 1945–1947," *Feminist Studies* 8, no. 2 (Summer 1982): 373–98.

52. See Milkman, *Gender at Work*.

53. I have uncovered no evidence of this for the auto industry specifically, but see Constance Green, "The Role of Women as Production Workers in War Plants in the Connecticut Valley," *Smith College Studies in History* 28 (1946): 64–65, who reports that ". . . most companies frankly admitted that, given full freedom of choice after the war, if only out of deference to prevailing male opinion in the shops, management would revert to giving men's jobs, so called, only to men. And employers generally assumed that labor would permit no choice." Regarding management's concern about postwar unemployment, see Harris, *The Right to Manage*, 95.

54. Patricia Sexton cites 1970 EEOC figures indicating that female employment in auto accounted for about 10 percent of the total—about the same level as twenty years earlier. See Patricia Cayo Sexton, "A Feminist Union Perspective," in B. J. Widick, ed., *Auto Work and Its Discontents* (Baltimore: Johns Hopkins University Press, 1976), 18–33. Figures on changes in women's employment at the Big Three auto firms over the 1970s may be found in the following publications: *General Motors Report to Stockholders; General Motors Public Interest Report; Ford Annual Report; Chrysler Report to Shareholders* (various issues).

# 7

## "The Man in the Middle": A Social History of Automobile Industry Foremen

### NELSON LICHTENSTEIN

The relative decline in the productivity and competitiveness of the U.S. auto industry has rekindled interest in the decisive role played by first line supervision in the industry's work process. Foremen are the linchpin in the structure of factory work and authority, the management representatives most directly responsible for actually making production happen. The costly proliferation of this supervisory group, combined with the realization that overseas competitors have organized work along more productive and less hierarchical lines, has focused attention on an organizational stratum that seems to stand squarely in the way of a less authoritarian and more efficiently organized workplace. After a forty-year hiatus, managers are again discovering that in the auto industry, as elsewhere in American manufacturing, foremen and forewomen are the "men in the middle" of the workplace hierarchy, "marginal men of industry" whose jobs are in desperate need of reform.[1] "They aren't going to control people anymore," declared one management consultant in *Business Week*. "They have to coach them, help do the planning, approve organizational direction and make sure the directions are clear."[2]

Unfortunately, much of this discussion, largely in the industrial relations literature and the business press, has had an ahistorical quality assuming that the traditional role played by foremen has been determined exclusively by either the technology of production or the structures of management. These have been important, of course, but they cannot be divorced from either the larger politics of production or the changing consciousness of foremen themselves in the first half of the twentieth century. This essay seeks to uncover a slice of this complex history by emphasizing the way in which cultural and political forces, as well as structural changes in the organization of work, shaped the role foremen played in the factory hierarchy. During the late 1930s and early 1940s the changing collective identity of this stratum not only sustained a brief experiment in foreman unionism but also challenged the structure of authority inside the production facilities of the nation's premier industry; in the process foremen began to explore and expand the definition of what constituted a self-conscious working-class identity at midcentury.

## Foremen in the Mass Production Factory

In recent studies of the early twentieth-century factory, historians Daniel Nelson and Stephen Meyer have demonstrated that Taylorized management was only possible with the virtual destruction of the shop floor "empire" commanded by many nineteenth-century foremen. The power, autonomy, and prestige of both "inside contractors" and skilled mechanics could not survive where both the technology and organization of production were geared to scientifically managed mass production facilities. As factories became larger and work more compartmentalized and as production became standardized and coordinated, the foreman-contractor—who bid on a job, hired the workers, and then determined the pace, layout, and methods of work—vanished from the factory. Likewise, the skilled worker, who at one time might have employed a couple of helpers out of his own pay, became a tool maker or repair man who served a vital though auxiliary role in the mass production facility.[3]

Much of the skilled work was taken over and systematized by a burgeoning managerial stratum, including a growing corps of engineers, accountants, clerks, inspectors, and personnel managers. In those industries that began to approach the ideal of mass production—rubber, meat packing, oil, chemicals, automobiles—production line foremen had little say in scheduling or engineering and only a slight voice in the maintenance of the production facility or the control of product quality. Foremen did have some responsibility for cost control, and they sometimes kept rudimentary production and personnel records; but these tasks were often taken over by specially trained clerks in the larger factories.

With technical production decisions centralized, the foreman's role in recruiting, promoting, and firing his workers also underwent a dramatic transformation. Managerial awareness of the large cost of worker turnover, especially during World War I, led many firms to set up personnel departments which did much of the recruiting, testing, and assignment of the workforce.[4] By the end of the 1920s about 65 percent of some 224 large factories surveyed by the Department of Labor had a central employment office handling hiring for the plant. All the major automobile companies recruited through a central office in 1930, and more than 80 percent of the surveyed firms in the iron and steel, petroleum, refining, and food processing industries did as well. Centralized hiring enabled large firms to more easily maintain age and health standards, establish more uniform wage rates, and screen unionists and other undesirables. Foremen still had the right to reject a recruit in their department, and they could use their influence to facilitate the hiring of a friend or relative, but such action was the exception, not the norm, in the core firms of the auto industry.[5]

## "Getting Out Production"

Despite these genuine limitations on their power, foremen retained one essential function. They were responsible for labor discipline, for "getting out production" on time and up to standard. Style and technique might vary, but this would remain the first line supervisor's basic responsibility decade after decade. In 1912 an *Iron Age* correspondent noted that under Ford's new production set up, "the foreman in each department is purely a production man." His "particular duty" was "to see to it that the men under him turn out so many pieces per day and personally work to correct whatever may prevent it."[6] Forty years later foremen in a unionized auto plant told Yale University researchers virtually the identical story. "Ninety percent of my job is knowing how to break in and handle men," reported one foreman on the final assembly line. "It is very easy for the men to rebel, and then things go to hell before you know it. . . ."[7]

To maintain labor discipline production foremen held several social and organization weapons. First, the sheer number of foremen increased dramatically in the first two decades of the twentieth century. In auto plants and other continuous flow production facilities, the sequential and integrated character of production made the careless or recalcitrant worker a costly threat to overall efficiency, far greater than when small batch production was the norm. Close supervision was therefore essential. At Ford's Highland Park factory the ratio of foremen to production workers increased at a phenomenal rate. In 1914 one foreman directed an average of fifty-three workers; in 1917 each supervisor oversaw the work of only fifteen. In manufacturing industry as a whole the number of foremen increased more than 300 percent in an era when total employment did not quite double.[8]

Second, production foremen still held almost unlimited authority over the work lives of the men and women they supervised. Foremen had the unfettered right to assign jobs of varying levels of pay, difficulty, and pleasantness, and their voice went far beyond their jurisdiction in determining promotions or transfers. While establishment of central personnel offices had deprived foremen of their ability to hire workers off the street, managers were still extremely reluctant to deprive first line supervisors of the right to discharge. As one manager put it in 1926, the "foreman in the last analysis cannot help being a personnel man."[9] In the auto industry, employment managers and higher officials retained the sole right to discharge a worker in almost three-quarters of all firms surveyed in 1930, but this formal authority was rarely used to countermand a foreman's disciplinary action for fear of "demoralizing" the workers in his department. In this industry, reported economist W. Ellison Chalmers in 1932, "a strong position in favor of keeping the authority in the hands of the foremen" meant that employment managers "very seldom straighten the case out for the worker unless the foremen and superintendent agree on giving the man another chance." Most large auto firms declared a commitment to "adjust difficulties" between worker and foreman, but in few cases did higher level management make a foreman work with an employee he sought to discharge. At Ford workers had the right to petition a discharge to the Employment Office, but even if they were vindicated there such workers were always transferred to another department.[10]

When it came to layoffs, foremen had even greater unilateral power. In theory, some combination of efficiency, seniority, and family responsibility determined the layoff order during slack times, but in practice foremen had enormous discretion in making the individual selections. During the brief recession in 1927, for example, the Conference Board found that 90 percent of the firms it surveyed allowed their foremen to make the initial evaluation of who would be laid off; 60 percent left the layoff decision entirely up to the foremen.[11] Auto worker Clayton W. Fountain recalled in later years how application of this power looked to the average worker:

> The annual layoff during the model change was always a menace. . . . The bosses would pick the men off a few at a time, telling them to stay home until they were notified to come back. . . . The foremen had the say. If he happened to like you, or if you sucked around him and did him favors—or if you were one of the bastards who worked like hell and turned out more than production—you might be picked to work a few weeks longer than the next guy.[12]

On the assembly line, and in closely related departments where semiskilled labor predominated, a foreman's authority was further advanced through the intermediators he chose among the workforce itself. These were the variously named petty functionaries—crew chief, lead man, pusher, set-up man, gang boss, and straw boss— who, in contrast to the foreman, spent most of their time in actual production. Foremen selected these workers to see that their orders were actually carried out and the pace of production maintained. Set-up men were generally experienced or clever workers who made the initial adjustment when a machine was installed or its work load altered. Paid a nickel or so more than production workers, set-up men were also responsible for determining, in consultation with the foreman, the pace or quota of the new machine operation. Pushers and lead men, also paid a few cents an hour above the norm, were selected because of their loyalty and propensity to hard work. They were placed in those strategic locations in the production process, such as the first man on a sub assembly crew, where their own work rhythm could automatically set the pace for the rest of the working gang.[13]

Finally, the straw boss played a key role. Straw bosses, sometimes called working leaders or speed bosses, were combination pusher, relief man, spy, and all around foreman substitute. "What we call a straw boss," reported the Communist militant Bill McKie in 1934, "is a man who is not officially recognized as a foreman in the Ford plant, but is usually appointed by the foreman himself to look after particular gangs."[14] They were often chosen because they were of the same ethnic or language group as their work crew, thus enabling them to more effectively transmit the foreman's orders. Unlike lead men, straw bosses might not be continually engaged in production, but their responsibility for hurrying the work was still at the core of their duties. When the Ford Motor Company was struggling out of the postwar recession in 1922 management doubled the number of straw bosses to intensify the work pace.[15] Indeed, straw bosses could be difficult taskmasters, as Frank Marquart remembered from his stint at Chevrolet Gear and Axle: "One night I had machine trouble and fell behind in production. The straw boss, a sub-human pusher who had the authority to hire and fire, bellowed like a bull. When I tried to explain that I had machine trouble, he roared: 'I don't give a damn what you had, you get out production or you get fired—That's the rule around here, and no goddamn excuses.' "[16]

## Interwar Cultural Values

A foreman's power and his sense of social identity were also sustained by a set of social and cultural expectations largely intact until the 1940s. Most auto industry foremen took home wages about 25 percent higher than the men they supervised. More important, their paycheck was a good deal more predictable because managers sought to keep a core of experienced men employed even during large layoffs. Such employment stability enabled foremen to purchase solid houses in the better working-class neighborhoods and maintain a standard of living that approached that of the lower middle class. The overwhelming majority were married, and their children had good prospects of completing high school. Compared with the average production worker, who frequently changed jobs and firms during layoffs and recessions, foremen stayed put, and amassed some of the greatest seniority of any group in the midcentury industrial plant. In one survey conducted in the 1940s, foremen were found to be about fifteen years older than even the average member of the white-collar staff and had a turnover rate about one-third as high.[17]

A Protestant, lower middle-class outlook was one of the most distinctive elements of the foreman's worldview in this era. In the prosperous 1920s, when ethnic cleavages were most manifest, first line supervisors easily maintained a set of values that, on the surface at least, emphasized self-improvement, organizational loyalty, and unhyphenated Americanism. This outlook served to distance this overwhelmingly Anglo-Saxon and German group from the heavily Catholic, immigrant working class, and linked them, if somewhat tenuously, to the white-collar workers and the bureaucratic culture of corporate America. Advancing this orientation were the popular foremanship training classes offered by the YMCA in the first four decades of the twentieth century, and the company and community foremen's clubs that proliferated throughout many of the middle-sized, industrial cities of the Midwest. Part social club and part business association, the management-dominated National Association of Foremen emphasized education, self-advancement, and social intercourse between foremen in different industries and between foremen and top management.[18]

As both ideology and social network, Freemasonry played a particularly influential role in sustaining this supervisory work culture. Reaching its greatest popular influence in the 1920s, Freemasonry stood for brotherhood and respectability and propagated a creed of sober self-improvement, conventional morality, and class harmony. Lower middle-class white-collar workers composed about half its membership, and skilled craftsmen accounted for another 15 percent. Masons maintained an elaborate ritual, reinforcing a sense of social selectivity, but the quasi-religious elements which had infused nineteenth-century Freemasonry gave way to a more secular content that easily accommodated itself to the commercial culture and respectable evangelicalism of urban white-collar workers and small businessmen. It is not surprising therefore that many foremen joined the order: Masonry's anti-Catholic, Americanist flavor strengthened the lines that divided them from much of the factory workforce; moreover, its emphasis on the social and moral links between men of divergent occupations and class standings gave credence to top management's insistence that once promoted out of the workforce, foremen were now part of the company's "management team."[19]

Aside from its ideological message, Masonry served as a factory social network that partially overlapped the formal hierarchy of management's power and authority. At the Ford Motor Company, Protestant workmen proudly wore their Masonic rings in the expectation that membership in the organization would win them a promotion to foremen or at least protect them from the sometimes capricious discipline meted out by the company's infamous service department. Since Ford boss Harry Bennett was an active Mason, there was indeed some validity to the anti-Masonic charge that it was "not what you know, but who you know" that won advancement in the Ford organization. As foundry foreman Roy Campbell remembered the mid-1930s, "If you wanted to get any place or hold a job with any responsibility you better be a Mason." Almost all general foremen there were Masons, and although some particularly bright and ambitious Catholic workmen were promoted to the supervisory ranks these foremen remained under considerable pressure to join the order. Masonic influence was also pervasive among supervisory employees at Kelsey-Hayes, Packard Motor Company, and Cadillac in Detroit and at General Motors–controlled North American Aviation in California.[20]

## The Wrong Side of the Collar Line

By the end of the 1920s automobile industry foremen seemed to have found their place as tough, loyal sergeants in the management hierarchy. Yet auto industry foremen would soon demonstrate that despite their formal role in management they were in fact an integral part of the working class itself. This was true in two ways. First, foremen were subject to a wide set of social and organizational influences that brought their interests into a parallel relationship with that of their subordinate workmates. Foremen had higher wages and more authority, but, as we shall see, their factory role was far closer to that of a semiautonomous skilled worker than a management official. Second, their consciousness was never a simple reflection of their place in the factory hierarchy. When a mobilization of rank-and-file workers broke open the social mold of the traditional factory in the late 1930s, foremen became subject to a dynamic set of pressures propelling them into a de facto alliance with the brand of militant industrial unionism then sweeping the auto industry.

Foremen stood on the wrong side of the collar line: they got their hands dirty, they were recruited directly out of the workforce, were rarely salaried, and wore work clothes almost indistinguishable from the average worker. At Ford foremen wore the same numbered badge as did other workers in the plant: the great social dividing line there was drawn between those who were on salary—they had a star imprinted on their metal badge—and the vast majority of hourly workers. At the Rouge foremen had neither desks nor telephones; they kept their few records at little stand-up "pulpits" close to the department they supervised. They were not often skilled craftsmen, but their work values had much in common with such workers. They took enormous pride in the efficient, autonomous operation of their department. At Ford and Chrysler foremen were routinely expected to know how to set up and run the machines of all the workers they supervised, and they were proud of their ability to solve production problems without assistance or interference from higher levels of plant supervision.[21]

The production-oriented outlook of such foremen had a Veblinite flavor when they came into conflict with higher management, especially the college-educated, and sometimes condescending, white-collar staff. These staff specialists were frequently resented, not only by foremen but also by general foremen and plant superintendents. Sociologist Melvin Dalton found that such line personnel shared a blue-collar production culture. They referred to their white-collar superiors as "college punks," "sliderules," and "chairwarmers." "First line foremen were inclined to feel that top management had brought in the production planning, industrial relations and engineering staffs as clubs with which to control the lower line," concluded Dalton. "Hence they frequently regarded the projects of staff personnel as manipulative devices and reacted by cooperating with production workers . . . to defeat insistent and uncompromising members of the staff."[22]

Although foremen were responsible for labor discipline, even this task was full of ambiguity. They themselves were the objects of a managerial effort to rationalize and intensify production, but first line supervisors were also subject to the intimate and unremitting social and psychological pressure generated by the workers under them. In the 1940s it became a passionately held axiom of corporate spokesmen that foremen were part of management, but executives as early as 1926 recognized that "the foreman stands on the middle ground between management and employee. . . ." He had a "dual personality: to the company he represents the workman, to the workman he is the company."[23] This tension made foremen both the "master and victim of doubletalk," concluded the famous industrial psychologist,

Fritz J. Roethlisberger. "The foreman is management's contribution to the social pathology of American culture." [24]

The pressures generated by the daily world of work sucked foremen into a degree of informal accommodation with their subordinates. Foremen spent the bulk of their workday not with higher level management or other foremen but with a production crew upon whose efforts the foreman's own success depended. A measure of friendly cooperation was therefore essential to efficient production, and a degree of psychological accommodation was vital if foremen were to avoid the isolation and ostracism of which even a nonunion work crew was capable. Thus, foremen often shared many of the same attitudes toward their job as did ordinary production workers. They wanted predictable work quotas, stable piece rates, and steady work. They wanted a smoothly running department, which meant they wanted to avoid conflict with either management above or workers below.

When Stanley Mathewson took his working tour of industrial America in 1930, he found numerous instances in which foremen or straw bosses "conspired" with their workers to thwart the will of the managerial staff. "They don't want the rate cut any more than we do," one worker told Mathewson. "It just makes the men sore and causes a lot of trouble." [25] Fifteen years later sociologist Donald Roy found foremen just as hostile to time-study people, "the true hatchet men of upper management." In the Chicago machine shop he studied, Roy found that foremen tolerated the elaborate stratagems workers devised to bend the piecework rules. "You've got to chisel a little around here to make money," one foreman asserted. [26] And in the more authoritarian setting of GM's Framingham assembly plant a postwar foreman defined one of his prime duties as that of social "shock absorber," with the "ability to take pressure from above, but not pass it on." [27]

A region of chronic conflict between foremen and their supervisors came in the realm of manpower management. Unforeseen equipment breakdowns, schedule changes, and absenteeism always seemed to keep foremen on the short end of the manpower stick—or so it seemed to them. This made the foremen's job much more difficult: sometimes they had to do the production work themselves, but more often it forced them to drive the men harder or scurry around in search of stray workers in other departments to fill the gaps. Thus, foremen were often reluctant to grant workers adequate relief time on the job, and they could be harsh disciplinarians when it came to unauthorized absences. But by the same token, foremen sought to maintain a certain "fat" in their manpower roster, ready for use when the inevitable emergency arose. In the early 1930s W. Ellison Chalmers was surprised to find that many workers considered themselves in alliance with their straw boss or foremen against the plant superintendent and the company's notorious service department. Foremen penalized obvious idleness, he reported in 1934, but they also told workers that any loafing should be done by leaning against the inside of a car body, where they would not be spotted by the service personnel. This subterranean conflict between foremen and managers was more systematically confirmed after World War II.[28] Charles Walker and his team of researchers from Yale found that absenteeism, along with quality control, was the most vexing problem faced by foremen at GM's Framingham plant. "It seems to me that if I can't be trusted to judge how many men I need, I shouldn't be a foreman," reported one first line supervisor in final assembly. "We just get treated as if we can't be trusted."[29]

## The Impact of the CIO

Given the conflicting pressures under which foremen functioned during the interwar era, the organization of strong industrial unions in the late 1930s was bound to precipitate a major crisis for first line supervisors. The empowerment of workers at the shop floor level proved the central thrust of the union movement in its early years. Almost by definition, therefore, the success of this effort required the diminution or elimination of the power traditionally exercised by foremen. "With the coming of the Union, the foreman finds his whole world turned upside down," asserted a United Automobile Workers (UAW) stewards manual. "His small time dictatorship has been overthrown and he must be adjusted to a democratic system of shop government."[30] The transformation in power relationships could be dramatic. "First we had to cut down the size of those hard boiled foremen," recalled a Dodge worker. "Sometimes foremen would jerk up the automatic conveyor a couple of notches and speed up the line. We cured them of that practice: we simply let jobs go by half finished."[31]

A more subtle but hardly less important erosion of foreman power

took place as the new unions developed a set of uniform regula-
tions to govern shop floor working conditions. Seniority rules, job
bidding, and grievance procedures gave workers an elementary sense
of job security because these contractual devices sharply limited the
foreman's ability to either reward or punish his subordinates. In the
early years union shop stewards often patrolled their department to
police the contract and maintain informal contact with their men.
When grievances arose, most contracts insisted that stewards first
take these up with the foremen for immediate resolution. But in a
situation where the union's shop floor strength was clearly manifest,
stewards often "short circuited" the foremen, taking their grievances
directly to plant management where the real power lay. Executives
and superintendents frequently cooperated in this operation; either
they doubted the loyalty of the foremen, or they considered union
problems far too important to be left to the lowly foremen.[32] "Sometimes the employer stands behind the foreman," complained a Murray Corporation supervisor in 1943, "but more frequently the foreman
is thrown to the wolves."[33]

Unionism in the automobile industry also had the effect of strip-
ping foremen of the lead men, pushers, and straw bosses who projected their authority in the shop. Most workers hated these petty
tyrants, and the new UAW insisted that any individual who worked on
production had to be a union member; therefore, these intermediate
categories were either upgraded to full foreman status, eliminated, or
refined. Set-up men became "special operators," while straw bosses
lost their disciplinary and production control function, becoming instead the slightly higher paid "relief" or "utility" workers who rotated
jobs as members of the work crew took their breaks. At the Rouge
foundry the very second grievance handled by committeeman Shel-
don Tappes involved the status of some ninety straw bosses there.
Forty-two were upgraded to foremen, but the rest lost their quasi-
supervisory status and were returned to production worker rolls.
Working leaders were also eliminated in most production departments or made part of the union where they still played a functional
role, as in tool and die work.[34]

As shop stewards exhibited their power and foremen lost their departmental corporals, managers compensated for the changing equa-
tion of shop floor power by substantially increasing the number of
first line supervisors. For example, in the railroad operations of the

River Rouge plant, unionized yardmasters assigned switch orders to the crews and oversaw their execution. By 1945 Ford management had concluded that supervision needed to be tightened up. The existing foremen, spread over three shifts, were inadequate for the job. So Ford eliminated the yardmaster job and assigned twelve additional foremen to the yard.[35] In like manner foremen/production worker ratios, which had ranged as high as fifty-to-one on line operations, were now sharply reduced. At the Rouge 2,226 foremen supervised 67,360 workers in July 1935; eleven years later 3,020 supervised a workforce that had shrunk by 3,853. Thus, Ford's foreman/worker ratio increased about 50 percent.[36]

Indeed, the 1940s was an era of large increases in both the absolute numbers and in the proportion of American manufacturing foremen. While the ratio of foremen to production workers had remained static between 1920 and 1940, the next decade saw a 70 percent increase in the number of foremen and a 21 percent increase in the ratio of first line supervisors to the production workforce. This phenomenon was not merely a product of the conversion and reconversion of U.S. industry to war production, for the foreman/worker ratio continued to increase in the next few decades as well (see Table 7.1).[37]

## Foreman Unionism

Although rank-and-file militancy eroded the power enjoyed by manufacturing foremen, the union idea also promised fundamental changes in the role foremen would play in the twentieth-century factory. During the next decade many foremen sought to win for themselves some of the same protections against managerial authority that the unionized rank and file had already begun to secure. This meant that foremen would enjoy the protections of a seniority system, a grievance procedure, and a rationalized wage structure. But beyond this, foreman unionization also held out the vision of a more radical transformation of the way in which work and authority would be organized in the midcentury factory. Foremen, after all, were the linchpins of a hierarchical, bureaucratic work process, and any fundamental change in their status necessarily reverberated throughout the factory social structure.

Foreman unionism arose in those places where the new CIO unions had proven most disruptive to the old order. At the Kelsey-Hayes

**Table 7.1.** Foremen as a Proportion of Workforce

| Year | Foremen (in thousands) | Manufacturing Payroll (in thousands) | Foremen (in percentages) | Foremen Auto (in thousands) | Total Auto Employment (in thousands) | Foremen (in percentages) |
|---|---|---|---|---|---|---|
| 1900 | 90 | 5,468 | 1.64 | | | |
| 1910 | 164 | 7,828 | 2.09 | | | |
| 1920 | 296 | 10,702 | 2.77 | | | |
| 1930 | 293 | 9,562 | 3.06 | | | |
| 1940 | 310 | 10,985 | 2.82 | | | |
| 1950 | 525 | 15,241 | 3.44 | 31.6 | 863.4 | 3.66 |
| 1960 | 756 | 16,796 | 4.50 | 39.4 | 838.9 | 4.70 |
| 1970 | 938 | 19,369 | 4.84 | 52.0 | 1,033.3 | 5.02 |
| 1980 | 1,754 | 21,942 | 7.99 | 70.1 | 1,171.1 | 5.98 |

*Note:* 1980 foremen data is listed as "Blue Collar Worker Supervisors," a category which differs somewhat from earlier "foremen" category.

*Sources:* U.S. Bureau of the Census, *Historical Statistics of the United States, Colonial Times to 1970*, part 1 (Washington, D.C.: GPO, 1975), 137, 138, 142; U.S. Bureau of Labor Statistics, *Labor Force Statistics Derived from the Current Population Survey: A Databook*, vol 1, Bulletin 2096, Tables B-19, B-20.

Wheel Company, a labor intensive parts plant, shop conditions were revolutionized by UAW Local 174, a militant union led by a coalition of radicals that included the famous Reuther brothers. Within a few weeks of the organization of the 5,000-worker plant in late 1936 wages almost doubled, and a strong steward system was installed. Swept up in this movement, Clarence Bolds, a veteran foreman with an older brother active in the International Typographical Union (which had long organized pressroom foremen), began urging foremen to join Local 174. Bolds's efforts were encouraged by the UAW—he spoke at the Local's joint council meetings—but his work first bore fruit during the recession of 1938 when Kelsey-Hayes forced foremen to take a 10 to 15 percent salary reduction and a two-week stretch of work at half-pay. Since the wages of the company's production workers were protected by a contract, the benefits of unionism seemed manifest.

In December 1938 Bolds and a group of Kelsey foremen won a charter from the CIO as United Foremen and Supervisors, Local Industrial Union 918. Although Bolds had lobbied for direct affiliation with the UAW, auto union activists in Local 174 were not entirely convinced that the foremen might not be or become corporate pawns. In any event the independent union expanded rapidly, recruiting almost 100 percent of the Kelsey workforce in a couple of weeks and then winning a cancellation of the wage cut. Local 918 won few written contracts but nevertheless soon expanded to at least sixteen other Detroit plants and enrolled over 900 foremen.[38]

In practice Local 918 functioned in a close alliance with the UAW. For example, at the Universal Cooler Corporation, the local negotiated a contract, really a supplement to the UAW agreement there, which provided foremen with grievance adjustment, seniority protection, and a two-week vacation. But the clause foremen pointed to with at least equal satisfaction read: "It is mutually agreed and understood that the Universal Cooler Corporation will not demand or request any act or action whatever of its supervisory employees which would tend to strain or break the existing harmonious and fraternal relationship between United Foremen and Supervisors and the UAW and Local 174." To one foreman, this simply meant: "No longer are we to be forced to treat employees like heels."[39] Bolds himself cast the cordial relationship he expected to build with the production worker unions in a radical light. "With the organization of foremen and supervisors into a bona fide labor union," Bolds asserted in the *Michigan CIO News*, "management loses its last outpost in the plants, and organized labor gains a valuable ally":

> Management loses its cat's paw, the one it always used to pull its chestnuts from the fire. . . . It loses the group it used as a union busting, union baiting force and through which it spread false rumors to cause internal dissention in labor's ranks. . . . The threat of strikebreakers becomes less than nothing, for without supervision to show them how and what to do, they are helpless.[40]

An early conflict involving CIO foremen occurred at Chrysler during the UAW's long, bitter strike in the fall of 1939. The central issue in this work stoppage was the union's effort to win joint control of production standards at the corporation's Dodge Main, Dodge Truck, and Jefferson Avenue plants. After the UAW swept Chrysler's NLRB elections in the spring, Chrysler locals had orchestrated a series of slow-downs and stoppages to demonstrate union strength. With some 500 "white button" stewards at Dodge Main alone, the UAW maintained a powerful shop floor presence to neutralize the power of management's lower level officials and spread union influence throughout all phases of the production process. Chrysler replied by firing some 150 union activists in August, which in turn precipitated a corporation wide lockout-strike two months later.[41] "Production schedules are the management's function," declared Chrysler spokesmen. "You may as well know now that we do not intend to give your union control of production."[42]

Foremen were caught squarely in the middle of this battle. Local 918 had a substantial, but unrecognized organization in the Chrysler plants, and top management there suspected, with some justification, that these foremen were unreliable sergeants in the struggle against the union. In mid-November, therefore, Chrysler fired forty-eight Dodge Truck foremen, all members of Local 918. Bolds shortly thereafter petitioned Chrysler for a formal bargaining session so that, upon the corporation's refusal, Local 918 could file an unfair labor practices charge with the NLRB. But Chrysler now used the foreman's petition to assert that the CIO "wanted to sit on both sides of the bargaining table." Widely publicizing the incident, Chrysler called off negotiations with the UAW, threatened a back-to-work movement, and demanded that the CIO repudiate the foremen's group.[43] CIO officials

did little to resist Chrysler's new demands. The long strike, over issues not readily comprehensible to the public, was proving an embarrassment; furthermore, the status of foremen under the Wagner Act
was a subject of much controversy. Thus, in the final strike settlement
the CIO agreed to disband Local 918 in all Chrysler plants, and in
effect repudiated any immediate effort to organize foremen in heavy
industry.[44]

The Chrysler fight had a threefold legacy. First, managers in large
corporations were sensitized to the potential defection of their first
line supervisors, especially to any organizational links they might
forge with unions of production workers. At the same time, the CIO,
increasingly attuned to the growing conservative backlash of the late
1930s, sought to avoid opening a new battlefront with management,
and quite possibly with the government, by taking a hands-off attitude toward foreman unionization. And finally foremen themselves
seemingly recognized that direct affiliation with the industrial union
might carry an unexpectedly heavy public relations and organizational burden. Thus, when the next round of auto industry supervisory unionism began in late 1941, its institutional form would be
independent of the union composed of the production workers themselves.

## The Foreman's Association of America

World War II economic mobilization increased supervisory disenchantment with existing factory arrangements. In the new full employment economy, the foremen's tradition of employment security
was of much less value, but supervisors found that many economic
benefits of the wartime boom were passing them by. With their pay
constrained by the government's wage and salary controls, but without the plentiful overtime pay enjoyed by production workers, many
foremen found their wartime wage hovering little above that of the
men and women they supervised.[45]

Furthermore, the ranks of supervision were greatly diluted by
the rapid upgrading of production workers, given crash courses in
basic foremanship by individual companies and the federal Training
Within Industry organization. At General Motors 42 percent of its
19,000 foremen had been on the job less than one year in 1943. At
Chrysler's De Soto Wyoming Avenue Plant, the number of foremen

tripled in the three and a half years after mobilization began in early 1941. Fully 85 percent of the new foremen had been recruited from the ranks of the plant's unionized workforce.[46] Wartime foremen were thus likely to have had a direct personal experience with the industrial unions during their most aggressive phase, although it would prove to be the old time foremen, not the new recruits, who would spearhead the efforts toward foremen organization. Regardless of their tenure, many wartime foremen could expect to return to the ranks once the war ended, the veterans returned, and industry's manpower needs shrank. As a result, they were preoccupied with job security and naturally considered unionism the way to get it. "They have not been properly trained or instructed in order to function efficiently, " complained a middle-level manager at Packard, "nor have they the proper viewpoint of management toward their jobs."[47]

The Foreman's Association of America built its spectacular wartime growth upon this disenchantment. The new organization took much of its character from its place of origin and largest organizational base: the 4,000-member supervisory force employed at Ford's giant River Rouge complex. Although prewar supervisors at Ford were noted for their hard driving manner, these same foremen also inhabited a world of insecurity and fear. Under Harry Bennett the company was notorious for its administrative disorder and brutality. Service department personnel harassed foremen as well as their subordinates, lines of authority were indistinct, and employment records were often incomplete. Supervisory pay varied considerably between the nineteen separate buildings at the Rouge; for example, when a seniority and classification system was later established, many foremen found that they had for several years been assigned supervisory tasks but listed on the employment role as mere working leaders.[48]

The union breakthrough at the Rouge struck this archaic supervisory structure like a whirlwind. During the summer and fall of 1941 production standards everywhere were cut back, and petty shop rules ignored. In many buildings UAW committeemen won the de facto right to veto supervisory decisions. "We noticed a very definite change in attitude of the working man," recalled one supervisor some years later. "They got very independent. It was terrible for a while, just awful. . . . The bosses were just people to look down on after the union came in. We were just dirt after that."[49] Many foremen sought to join Local 600 immediately after it won recognition in May 1941, but the union rejected their affiliation after it signed a contract with Ford that limited its membership to nonsupervisory blue-collar workers.

Rouge foremen would have to undertake their own organization; it began soon in the newly built Pratt and Whitney Aircraft building. In this massive but still incomplete facility, the technical landscape was as chaotic as the shop floor social relationships were explosive. To staff the new facility Ford managers had recruited 500 foremen from throughout the Rouge complex itself. These men were the pick of the supervisory staff: experienced but still ambitious, technically competent, many with skilled trades backgrounds. But in the summer of 1941 they found no roof over much of the new building, machine tools scattered everywhere, and layout plans that required clever modification before actual production of the complicated, precision-tooled Pratt and Whitney engines could begin. To get their newly hired workforce into shape most foremen were working seven days a week, ten hours a day. Their pay, they soon found, varied not according to their work responsibility but remained linked to their prewar assignments.[50]

All this put aircraft building foremen under enormous pressure, deeply offended their sense of order and efficiency, and sparked the first informal group meetings. Led by twenty-eight-year-old Robert Keys, a few aircraft unit foremen met as a "social club" in August and September, but in October they held a joint meeting with the foundry unit foremen, attended by about 350. By this time Keys and the other foremen activists were being swamped by inquiries about the new organization; they found it easy to pull together a plantwide meeting of 1,200 at Fordson High School the next month, formally establishing the Foreman's Association of America and electing a set of officers. By the end of the year the FAA had 4,020 members in six Ford chapters.[51]

Early efforts to communicate with Ford management were unsuccessful until May 1942 when Ford discharged an FAA building chairman who sought to represent another foreman on a grievance. After 169 fellow foremen in the spring and upset building stopped work to protest, Ford dismissed them all. At this point the FAA, then representing more than 3,700 members at the Rouge, threatened a strike, which finally forced Ford's top management to take notice of the new organization. All foremen were reinstated and a joint committee established to negotiate a new wage scale and grievance procedure.

In November, the FAA concluded a fairly elaborate agreement with Ford that boosted wages 15 percent and began a process that would rationalize supervisory job classifications. At the same time Ford created a Foreman's Personnel Office to handle supervisory grievances and administer the reclassification scheme.[52]

During 1942 the FAA spread to Packard, Chrysler, Briggs, Hudson, and Kelsey-Hayes, where the CIO had once enrolled foremen, and then to other plants in the Detroit area. By the end of the year the association had eight chapters in thirty-two different plants for a total membership of some 9,000. When a chapter was organized, it took in not only the foremen but also most of the general foremen above them. Among the production line supervisory staff there was extremely little opposition to the new organization; thus, when the NLRB began to hold certification elections in 1944 and 1945, pro-FAA votes usually ran about nine-to-one, higher even than that of the CIO unions in their most dynamic phase.[53] With no paid staff or organizing department, the FAA "comes as close to being a spontaneous development as anything that requires organization can be," admitted *Business Week* in late 1942. The next year the FAA doubled its membership and began to spread beyond the Detroit area, enrolling supervisors in the rubber, steel, and aircraft industries. By early 1945 the FAA had enlisted 33,000 foremen in 152 chapters, largely in the Midwest and almost always in mills or factories first organized by the new industrial unions.[54]

## The Foreman's Association: Ideology and Politics

The early FAA activists shared several important social characteristics. Almost all were veteran foremen. Youthful Robert Keys, the FAA founder and first president, had been a Rouge foreman since 1935, and his father had almost thirty years of supervisory experience at Ford. Carl Brown, the FAA's first paid organizer, had made foreman at Ford's Highland Park factory in 1924, and Ford activist Bertram Fenwick was promoted to foreman in 1927 and general foreman in 1929. At Packard FAA chapter chairman Prosper Traen had been promoted to foreman in 1932 and later made general foreman, and Chrysler leader Frank Elliott had almost as many years supervisory experience. DeSoto FAA activist Roger Erickson had been a foreman since 1937. Production workers recently upgraded to foreman rank undoubtedly made up a substantial portion of the FAA rank and file, but the association cadre was almost universally prewar foremen of several years' experience.[55]

FAA leaders were proud of their technical proficiency and appalled at what they viewed as managerial confusion and inefficiency. Few association leaders seem to have won their posts through Masonic or other "inside" connections: the activists in the organization were typically ambitious and highly competent Catholics who had been promoted from the production worker rank and file despite their religious background. Keys and Theodore Bonaventura, another aircraft building pioneer, had graduated from the Ford Trade School, the rigorous high school located in the Rouge itself. Bonaventura, an instructor there for several years until he was put in charge of sixteen other foremen in the aircraft building, was disgusted with wartime cost-plus waste and saw the FAA, among other things, as a vehicle for putting some "backbone" in the Ford organization. Fred Temple, another FAA pioneer, had moved rapidly from a skilled trades apprenticeship to foundry foreman at age nineteen, with responsibility for technically difficult castings. Fenwick had not taken apprenticeship training, but he was an effective and resourceful supervisor of more than 1,200 workers in the stamping plant, and on at least one occasion he had assisted Henry Ford in experimental work on an early V-8 engine. He was contemptuous of those plant superintendents and managers who had won their posts through the connections they enjoyed with Harry Bennett and other high Ford officials. Keys spoke for many of these production-minded foremen when he later told a House Committee, "We are trying to establish a program in the plants where we work that the employers themselves have failed to established—a program of harmony, cooperation and efficiency."[56]

The social ideology put forward by the Foreman's Association was one of inherent ambiguity. Unlike the CIO supervisory union, the FAA sought to maintain an institutional distance between itself and the UAW, but its independence was continually undermined by the growing hostility of the employers and by the everyday alliances association members forged with rank-and-file workers. As the FAA constitution's preamble announced: "The foreman fits between two enormous powers: ownership and management on top; and labor unions with enormous numbers, on the bottom . . . in the ceaseless struggle between ownership and wage labor the foreman will become a victim

unless all foremen are organized. . . ."[57] The FAA's effort to carve
out a separate identity for itself was in part a calculated effort to as-
suage the fears of employers like Ford, Packard, and Chrysler, who
suspected, rightly as it turned out, that no supervisory union could
long exist without the tacit support and cooperation of the industrial
workers themselves. But the FAA's adoption of the view that its members were the "men in the middle" also reflected a certain resentment
foremen felt toward the newly empowered rank-and-file workers.
Foremen were genuinely upset when even a small minority of their
subordinates earned more than they, for such a discrepancy seemed
to mirror in a highly visible form the changing power relationship in
the factory. As the veteran Packard foreman Alfred Bounim put it in
1944, "We want to be honored men among honored people. This is
why we are fighting. . . . The rank and file gets [pay] increases all the
time. All the CIO has to do is to make a serious complaint and they
get it; they are even successful in getting foremen removed."[58]

But as much as individual foremen might feel a personal sense of
anxiety, the actual process of building a union drove the FAA, despite
its formal ideology, into an increasingly intimate collaboration with
the CIO as an institution and with rank-and-file workers as individuals. Because executive management fiercely resisted the organization
of foremen, the FAA had to define itself as an opponent of top management and search for other allies in its battle for survival. With
public opinion generally hostile to foreman unionization and with
the government labor relations agencies unreliable, the FAA turned to
the UAW and other industrial unions for aid and encouragement. On
one level this informal alliance represented a practical recognition
that the new trade unions were the only force powerful enough to
enable the FAA to survive in its struggle with the corporations; but on
a deeper social and psychological level, the foremen's union orientation proved a tribute to the ability of a newly mobilized working
class to sweep into its orbit whole social strata that in more socially
quiescent times might have opposed it.

In the 1940s unionizing foremen increasingly rejected the role of
labor disciplinarian. This attitude reflected the social pressures generated by a militant stewards organization, but it was also part of the
changing consciousness of foremen themselves. "Let the employer
quit issuing trouble-making orders through foremen to the rank and
file with the purpose of testing out how far he can push labor around

without backwash," complained FAA President Keys in 1944.[59] Instead, argued FAA membership director Harold M. Kelley, the association sought "harmony and good fellowship . . . making working conditions much more pleasant for all."[60] At Ford, where a collective bargaining contract was eventually worked out with the corporation, the association demanded strict adherence to seniority in all promotions and demotions, not simply as an equitable way to handle the postwar layoffs but as a shield against management's ability to select and assign new jobs to the "red apple boys" and "company men" within the supervisory ranks themselves. Foremen saw their work as production, not general labor discipline, and they resisted those traditional policing functions expected of first line supervisors, such as searching the washrooms for loafers and penalizing workers who left work early or rang each others' time cards. Foremen also refused to discipline UAW committeemen who did union business on company time because FAA officials sought to exercise this right as well.[61]

Organizational necessity and shop floor social pressure forced the association to develop close ties with the unions representing production workers. Most individual foremen were New Deal Democrats, and the FAA generally endorsed the CIO's social and economic agenda. The association considered itself part of the "labor movement as a whole," and the CIO in turn welcomed the organization of first line supervisors.[62] Despite repeated public protestations of their mutual independence, foremen and production workers were drawn into an increasingly intimate alliance. As even Chrysler attorney Theodore Iserman admitted, " 'Solidarity of labor' is not an empty phrase, but a strong and active force. . . ."[63] Many UAW locals helped the FAA organize their plants: foremen at Murray and Briggs met in the UAW local halls near these factories; at out-of-state plants—such as North American Aviation in Inglewood, Glen L. Martin in Omaha, and John Deere in East Moline—UAW officials helped spark FAA organizational activity.[64]

The collaboration between organized foremen and the UAW proved most apparent in a series of strikes called by the FAA in 1943 and 1944. These work stoppages—first at Ford and then at Chrysler, Briggs, Packard, Hudson, Murray, and other Detroit area firms—were designed to demonstrate the strength of organized foremen and to force government labor relations agencies to adopt a less hostile view of foreman unionization. In particular, the FAA sought to reverse the

NLRB's 1943 Maryland Drydock decision, denying foremen the protection of the Wagner Act. In May 1943 Keys won from CIO leaders the assurance that, although rank-and-file workers would pass through FAA picket lines, they would refuse to take foremen's jobs once inside the factory. As things turned out foremen received much more than this support, and their strikes, especially the multiday walkouts called in May 1944, proved exceptionally effective. Rank-and-file workers let production slide, refused to cooperate with working foremen and in some instances, as at Packard and Briggs, joined the FAA picket lines.[65]

Many businessmen had hoped that the end of the war would ease the pressure for organization of supervisory personnel; they thought that unreliable temporary foremen would now revert to production line jobs and that the end of wartime wage and salary controls would rebalance take-home earnings of first line supervisors and production workers. As war plants closed FAA membership did decline, but the vitality of the association was actually enhanced as seniority protections and grievance procedures became more important to foremen threatened by postwar factory reorganization. As *Business Week* put it in May 1946, "It seems clear that a few dollars more or less in the pay envelope will not determine the success or failure of efforts to build unions of foremen." The FAA had chapters at more than 100 worksites, bargained informally with an increasingly large number of companies, held annual conventions, and leased a country club for its members' exclusive use.[66]

Foreman unionization seemed to be making headway on the legal-political front as well. The strikes the FAA had waged in 1943 and 1944 had forced the National War Labor Board to hold a series of well-publicized hearings substantiating foremen's claims that their power and status had fallen in recent decades. More importantly, the NLRB, also reading the newspaper headlines, first modified and then reversed its 1943 Maryland Drydock decision which had consigned foremen to a nonunion managerial realm. In its March 1945 Packard case, the board used the same criterion advanced by the Foreman's Association in distinguishing first line supervisors from top management: they were employees under the Wagner Act because they did not set policy. The next year the board went further and ruled in a case involving coal mine supervisors at the Jones and Laughlin Steel Company: foremen could not be barred from membership in a rank-

and-file union if the employees' freedom of choice under the Wagner Act were not to be abridged. The FAA won NLRB elections at Hudson, Chrysler, and Packard and secured a ballot slot at twenty-five additional factories. Encouraged by the Packard and Jones and Laughlin decisions, both the CIO and the AFL became more active as organizers of first line supervisors, usually in separately chartered locals. By the early postwar years an estimated 100,000 foremen were organized into some sort of collective bargaining unit.[67]

## The Managerial Vision

Corporate management never reconciled itself to the unionization of first line supervisors. Because most American managers defined the structure of industrial enterprise as one necessarily hierarchical and authoritarian, the independent organization of foremen seemed to deprive them of the essential instruments by which they confronted and controlled the newly empowered but still "undisciplined" rank-and-file workers. By the end of the war most managers in the auto industry had concluded that "containment" was the most realistic policy to adopt toward the new industrial unions, especially on issues involving power relationships and management prerogatives at the shop floor level. There management would fight to retain or regain control of work standards, manpower allocation, and discipline, but to conduct this struggle with any chance of success managers needed loyal first line supervisors in numbers sufficient to compete with union stewards and committeemen.[68] "We must rely upon the foremen to try and keep down those emotional surges of the men in the plants and urge them to rely on the grievance procedure," argued a Ford Motor Company spokesman. "If we do not have the foreman to do that, who is going to do it?"[69]

Management feared industrial anarchy. Seniority rights, grievance procedures, and union representation by foremen were subversive because if supervisors themselves felt less threatened by orders from above, then the immense social and psychological pressures generated from below would surely turn them into unreliable agents. Hence corporate rhetoric often used the military analogy. For example, a Detroit machine shop executive in 1943 asserted, "Picture if you can the confusion of an army in the field if the non-commissioned officers were forced to listen to the commands of the men

in their ranks as well as those of their superior officers." Similarly
a Hudson manager insisted that foreman unionization would force
industrial corporations to downgrade first line supervisors because
"no army can risk granting a commission to one who holds partial
allegiance to another country."[70] If foremen were organized, decried
the president of the Automobile Manufacturers Association, "mass
production" would go "into just sheer mob production."[71]

These alarming predictions were surely exaggerated. Foreman
unionization had existed for decades in 'he printing and building trades and in many shipyards and machine shops. And as the
Foreman's Association and other organized supervisory groups repeatedly pointed out, production did not collapse in those newly
organized factories and mills where management recognized unions
of foremen. For the most part first line supervisors still obeyed orders
from above, disciplined production workers when necessary, and
produced the work in reasonable time. In fact, many FAA foremen
argued that factory efficiency rose when foremen unionized because
work could now proceed in an "atmosphere cleared of treachery and
political intrigue."[72]

Yet the stakes were high in the battle over foreman unionization
because this fight was central to the larger conflict over the legitimacy and limits of corporate power in the 1940s. Foreman organization did not just threaten to weaken management authority at the
point of production; rather it eroded the vitality of corporate ideology
in society at large by shattering the unitary facade of management
and opening the door to a much larger definition of what constituted a self-conscious working-class identity. Thus, General Motors
President Charles E. Wilson thought foreman unionization "one more
step toward participation in management by labor organizations, one
more serious encroachment upon management."[73]

The loyalty of a whole middle stratum of white- and gray-collar
workers seemed at issue in the wake of the powerful social currents
set in motion by the rise of supervisory unionism. "The Foreman
Abdicates" ran a *Fortune* headline in 1945, but the larger issue was
whether or not the lower middle class—clerical workers, salesmen,
store managers, bank tellers, engineers, and draftsmen—would also
abandon their identification with the corporate order. "Where will
unionization end?" asked Wilson. "With the vice presidents?" As al-

most all managers recognized, a militant breakthrough by organized foremen promised to accelerate this mutiny.[74]

## Demise of the Foreman's Association

The decisive battle over foreman unionization came at the Ford Motor Company in the late spring of 1947. Ford had bargained with the Foreman's Association since mid-1942 and actually signed a contract with the association in May 1944. Although the new management team which took over at Ford in 1945 and 1946 was among the most liberal and progressive in heavy industry, Ford Motor Company, like its more conservative and intransigent competitors, was determined to win back foremen to the "management team." Between 1945 and 1948 the corporation undertook administrative and organizational reforms designed to differentiate foremen from rank-and-file workers and bring them into a closer psychological and organizational relationship with top management. The corporation inaugurated a series of supervisory bulletins, gave foremen separate locker facilities, parking spaces, and cafeterias, and insisted they wear white shirts and ties on the factory floor. For the first time foremen were given name badges distinguishing them from rank-and-file workers. In early 1946 foremen at Ford were put on salary and given a 15 percent wage increase. A pay differential of at least 25 percent was mandated between foremen and the average pay of their top five subordinates. More frequent meetings were held with top management, and foreman training courses, emphasizing the human relations and leadership skills then popular among industrial psychologists, became mandatory. Even the leaders of the FAA admitted that Ford's personnel changes, and similar reforms undertaken at other manufacturing firms, had materially improved the conditions of first line supervisors, without really altering the basic relationship to top management.[75]

In the contract negotiations that began in early 1947, Ford did not initially seek the destruction of the FAA, but it was nevertheless determined to bring its foremen "closer to other groups in management." The probable enactment of the Taft-Hartley Act, whose section 2(3) included a redefinition of the term "employee" so as to specifically exclude all first line supervisors, greatly encouraged the company program. This section represented an important victory for those in management who had fought to deprive foremen of any protections of the Wagner Act so recently interpreted by the NLRB and the courts. Although Ford had not been active in this campaign, company negotiators used the more favorable legal and political climate to demand that general foremen be excluded from the FAA bargaining unit and that merit rather than seniority be more heavily weighed in promotions and demotions. In turn, the FAA insisted upon a union shop: first, it feared that the Ford reforms might in fact undermine the loyalty of the union foremen; and second, the association sought assurance that the corporation would not use Taft-Hartley as a club to break the FAA.[76]

With negotiations fruitless and FAA leaders feeling increasingly desperate, the association struck Ford on May 21, successfully pulling a large majority of the 4,000 man supervisory force out of the plant. The strike was not ineffective: FAA picket lines were spirited, rank-and-file workers entered the plant but refused to take over supervisory work (more than a thousand workers were laid off for laxity in the performance of their jobs), and production declined dramatically in several departments. But the strike was probably a tactical blunder. Not only did it give Ford the opportunity to use formal passage of the Taft-Hartley Act on June 23 as an occasion to simply cancel its recognition of the FAA and fire its leading activists, but also the association had done little to coordinate its activities with the UAW.[77] Any hope that the foremen might survive their strike floundered when the UAW denied the FAA request that rank-and-file workers respect the supervisory picket lines. UAW leaders recognized that if the FAA collapsed, foremen would again become "stooges" for management; but the faction-ridden UAW was then in the midst of its own negotiations with the company, out of which leaders of the Ford department hoped to bring a precedent-setting pension plan to boost their fortunes in the internal union scramble for power. Although active UAW support of the FAA would, of course, sidetrack this effort, in the larger sense UAW abandonment of the FAA was part of a general shift by new industrial union leadership—away from a contest with management over control of the shop floor work environment and toward a greater focus on wage and fringe benefits for their members. Ford management easily accommodated this shift: the contract signed with the UAW in August not only opened the door to a pension plan but also included a clause in which the union promised it would "not organize, or attempt to assist in the organization of supervisory employees."[78]

Defeat at Ford and passage of the Taft-Hartley Act effectively smashed the FAA in the auto industry. By the end of 1947 the association lost most of its other contracts, the NLRB dismissed some sixty-six cases the FAA had brought before the board, and important chapters like those at DeSoto, Packard, and Chrysler, which maintained shadow existences for some years, withdrew from the association. The FAA staggered on, sometimes negotiating "secret" agreements with supplier firms fearful of Big Three retaliation, but by the end of the 1950s little of the association remained in the industry.[79]

## Still the "Man in the Middle"

The shifting social terrain of most postwar auto factories helped reopen the social distance that had once existed between the supervisory strata and rank-and-file workers. In the quarter century after the end of World War II the gradual atrophy of the union shop steward system made it again possible for auto industry foremen to perform the disciplinary functions they had found so difficult in the 1940s. Thus, at Chrysler the strong tradition of shop floor activism that persisted until the managerial onslaught of 1957–1958 had forced supervisors into an accommodating, often cooperative relationship with rank-and-file work groups, while at the same time the tradition distanced foremen from top management. Thereafter, the Chrysler effort to recast its labor relations policy in the GM mold increased shop floor tensions and reduced the informal bargaining latitude enjoyed by first line supervisors. After that "we were puppets on a string," recalled one Chrysler supervisor.[80]

The cultural distance between foremen and workers also widened, especially in the 1960s and early 1970s. Although most foremen are still recruited from the ranks of the workforce, Ford and GM made an effort to hire college-educated foremen, making this job the first rung on the advancement ladder for about a quarter of the managerial workforce.[81] The new recruitment pattern increased social distance between workers and supervisors and dramatically reinforced the growing racial antagonism manifest in many auto plants in the 1960s. In most urban factories a cohort of older white foremen found them-

selves in command of a predominantly black and Hispanic workforce. Until top management began a forced draft effort to recruit
minority supervisors, the ethnic cleavage between workers and their
foremen could be stark, a distant reflection of the cultural polar-
ization that had once divided pre–World War II auto plants along
Protestant-Masonic and immigrant-Catholic lines. In the high employment years between 1967 and 1973 these tensions were quite
literally explosive.[82]

But despite these social polarities, the structures of work and authority that gave rise to supervisory unionism have remained remark-
ably unchanged in the last forty years. Thus, management consultant
John Patton could echo FAA complaints in 1973 when he argued that
the first line supervisor was "still being held responsible for functions over which he no longer has any real authority or control."[83]
Although auto management intensified training programs, expanded
career ladders, and increased status-building minor privileges, repeated surveys have found that a majority of supervisors continue
to resist full identification with higher level management. Given the
social and psychological tensions inherent in the job, almost half of
all rank-and-file workers promoted to supervisory ranks voluntarily
return to the shop floor. "One might say that supervisors are still back
where they started," concluded a recent study, "walking the tightrope
between management and workers."[84]

## NOTES

1. Among the classic essays on this subject are F. J. Roethlisberger, "The
Foreman: Master and Victim of Double Talk," *Harvard Business Review*
23 (1945): 283–98, and Donald E. Wray, "Marginal Men of Industry: The
Foremen," *American Journal of Sociology* 54 (1949): 298–301. For recent
evaluations of the status of first line supervisors, see Leonard A. Schlesinger,
*Quality of Work Life and the Supervisor* (New York: Praeger, 1982); William J.
Abernathy, Kim B. Clark, and Alan M. Kantrow, *Industrial Renaissance: Pro-
ducing a Competitive Future for America* (New York: Basic Books, 1983), 84–
93; and W. Earl Sasser, Jr., and Frank S. Leonard, "Let First Level Supervisors
Do Their Job," *Harvard Business Review* 58 (March–April 1980): 113–21.

2. *Business Week*, April 25, 1983, 73.

3. Daniel Nelson, *Managers and Workers: Origins of the New Factory
System in the United States, 1880–1920* (Madison: University of Wisconsin
Press, 1975), 34–78; Stephen Meyer III, *The Five Dollar Day: Labor Manage-
ment and Social Control in the Ford Motor Company, 1908–1921* (Albany:

State University of New York Press, 1981), 37–65; see also Thomas H. Patten, Jr., *The Foreman: Forgotten Man of Management* (New York: McGraw-Hill, 1968), ch. 2.

4. Nelson, *Managers and Workers*, 140–62; Sanford Jacoby, "The Human Factor: An Historical Perspective on Internal Labor Markets in American Manufacturing Firms," *Working Papers Series*, no. 21, Institute of Industrial Relations, University of California, Los Angeles, May 1980.

5. "Hiring and Separation Methods," *Monthly Labor Review* 35 (November 1932): 1005–17; Sanford Jacoby, *Employing Bureaucracy: Managers, Unions, and the Transformation of Work in American Industry, 1900–1945* (New York: Columbia University Press, 1985), 193–99.

6. As quoted in Meyer, *Five Dollar Day*, 58–59.

7. Charles R. Walker, *The Foreman on the Assembly Line* (Cambridge: Harvard University Press, 1956), 10.

8. Meyer, *Five Dollar Day*, 56; David M. Gordon, Richard Edwards, and Michael Reich, *Segmented Work, Divided Workers: Historical Transformation of Labor in the U.S.* (New York: Cambridge University Press, 1982), 135.

9. M. J. Kane, *The Relation of the Foreman to the Personnel Department*, Production Executive Series, no. 40 (New York: American Management Association, 1926), 4.

10. "Hiring and Separation Methods," 1010–11; W. Ellison Chalmers, "Labor in the Automobile Industry: A Study of Personnel Policies, Worker's Attitudes and Attempts at Unionism" (Ph.D. diss., University of Wisconsin, 1932), 171–72; Chen-Nan Li, "A Summer in the Ford Works," in Allan Nark and John B. Miller, eds., *Personnel and Labor Relations: An Evolutionary Approach* (New York: McGraw-Hill, 1973), 477–78.

11. Blanch Bernstein, "Hiring Policies in the Automobile Industry," Works Project Administration Report, January 1937, in W. Ellison Chalmers Collection, Box 1, Archives of Labor History and Urban Affairs, Wayne State University, Detroit, Mich. (hereafter ALHUA); Jacoby, *Employing Bureaucracy*, 193–95.

12. Clayton W. Fountain, *Union Guy* (New York: Viking, 1948), 41.

13. Author's interviews with Robert Robinson, Ford Motor Company salary specialist, October 9, 1983, Sterling Heights, Mich.; and Robert Durfee, Essex Wire Company foreman, April 30, 1982, Berkeley, Calif.

14. National Industrial Recovery Administration, "Hearings on Regularizing Employment and Otherwise Improving the Conditions of Labor in the Automobile Industry," Detroit, December 15, 1934, mimeo, 51, Department of Labor Library.

15. "Reminiscences of W. C. Klann," vol. 2, 153, in Ford Motor Company Archives, Henry Ford Museum, Dearborn, Mich.

16. Frank Marquart, *An Auto Worker's Journal: The UAW from Crusade to One Party Union* (State College: Pennsylvania State University Press, 1975), 31.

17. Stewart M. Lowery, *Selection and Development of Foremen and*

Workers, Production Series, no. 127 (New York: American Management Association, 1940), 7; author's interview with Bertram Fenwick and Roy Campbell, former Ford foremen, August 4, 1983, Livonia, Mich.; Melvin Dalton, "Conflicts between Staff and Line Management Officers," *American Sociological Review* 15 (June 1950): 344.

18. For a discussion of ethnic cleavages in the factory workforce during the interwar years see Peter Friedlander, *The Emergence of a UAW Local, 1936–1939: A Study in Class and Culture* (Pittsburgh: University of Pittsburgh Press, 1975), 3–37; Ronald Schatz, *The Electrical Workers: A History of Labor at General Electric and Westinghouse, 1923–60* (Urbana: University of Illinois Press, 1983), 80–99; William Kornblum, *Blue Collar Community* (Chicago: University of Chicago Press, 1974), 38–67; Meyer, *Five Dollar Day*, 149–94; Albert Sobey, *Foremen's Clubs*, Production Series, no. 45 (New York: American Management Association, 1926); William Musman, "Facts about Foremen's Clubs," *Management Record* (November 1946): 375.

19. Lynn Dumenil, "Brotherhood and Respectability: Freemasonry and American Culture, 1880–1930" (Ph.D. diss., University of California, Berkeley, 1981), 131–37, 269–76; Roy Rosensweig, "Boston Masons, 1900–1935: The Lower Middle Class in a Divided Society," *Journal of Voluntary Action Research* 6 (July–October 1977): 119–26.

20. Author's interviews with Fenwick, Campbell, and Robinson; Dumenil, "Brotherhood and Respectability," 379–84; see also Melvin Dalton, "Informal Factors in Career Advancement," *American Journal of Sociology* 56 (March 1951): 407–15. Dalton found Masonic membership a virtual requirement for worker promotion to supervisory ranks in the Chicago area factory he studied in the mid-1940s. In an overwhelmingly Catholic workforce, he found 75 percent of the foremen Masons.

21. Author's interview with Fenwick, Campbell, and Ford R. Bryan, Ford technician, May 27, 1983, Dearborn, Mich.

22. Dalton, "Conflicts between Staff and Line," 345, 348; author's interview with Theodore Bonaventura, former Ford foreman, February 12, 1984, Washington, D. C.

23. L. A. Sylvester, *The Foreman as Manager*, Production Executives Series, no. 38 (New York: American Management Association, 1926), 10–11.

24. Roethlisberger, "The Foreman: Master and Victim of Doubletalk," 283.

25. Stanley B. Mathewson, *Restriction of Output among Unorganized Workers* (New York: Viking Press, 1931), 45.

26. Donald Roy, "Efficiency and the Fix: Informal Intergroup Relations in a Piecework Machineshop," *American Journal of Sociology* 60 (November 1954): 261.

27. Walker, *Foreman on the Assembly Line*, 17. In the course of their famous Hawthorne observations, the Harvard University team headed by Elton Mayo also found this perspective common among first line supervisors whose work put them in intimate contact with the employees they supervised. See F. J. Roethlisberger and William Dickson, *Management and the*

*Worker* (Cambridge: Harvard University Press, 1939), 453–67.

28. Chalmers, "Labor in the Automobile Industry," 159–60; see also Chen-Nan Li, "A Summer in the Ford Works," 484.

29. Walker, *Foreman on the Assembly Line*, 47.

30. UAW-CIO, *How to Win for the Union: A Discussion for UAW Stewards and Committeemen* (Detroit: UAW, 1941), 8–9.

31. Marquart, *An Auto Worker's Journal*, 78.

32. Don Lescohier, "The Foreman and the Union," *Personnel* 15 (August 1938): 18–21.

33. Testimony of Walter Nelson in Murray Corporation vs. Local 34 Foreman's Association of America, November 4, 1943, 27, in Case 111-2882-D, National War Labor Board Collection, RG 202, National Archives, Suitland, Md.

34. Interviews with Durfree, Robinson, and Shelton Tappes, Rouge committeeman, October 7, 1982, Detroit.

35. Harry Shulman, "Elimination of Semi-Supervisory Job (Yardmaster)," Opinion A-220, April 8, 1946, in *UAW-Ford Arbitration Awards* (Detroit: UAW, 1947).

36. Ford Rouge Plant Factory Counts, July 7, 1935, October 29, 1946, in Box 196, Accession 157, Henry Ford Museum; author's interview with Robinson.

37. Some observers have argued that the increasing complexity of production technology has itself been responsible for a rise in supervisory overhead, but, as David Noble has recently shown, the character of workplace machinery cannot be divorced from the system of factory authority. See David Noble, *Forces of Production* (New York: Alfred A. Knopf, 1984), 265–323; and William A. Faunce, "Automation in the Automobile Industry: Some Consequences for In-Plant Social Structure," *American Sociological Review* 67 (October 1959): 401–7. Faunce found a sharp increase in the foreman-worker ratio after the introduction of motor block transfer lines; he ascribed that not so much to the increasing complexity of the machinery but more to the need for continuous production and greater collective work discipline.

38. Ira B. Cross, "When Foremen Joined the CIO," *Personnel Journal* 18 (February 1940): 274–78; "New Allies in Guise of Foremen Keep Rallying to CIO Banner," *Kelsey Hayes Picket*, June 6, 1939, in Box 10, Joe Brown Collection, ALHUA.

39. Cross, "When Foremen Joined the CIO," 279

40. Clarence Bolds, "Foremen Win Security, Labor Gains Ally in New CIO Union," *Michigan CIO News*, September 4, 1939.

41. Steve Jefferys, *Management and Managed: Fifty Years of Crisis at Chrysler* (Cambridge: Cambridge University Press, 1986), 91–103; "Union Striking, Chrysler Says," *Detroit Free Press*, October 9, 1939, in vol. 17, Joe Brown Scrapbooks, ALHUA.

42. "Chrysler Slowdown," *Detroit Free Press*, October 11, 1939, in vol. 17, Joe Brown Scrapbooks, ALHUA.

43. "Weckler and Thomas Hurl Strike Charges," *Detroit News*, October 26,

1939; "Chrysler Talks Hit New Snag," *Detroit News*, November 22, 1939; "New Issues Debated in Auto Talks," *Detroit News*, November 23, 1939, all in vol. 17, Joe Brown Scrapbooks, ALHUA.

44. "Wait Ruling on Foremen," *Detroit News*, December 9, 1939, in vol. 17, Joe Brown Scrapbooks, ALHUA; Cross, "When Foremen Joined the CIO," 280–82.

45. T. Carl Cabe, "Foremen's Unions: A New Development in Industrial Relations," *University of Illinois Bulletin* 44 (March 1947): 20–28.

46. U.S. House of Representatives, Committee on Military Affairs, Part 68, *Full Utilization of Manpower*, 78th Congress, 1st Sess., 375–78; Desoto Wyoming Plant, "Foremen on Roll, December 31, 1940 through May 31, 1944," in File 111-8243-D, War Labor Board Collection, RG 202, National Archives.

47. Ernest Dale, "The Development of Foremen in Management," *AMA Research Report*, no. 7 (1945): 9–59; Herbert R. Northrup, "The Foreman's Association of America," *Harvard Business Review* 23 (1945): 187–91; Packard supervisor quoted in U.S. Senate, Special Committee to Investigate the National Defense Program, Part 28, *Manpower Problems in Detroit*, 79th Congress, 1st Sess., 13730.

48. Author's phone interview with Fred Temple, February 12, 1985; Fenwick and Campbell interview.

49. George Heliker, "Ford Labor Relations," 323, unpublished manuscript in Frank Hill Papers, Henry Ford Museum.

50. Charles P. Larrowe, "A Meteor on the Industrial Relations Horizon," *Labor History* 2 (Fall 1961): 259–87; author's interviews with Bonaventura, Fenwick; testimony of W. Allen Nelson, *Full Utilization of Manpower*, 496.

51. Robert Keys, "Union Membership and Collective Bargaining by Foremen," *Mechanical Engineering* 66 (April 1944): 251–52; Philomena Marquart, "Foreman's Association of America," *Monthly Labor Review* 62 (February 1946): 241–44.

52. Testimony of Carl Brown, U.S. House of Representatives, Committee on Education and Labor, *National Labor Relations Act of 1949*, 81st Congress, 1st Sess., March 21, 1949, 1232–33.

53. Keys, "Union Membership and Collective Bargaining," 251; Larrowe, "A Meteor on the Industrial Relations Horizon," 270–85.

54. "Foremen Warm Up to Union," *Business Week*, November 17, 1942, 108; Foremen's Cases, *War Labor Board Reports* 26 (July 23, 1945): 657–60.

55. "The Foreman Abdicates," *Fortune* 32 (September 1945): 38; Carl Brown interview with Howell Harris, Detroit, November 13, 1974, ALHUA; author's phone interview with Raymond Erickson, March 13, 1985; author's interview with Fenwick; Trial Examiner's Transcript, Packard vs. FAA, December 18, 1944, 36, 423, Box 8314, RG 25, National Archives; National War Labor Board Panel Hearings, Chrysler Corporation (Case 111-4747-D), June 14, 1944, 35, RG 202, National Archives.

56. Author's interviews with Temple, Fenwick, and Bonaventura; Testi-

mony of Robert Keys, U.S. House of Representatives, Committee on Education and Labor, 80th Congress, 1st Sess., *Hearings on Bills to Amend and Repeal the NLRA*, vol. 2, February 1947, 868.

57. As quoted in *Hearings on Bills to Amend and Repeal the NLRA*, 883.

58. National War Labor Board Panel Hearings, Packard Motor Company (Case 111-5436-D), June 14, 1944, 157, RG 202.

59. Robert Keys, "Foremen Have Organized," Radio Broadcast of March 16, 1944 (printed), FAA pamphlet in Sumner Slichter Papers, Baker Library, Harvard Business School.

60. "Membership Director's Column," *Supervisor* 2 (June 1944): 3.

61. Testimony of John Bugas, U.S. House, Committee on Education and Labor, 83rd Congress, 1st Sess., *Hearings on Matters Relating to Labor Management Relations Act of 1947*, Part 7, April 16, 1953, 2492–96; "Foremen Challenge Ford II 'Human Relations' and Win," *Wage Earner*, October 11, 1946.

62. Author's interview with Bonaventura; Bugas testimony, *Hearings*, 2493.

63. U.S. House of Representatives, Committee on Education and Labor, 80th Congress, 1st Sess., *Hearings on Bills to Amend and Repeal the NLRA*, vol. 2, March 7, 1947, 2711.

64. Ibid., 2712–14. Similarly, in shipyards and in many steel mills, foremen and subforemen simply affiliated directly with the CIO unions in those industries. In the coal fields, an independent organization of mine foremen joined District 50 of the United Mine Workers of America. The International Association of Machinists organized several foremen's lodges, sometimes in CIO-represented factories but more often in facilities where the IAM had already organized the production worker rank and file.

65. "Summary of FAA Strike," *Supervisor* 2 (June 1944): 10–11; "Foremen's Cases," *War Labor Board Reports* 26 (July 23, 1945): 661.

66. "Union Wins More Foremen," *Business Week*, May 18, 1946, 95.

67. Virginia A. Seitz, "Legal, Legislative and Managerial Responses to the Organization of Supervisory Employees in the 1940s," *American Journal of Legal History* 28 (January 1984): 218–35; Larrowe, "Meteor on the Industrial Relations Horizon," 285–87. General Motors succeeded in resisting large scale foreman organization: first, the corporation had reformed its supervisory program and raised foreman pay in prewar years; and second, in General Motors UAW shop floor organization was somewhat less aggressive than at Ford, Chrysler, and the auto independents.

68. Howell John Harris, *The Right to Manage: Industrial Relations Policies of American Business in the 1940s* (Madison: University of Wisconsin Press, 1982), 84–87, 95–104.

69. William T. Gossett, Ford Motor Company counsel, as quoted in Harris, *Right to Manage*, 85.

70. Testimony of Edward Butler, *Full Utilization of Manpower*, 91; "Company's Comments on Panel Report," 33, in Hudson Motor Company vs. FAA, NWLB Case No. 111-85-14-D, RG 202, National Archives.

71. Testimony of C. C. Coulton, *Full Utilization of Manpower*, 110.

72. Testimony of Walter McNally, Murray Corporation, *Hearings on Bills to Amend and Repeal the NLRA*, 717.

73. "The Foreman Abdicates," *Fortune* 32 (September 1945): 150.

74. Ibid., 150. See also Jürgen Kocka, *White Collar Workers in America, 1890–1940: A Social-Political History in International Perspective* (Beverly Hills: Sage Publications, 1980), 200–50. Mark McColloch, "White Collar: Electrical Machinery, Banking and Public Welfare Workers, 1940–1970" (Ph.D. diss., University of Pittsburgh, 1975); C. D. Snyder, *White Collar Workers and the UAW* (Urbana: University of Illinois Press, 1973).

75. "Ford Gives 15% Raise to Foremen," *Supervisor* 4 (February 1946): 1; author interview with Bonaventura.

76. "Major Issues in Foremen's Strike at Fords Are Listed," *Supervisor* 5 (May 1947): 1; David Levinson, "Wartime Unionization of Foremen" (Ph.D. diss., University of Wisconsin, 1949), 298–302.

77. Levinson, "Wartime Unionization of Foremen," 303–307; author interviews with Fenwick, Campbell, Bonaventura. On the grounds that they had engaged in strike violence, Ford fired thirty-two FAA activists. Most were blacklisted throughout the industry, and many never worked as foremen again.

78. Robert Keys to Walter Reuther, June 17, 24, 1947, in Box 96, Walter P. Reuther Collection, ALHUA; Special Session, UAW International Executive Board, July 1, 1947, in Box 1, IEB Collection, ALHUA; Seitz, "Legal, Legislative and Managerial Responses to the Organization of Supervisory Employees," 239–41. The same trade-off took place in the coal industry where John L. Lewis abandoned any effort to organize mine supervisors in return for industry funding of a health and welfare fund. In the UAW the situation proved more complicated because a referendum of Ford workers rejected the 1947 pension plan, but it was successfully renegotiated in 1949. For more on UAW bargaining strategy see Nelson Lichtenstein, "UAW Bargaining Strategy and Shop-Floor Conflict: 1946–1970," *Industrial Relations* 24 (Fall 1985): 360–81.

79. Larrowe, "A Meteor on the Industrial Relations Horizon," 289–92; Levenson, "Wartime Unionization of Foremen," 308–27.

80. Jefferys, *Management and Managed*, 127–45; author's interview with Roger Erickson, Chrysler worker, May 13, 1985, Dearborn; Chrysler locals demanded the right to "discipline" authoritarian foremen when, during slack production, they returned to rank-and-file status. See "Foreman Tussle," *Business Week*, May 22, 1954, 151.

81. Author's phone interviews with Gary Bonaventura, former Ford foreman, January 23, 1985, and Wendy Thompson, GM committeewoman, May 31, 1985; Kenneth Hopper, "The Growing Use of College Graduates as Foremen," *Management of Personnel Quarterly* 6 (Summer 1967): 2–12.

82. For a history of black power politics in the workplace see Don Georgakas and Marvin Surkin, *Detroit: I Do Mind Dying* (New York: St. Martin's Press, 1975); James Geschwender, *Race and Worker Insurgency: The League*

*of Revolutionary Black Workers* (New York: Cambridge University Press, 1977).

83. John A. Patton, "The Foreman: Most Mis-Used, Accused and Abused Man in Industry," speech delivered before National Machine Tool Builders' Association, October 11, 1973, in "Foremen," Vertical File, ALHUA. See also, "As a Ford Foreman, Ed Hendrix Finds He Is Man in the Middle," *Wall Street Journal*, August 9, 1973; and Daniel Cook, "Foreman: Where Theory Collides with Reality," *Industry Week*, April 6, 1981, 74–80.

84. Leonard A. Schlesinger and Janice A. Klein, "The First-Line Supervisor: Past, Present and Future," working paper, Harvard Business School, April 1983, 29.

# 8

# Triumph of Industrial Orthodoxy: The Collapse of Studebaker-Packard Corporation

## STEPHEN AMBERG

Studebaker Corporation's abandonment of the automobile market in the early 1960s demonstrates both the power and limits of what social scientists and historians have come to call the Fordist model of production. With the cooperation of the United Auto Workers (UAW) and the encouragement of outside management consultants, Studebaker managers in the 1950s sought to transform their firm into one whose labor relations and market strategy conformed to those of industry leader General Motors. Their failure to do so sheds light on one of the key industrial dilemmas of our time: Can firms construct an alternative form of work organization capable of producing an economically viable, flexible response to the stagnant or unstable mass markets characteristic of much American manufacturing? Or are mass production firms in high-wage regions doomed to lose out to companies that reap cost advantages by producing for mass consumption in world markets and locating their factories in low-wage countries?

This study of Studebaker Corporation, a small firm in a mass production industry dominated by giant organizations, claims that pieces of an alternative "flexible-specialization" industrial strategy were already in place when financial crisis enveloped the firm in the 1950s.[1] A fully realized flexible-specialization strategy combines a flexible production process with a product strategy aimed a filling market niches overlooked by mass producers. As a locally controlled producer with a long history of production in South Bend, Indiana,

Studebaker might have been able to capitalize on the growing segmentation of the auto products market and the high degree of labor solidarity in its plants. Such a strategy would have avoided a head-on clash with Ford and GM and concentrated the firm's energies on a more viable strategy when the first wave of small car imports arrived. But the political and institutional formulas governing postwar production politics foreclosed an exploration of any such unorthodox solution to Studebaker's dilemma. To the contrary, the firm's effort to mimic GM and Ford locked its managers, workers, and bankers into an insoluble conflict that reduced Studebaker to near bankruptcy. As this strategy backfired, management pursued the orthodox alternative: disinvestment and diversification into other products. Studebaker became a successful conglomerate in the 1960s, but only after it closed its South Bend factories and left the auto business.

### Fordism and Flexible Specialization at Studebaker

The quarter century following World War II represented the high noon of American Fordism—a production system characterized by long production runs, mass markets, relatively high wages, and low unit costs. The pattern setting UAW-GM contract settlements of 1948 and 1950 helped codify the new order by establishing wage rules that linked workers' purchasing power to the rising prices and productivity of the U.S. economy. These formulas stabilized class relations in the industry and spurred managerial efforts to reassert its sovereignty in the workplace. Although an increasingly elaborate set of work rules and grievance procedures protected workers from the foreman's full authority, the postwar era also saw the gradual reassertion of management's "right to manage." Legal limits on the scope of collective bargaining, the "management rights" clauses inserted into the manufacturing industry's union-management contracts, and the accommodative policies pursued by the leadership of most large trade unions laid the groundwork for resurging management power in the 1960s.[2]

This system of production was linked to the political coalitions established in the New Deal era. After a few brief years of experimentation in the 1940s, corporatist planning efforts were abandoned, and the government allowed unions and corporations to settle their disputes largely by their own means. Although the federal government gradually adopted a liberal program of Keynesian demand management and free trade designed to spur economic growth at home and abroad, Congress and the president maintained an arm's-length involvement in the labor market at the same time the federal courts deferred judicial review of labor contracts to private arbitrators. Scanty welfare state benefits were supplemented by private programs of "social insurance," including livable pensions and health and welfare benefits.[3]

For producers like GM and Ford, the system was a boon. Government macroeconomic demand stimulation and pattern increases in wages guaranteed a mass market for standardized products and a payoff for expensive labor-saving investment. GM produced 3.4 million cars and trucks a year during the mid-1950s, and its most popular model, Chevrolet, sold over a million and a half units during each year of the decade. In 1955 its market share stood at over 50 percent; its return on investment was more than 30 percent during 1953–1957.[4] Given its enormous market strength GM adopted product innovations only after they had proven themselves elsewhere; instead, it focused its resources on improving production methods and passed on any increased costs to consumers.

In contrast, Studebaker had a radically different relationship to its market. Its market share was 2.6 percent in 1946 and 4 percent in 1950 when it sold 268,000 cars. Its share declined to 2.4 percent in 1954, 2.1 percent in 1955, and 1.1 percent in 1957.[5] As a consequence, small changes in the quality of demand could have a large impact on its cash flow and profitability. To shift flexibly with changing markets and efficiently produce comparatively small batches of products, its employees took on a broader range of work tasks and responsibility. Rather than driving to standardize products and the production process, Studebaker management emphasized distinctive product design and quality.

Studebaker had an incipient flexible specialization strategy. Crucial to successful flexible specialization is that the production process and market strategy depend on each other: filling product niches as they develop requires that process technology and labor-management relations adjust flexibly to accommodate new products. Studebaker had first adopted a specialist strategy in the early 1920s with production of the Light Six, a high-quality low-priced car of distinctive styling; yet a disastrous policy of liquidating operations to maintain dividends bankrupted the company early in the depression. But after coming out of receivership in 1933, the company again sought a market niche. Studebaker's strategy proved very successful in the 1930s, and, except during 1938, the company made money. Strong sales of its new economy Champion model in 1939 promised growing success on the eve of World War II. During the war Studebaker built amphibious vehicles, big trucks, and aircraft engines. Government officials even suggested that Studebaker management take over Ford, which was faltering on its production commitments.[6]

In the postwar consumer market, Studebaker was first among all companies with a new model. Market share stood at 5.4 percent in 1951—its best year ever. Studebaker also expanded abroad to broaden its sales base; it sold cars in dozens of countries in 1953 and operated or licensed manufacturing facilities in twelve in 1955. In 1953 Studebaker also set the new car pace in the industry by adapting Chrysler's novel power steering to its model line and introducing the long, low body style later dominant in the industry. In 1953 its sales were $594 million. Moreover, the company had invested in new plant and machinery at a rate equal to the Big Three after the Second World War, providing up-to-date facilities.[7]

Paul Hoffman, a star salesman for the company in Los Angeles and its vice-president for sales, presided over the rebirth of Studebaker after its depression era bankruptcy. Taking over in 1935, Hoffman sought to capitalize on the company's tradition of product quality and historical roots in the South Bend community. According to Hoffman, the company could only compete in the larger auto market if it took full advantage of the "intangibles entering into value—and particularly those which did not cost us money. Morale and good will of the working force were two such intangibles." Under Hoffman, Studebaker emphasized pride of workmanship in its product marketing and traded on its 100 years of manufacturing experience in South Bend. The company boasted that over one-third of the workforce were father-son-daughter "teams."[8] This was more than advertising gimmickry, for Studebaker's economic position was too precarious after 1933 to withstand the strikes and job actions characterizing auto industry labor relations during the late depression years when the UAW established its position at GM, Chrysler, Briggs, and other major producers. Thus, Studebaker readily accommodated itself to the rise of industrial unionism in the 1930s. It bargained with an AFL federal local in the mid-1930s and recognized without a strike UAW Local 5 in 1937.

Hoffman's politics also differed markedly from those held by most other automobile executives in the 1930s and 1940s. He was a leading internationalist Republican and served as first chair of the Committee for Economic Development, the influential group of businessmen who favored moderate national economic planning and cooperative union-management relations in the postwar years.[9] By 1948 Hoffman's stature was such that President Truman appointed him director of the European Recovery Program. In the early 1950s he was president of the Ford Foundation and a founder of the liberal Fund for the Republic.

In the immediate postwar era Studebaker's unique style of labor management seemed to provide a basis for a flexible-specialization manufacturing strategy that might enable the company to compete with its larger rivals. The company did not fight the union over wages or institutional security. Studebaker had historically followed the wage pattern set in Detroit, and in 1945 it willingly granted the union a 12.5 percent wage increase and promised to match any further increase won from GM. Although UAW Local 5 did not have a union shop, the company voluntarily agreed to a dues check off during the war; in fact, it encouraged workers to sign up with the union. And until the mid-1950s, no management rights clause existed in the short and generally worded UAW-Studebaker collective bargaining agreement.[10]

The scope of bargaining was "almost unlimited," remembered one local union president. Management could act unilaterally, though both sides consulted each other on important issues. For example, the company went to considerable lengths to accommodate union plans for revising wage rates and job assignments to achieve greater equity among local members. Disputes were handled by a grievance system, as elsewhere in the industry, but there were no written grievances, little adherence to "common law" precedent, and no arbitration. The company's top officials held a problem-solving, pragmatic approach to labor relations issues, which they saw as part of, rather than distinct from, production questions. Compared to GM, the firm had an extremely thin personnel department; its top management, including Presidents Hoffman (1935–1948) and Harold Vance (1948–1954), frequently bargained directly with union officials, "talking out" difficulties in a relatively flexible give-and-take fashion. "The logic of production has been the logic of industrial relations," reported two academic observers in 1947. "And the solution of production problems has been immediate, forthright and to the point." The system seemed to pay off in "mutual trust" and "glass-smooth labor relations." Surveys of grievance cases at Studebaker and General Motors in 1944 and 1945 found that 20 percent of grievances at GM were complaints about unfair treatment from supervisors compared to just 5.5 percent at the South Bend company.[11]

Studebaker workers combined a solidaristic tradition of active unionism with a strong sense of company allegiance. Their local had played a key role in founding the UAW International in the mid-1930s and had supported a farmer labor party in 1936. Democratic and highly participatory, Local 5 supported a wide range of cooperative or union sponsored social services in the following decade, including a credit union, food store, lending library, and housing cooperative. It was one of the few CIO locals to demand from management and win a union controlled pension fund in the 1930s.[12]

Although Studebaker workers would prove extremely militant when defending what they considered customary work norms, these same workers were intensely loyal to the company itself. Compared to Detroit area auto workers, they were an older and more often home-owning group who overwhelmingly thought Studebaker the best place to work in South Bend. Jealously guarding their autonomy, Local 5 conducted its affairs, including negotiations with Studebaker, almost entirely without aid or interference from the International UAW. During the 1930s the Studebaker local not only refrained from calling any strikes, but it kept discipline at work. In 1939 the union even did some independent advertising for the new Champion model. Then in 1946, when stoppages at auto supply factories threatened to disrupt Studebaker's effort to get a production jump on the Big Three, Local 5 used its UAW connections to provide the company with information about the timing and likely duration of these supplier strikes.[13]

On the shop floor level worker collaboration with management rested upon the local's extensive influence over operation of the company's group piece rate system and its control of an elaborate seniority scheme. Studebaker was one of a handful of auto industry companies that had kept a piece rate system rather than switch to measured day work (hourly rated). Although the International UAW had campaigned against the piece rate system in the 1930s and 1940s as a principal cause of "speedup" and unhealthy working conditions, Studebaker workers insisted on its retention because their influence in the factory enabled them to exercise control over the actual operation of the system. Workers ran the jobs themselves, a local member recalled, and supervisors were "just clerks." Studebaker workers regularly joined together to control the work pace, and their wages were higher and work effort lower than in Detroit factories.[14]

Local 5 shop stewards were the linchpin of this system; there were proportionately five times as many at Studebaker as at GM and Ford. It was standard practice for shop stewards to meet every morning to plan their approach to the day's work and to monitor the composition of work groups to ensure equitable individual effort, group morale, and pay.[15]

The seniority system was the second feature of shop floor union strength. Seniority rules at Studebaker, as elsewhere in mass production industry, were designed to provide an equitable method for deciding who should be laid off, recalled, transferred, and promoted, in such a way as to prevent political manipulation by supervisors favoring apple-polishers, rate-busters, or younger workers. To long-tenure workers, seniority rules also provided short-run job and income security.

Compared to other auto companies, seniority rights at Studebaker were unusually extensive. Workers in South Bend had the right to transfer to any job anywhere in the plant and "bump" a current job holder with less seniority; layoff and recall operated the same way. In contrast, seniority rights at the Big Three usually were limited to bumping only lowest seniority workers and bidding on jobs only within a given task or skill group ("non-interchangeable occupational classifications"). At South Bend and Detroit bumping rights could be exercised only if the worker could qualify for the new job, but at Studebaker workers had won generous qualifying periods and options for further bumps.[16]

## Toward Fordism

In the post–Korean War years a buyer's market returned, and the first casualties were firms in the auto industry. GM and Ford engaged in a market share and production war, and rapidly automated their plants, thus squeezing the so-called auto independents: Nash, Hudson, Willys, Kaiser-Fraser, Packard, and Studebaker. Except Nash and Hudson, which merged to form American Motors, all went out of business in the next ten years. As financial difficulties quickly mounted top Studebaker management came to believe that the company's problems were rooted in its insufficiently orthodox manufacturing strategy. There were two basic elements inherent in this analysis: first, they thought the company was too small to reap the needed economies of scale in the auto industry. It would have to increase production and sales and compete head to head with the other major auto producers in order to reduce unit costs. Second, labor practices and productivity would have to be brought into line with Ford and GM. Studebaker management had exhibited "poor judgment" in attempting a flexible accommodation with its workers, argued labor economist Robert MacDonald. Its "weak, complacent and short-sighted (managers) virtually relinquished control of their plants. . . ." The company, thought most observers, needed to adopt a Fordist strategy to survive in the more competitive auto market of the 1950s.[17]

Studebaker began a significant change in its long-time corporate strategy in 1953 and 1954. The company merged with the Packard Motor Company in June 1954, and under the presidency of Packard's James Nance, who had spent much of his career as a GM manager, began to shape Studebaker-Packard's labor and product policies to make the firm conform to a Fordist model. Major features of the new strategy included abandoning the distinctive styling required for a niche strategy, fielding a full line of cars to cover the entire market, expanding the dealer network, and integrating product components and production to gain better economies of scale.[18]

But rather than reviving the company, the new strategy was the beginning of the end. Although Studebaker-Packard's combined production capacity stood at 470,000, well above what most economists considered the minimum level necessary for efficient production, sales never came near this level. Studebaker-Packard's new product strategy followed the industry pattern by filling the market with thirty-three cosmetically different models of four basic cars in 1955 and twenty-five models in 1956 (up from seventeen models in 1953). Moreover, unlike a flexible-specialization strategy, the company did not produce small batches of different cars on the same production lines. Instead, it maintained financially draining multiple production facilities—Studebaker's plus Packard's. As one business editorialist observed, Packard was an "ex-car of distinction" and Studebaker designs were "dolled up" to industry norms. Studebaker's chief designer still argued for new products to meet the "market emerging for specialized cars," but Studebaker-Packard rejected his counsel. Its prices were slightly above those of its Big Three competitors in 1955; thus, without a distinctive product, the merged company lost $29.7 million on sales of 148,000 that year; when sales dived to 105,000 in 1956 red ink splashed to $103.3 million. These losses, combined with the large new debt taken on to deploy the full line strategy, contributed to the company's virtual insolvency by the end of that year.[19]

The strategic turnaround also disrupted the old Studebaker management hierarchy. Under Nance's presidency, a thorough corporate reorganization was begun. Arriving in South Bend, a phalanx of Packard managers split industrial relations from operations management and made rigid Studebaker's traditionally informal authority structure. Lower and middle level Studebaker managers resented and resisted the new regime, and Nance's relationship with Paul Hoffman, who had returned to the new firm as chairman of the board, quickly deteriorated. Finally, the new management focused its energy on production engineering and the rationalization of the production process.[20]

These difficulties made Studebaker managers more determined to impose GM-style shop discipline and convinced them that a radical reduction of labor costs was essential to corporate survival. In a report commissioned for the firm in the summer of 1953, Anna Rosenberg and Associates reported that Studebaker's labor relations system needed a thorough overhaul. Rosenberg, a former labor relations trouble-shooter for President Franklin Roosevelt, was among the influential group of New Dealers who had sought to end unpredictability in worker-management relations and replace their episodic confrontations with more routine contract negotiation and administration. Her report recommended stronger contract administration, a foreman training course, and a "communications" program aimed at production workers.[21]

Studebaker managers were determined to bring the firm's production standards "up" to those at GM. To do so the number of direct and indirect labor hours per car would have to be cut by 34 percent; this required a sizable reduction in the labor force and an increase in the amount of work performed by the remaining employees. Studebaker wanted a completely new labor contract that would include a management rights clause like that at GM, a union shop, a grievance procedure ending in arbitration, tough antiwildcat strike language, management-controlled production standards, and a pay cut of 10 to 20 percent.[22]

In its efforts to transform shop floor labor relations, Studebaker management considered abolition of the piecework system and a thorough reform of the local's elaborate seniority arrangement essential to its success. In 1954 management demanded that the local agree to replace the long-standing incentive pay system with a day work pay schedule. Under the day work arrangement, a worker, paid a basic hourly rate, is expected to meet a standard of production per hour, set by an engineering department time-and-motion study of the operation performed. Managers thereby gain much greater discretion to control the pace and volume of work. Note that the worker is paid in exchange for a "fair day's work," but the job itself is determined by management. In freeing wages from production of particular pieces and emphasizing production flow and time, management can easily change the process and the content of work.

Studebaker management also complained vigorously about the seniority system because it inflated employment and training costs and triggered great chain reactions of bumps during large layoffs. As manning levels in various departments were cut, workers bumped into jobs in other departments. Those who were bumped then bumped others, who bumped others, and this continued all around the plant. During the time workers had to qualify, jobs were double-manned. If the worker could not qualify for one job, he or she was allowed more bumps. Not surprisingly, people were "lost in the bumps": either management could not keep track of all the changes, or a department supervisor might ask a bumping worker to temporarily perform a different task, after which the worker would never return to the previous job. In the meantime workers drew more pay, holding their jobs, and management footed the bill. In 1954 management insisted that abuse of this system could only be curtailed if Local 5 agreed to limit job transfers: three per year interdepartmental and two intradepartmental.[23]

Officials of the International UAW, including Walter Reuther, had met with management over the winter of 1953–1954 and were convinced that Studebaker was in desperate straits. The International had studied Studebaker's market position and apparently accepted the view that only a Fordist strategy could insure the firm's survival under the new competitive conditions. Reuther argued before the Joint Economic Committee of Congress that the root problem was the rationalization of the industry: "automation in Detroit is creating unemployment in South Bend." The International agreed with Studebaker management that the company's contract should be put on an equal footing with the Big Three and that Studebaker workers' superstandard wages were keeping production costs uncompetitively high. This was consistent with the UAW's historic position favoring industry-wide standards, although applied for a novel purpose, and managerial initiative in work organization. Moreover, the International had long opposed piecework, and this was an opportunity to get rid of it at Studebaker. It put great pressure on the Local leadership to be accommodative and to sell the membership on the new contract.[24]

## Shop Floor Politics

The response Studebaker workers offered management and their own International tells us much about the consciousness and character of American workers in the early postwar era. On the shop floor level, these workers fought Studebaker to a virtual standstill. They used slowdowns, wildcat stoppages, official strikes, and "abuse" of the bumping system to resist the managerial work reforms. For five years in the mid-1950s they kept Local 5 in turmoil, but no alternative strategy emerged from any leadership faction that managed to control the local during this period. Some leaders upheld the International's position against their own private inclinations, although opponents promised only more vigilant bargaining. But when the opposition was elected to local office, their defensive posture proved ineffective against the company's long-term plan for further concessions.

The decline of "movement" unionism in the postwar era partly explains Local 5's inability to formulate a coherent response to the management onslaught. Organized by George Hupp, Ray Berndt, and J. D. (Red) Hill, a self-described "right-wing" faction took over the local in

1945 and thereafter dominated the local officialdom. It had a strong rank-and-file base among the workers added to the labor force during the war, and it probably relied heavily upon Catholics for much of its support. Red-baiting their opponents, the Hupp faction had attacked local president Bill Ogden for splitting his time between the local and the state capitol, where he sat in the legislature, and they campaigned successfully to purge the regional UAW staff of "Communist" supporters of the George Addes group in the International.[25] They became influential in city and county politics, but less so statewide. In the state CIO (and later AFL-CIO) Council, they were largely unsuccessful at uniting the labor movement behind a liberal program, largely because AFL and some CIO unions would not participate in a common political organization with UAW militants.[26]

The right-wing program centered on defending and extending workers' job rights, which it believed communists were willing to sacrifice for labor participation in corporatist planning schemes. Yet personality and fiefdoms characterized Local 5 politics after the victory of the right wing. One right-wing stalwart volunteered that they dominated the local "like the one-party South." And in fact, like one-party regimes, the local opposition was reduced to a rump organization, gathering at local election time to set a slate of the "outs" against the "ins." Shop stewards became practically autonomous in their attention to ad hoc deal making with shop management; they were uninterested in a debate on the larger purposes the union might play in production. One local president recalled that departments were "unions unto themselves."[27]

Although union officials adopted a generally defensive posture toward managerial reform initiatives in the late 1940s, they were not unwilling to make some concessions. Hupp and other local officials counselled the company to take a more principled stand in grievance bargaining and maintaining work standards. They were also willing to entertain some reform of the union's complex seniority system, if only to protect many workers from too frequent job changes. But in fact these local officials could offer Studebaker little cooperation without appearing to "give in" to management. Their claim to legitimate power rested on defense of workers' job interests. Indeed job control was an important source of union solidarity, especially after 1950 when employment at Studebaker became increasingly erratic.[28]

Although Local 5 members had agreed to reopen the contract in

1954, union leaders were very apprehensive about the reception the rank and file would give the company's proposals. After reaching a tentative agreement with the company in August, local president Louis Horvath simply dumped the detailed contract reforms in workers' laps and called for a "yes" vote; the members rejected it. When the company immediately announced it would lock out the workers, local leaders quietly encouraged rank-and-file petitions for a new vote. At a massive school field rally held to reconsider the concessions later in August workers passed the new contract on a voice vote.[29]

During the next year workers refused what they had ostensibly voted for—namely, management's sole control over the organization and content of work. Studebaker workers were willing to take a pay cut—they already were working only every other week—but they balked at the newly asserted management rights over working conditions, effort norms, and job transfers. A steward later charged that these would "tear the heart out of the union."[30]

At first local and international leaders were able to convince the rank and file to avoid resistance and see how the system would look once in place. Then in January 1955, the company began to build up its inventory as it anticipated a strike later in the year when new contract talks were scheduled and further concessions would be demanded. Workers began wildcat strikes, and the stewards organized a slowdown to the old rate.[31] The management sent the whole line home January 6, asserting that "operating schedules" were a "management function." The stewards replied that management should "cooperate" with the union and negotiate the standard or the workers would set it unilaterally. The company refused and for several days mass one-day suspensions followed slowdowns. On January 17 the local voted strike authorization 7,188 to 806 and prepared for an actual strike. Studebaker began intensive negotiations that led to modification of the standard in the union's favor.[32]

A few months later the company girded itself for new negotiations, fully expecting a strike. President Nance talked to Reuther several times in advance to reconfirm the International's perception that the company needed concessions. At the same time, the company began a systematic department-by-department program of standards enforcement and "force reductions." The number of man-hours per unit fell from 160 to 122.5. Workers resisted with a one-day plant shutdown in mid-May after the union refused to order an absent worker back to work when there were no relief workers to replace him. Ten days later there was another plant shutdown.[33]

By early July 1955 the International UAW had to send Studebaker department representatives to South Bend to prevent a breakdown of local negotiations over "speed up and layoffs." On July 8 the company laid off 1,700 workers, about 17 percent of the workforce, and cancelled all bumping rights. The next day workers voted to take a strike vote. The UAW Studebaker department and local president Horvath criticized the company but wanted to continue negotiations; they opposed a strike over the layoffs and cancelled rights and successfully, if "narrowly," defeated the motion to strike.[34]

Local union elections scheduled for that same July were a kind of referendum on the new industrial relations, but it offered only one choice: to ratify rank-and-file frustration with their impotency. Local politics were constrained by the fact that Studebaker had already decided to pursue the new strategy without local consultation. A second constraint was the opportunistic character of Local 5 factionalism. Thus, although the workers believed that both their stake in the company was threatened and management had broken its trust, the election simply led union leaders to fight over local office and a militant defense of contractualism. In effect the union had accepted the parameters of postwar Fordism.

The right-wing faction maneuvered to avoid responsibility for concessions and to keep control of the local by slating Les Fox for president, a right-winger who had singularly opposed the concessions. But Local 5 members were so provoked by the new work regime that they rejected this ploy and decisively defeated Fox and most of the rest of the right-wing slate in favor of Bill Ogden. Yet the former oppositionists, offering no coherent plan to change the situation, now tried to stick to the contract. Rank and filers continued their own opposition, now with help from the right-wing faction, and they rejected Ogden's plea to avoid wildcat strikes, act "responsibly," and use the grievance procedure.[35]

When official contract talks began August 5, 1955, the company again demanded major changes which would bring Studebaker-Packard's internal plant regime closer to that of General Motors. Their proposed demands included stipulations to: reduce the number of stewards by two-thirds; restrict seniority bumping to noninterchangeable occupational groups with no bumping at workers' discretion; create a divisionwide (all South Bend) unskilled labor pool; provide companywide social insurance (i.e., merge Studebaker's plan with Packard's inferior one) with joint control (instead of unilateral union control at Studebaker); deunionize plant guards; allow foremen to re-assign workers within job categories out-of-seniority; limit seniority in layoff and recall; reduce relief time; and eliminate contractual standards for break-in time on new jobs.[36]

Members put intense pressure on the union negotiators to resist management demands and contract talks reached an impasse in September. However, the International would not authorize a strike and, after the negotiations dragged on for another three months, it took over from the local. The Studebaker department, with a new director, Norman Matthews, agreed with the corporation to most of the changes. The new contract was narrowly ratified in January 1956— 2,456 votes to 2,139.[37]

Management believed it had a very good contract. President Nance reviewed for the board of directors the "successes" of 1955. Studebaker had made its labor costs competitive with the industry. Labor hours were down to ninety-six per unit in January. The "right of management to manage" had been won. Studebaker had adopted the GM-style divisional management structure, and it had restyled its product lines. "Now our problems are the problems of the industry," he asserted.[38]

For Studebaker workers the big fight was seriously undermined, but not over. Although more than 3,600 workers had been cut from the payroll and standards had increased, the workers' power to claim job rights was not completely lost. Throughout 1956 wildcats continued, especially over the revision of clean-up and relief time. Stewards from all departments organized "mass relief" in defiance of the contract. When one department continued wildcatting and supervision discharged them, laid-off workers refused to hire-in to replace them. Stewards refused to follow the griever model, according to which workers must follow orders until grievances are settled. They argued that the company should write a grievance if it disputed the workers' application of the contract: the company was forced to back down, at least temporarily.[39] Over the next several years Studebaker's labor relations settled into an adversarial pattern typical of unionized heavy industry.

The electoral merry-go-round continued. Ogden was defeated for reelection in 1957 by Forrest Hanna, a former vice-president under Horvath, who split off temporarily from the right wing. Yet Hanna also lost a reelection bid in 1959 and was replaced by Fox who, as vice-president from 1961 to 1964, became a chief negotiator. On the one hand, the new management's hardball tactics created lasting bitterness among the rank and file and stewards. Fox argued that the union's financial "sacrifices" were not appreciated and workers simply ended up "sharing scarcity and misery" and "subsidizing" the company. On the other hand, Ogden claimed that "mismanagement" and management "cronyism" caused Studebaker's plight, including the "loose production standards." Fox and Ogden each later explained that production standards were a "power situation" in which stewards represented workers' demands to protect jobs and income by keeping the pace of work reasonable; it was management's "responsibility" and "right" to resist them and tighten standards, said Fox. But management's new wage system changed the local leaders' situation by removing problem solving from the shop floor. Attempts by stewards to leverage influence through militant job control tactics were unavailing with the new authority structure and without international support.[40]

## National Industrial Politics

UAW strategy in this crisis was twofold. First, the International Union used collective bargaining to win fair distribution of gains from the rationalization of production at GM and Ford. In the 1930s and 1940s the UAW had insisted on better production planning to stabilize employment in what was a notoriously seasonal industry. The UAW demanded a guaranteed annual wage in the early 1950s, hoping it would provide a financial incentive for employers to regularize employment. The companies retained control of manning schedules, but the UAW did win employer-paid supplementary unemployment benefits (SUB) in the 1955 national contract negotiations. By the 1960s and 1970s SUB had become very generous for individual workers who qualified, but it did little for Studebaker workers. Benefit levels in the 1950s were too low; they did not help high-seniority workers, especially at Studebaker where SUB was paid to both laid-off and short-week workers; Indiana disqualified SUB recipients from unemployment compensation until 1957; and in 1958 the UAW agreed to let Studebaker defer its SUB contribution for fifteen months.[41]

Second, as it cooperated to make Studebaker competitive, much as it did at American Motors and Chrysler in 1958, the UAW sought to transform the workers' demands for job security and local control into a public welfare obligation for local redevelopment aid and evidence of the need for vigorous Keynesian growth policies. The UAW attempted to attract national attention to unemployment and community disinvestment during the 1950s. But the union effort was inconclusive because of uneven AFL-CIO interest, congressional factionalism, and Eisenhower administration opposition.

In the late 1950s Senator Paul Douglas—a Democrat from Illinois and a prominent spokesman for the liberal coalition that supported moderate Keynesianism, free trade, and progressive unionism —introduced legislation, supported by Reuther and the AFL-CIO, to provide capital and planning for "distressed" high unemployment communities. A federal loan and grant fund would buy land and machinery and provide public works and manpower training assistance. In conjunction with local "public advisory committees," a new federal agency would be in charge of administration. In South Bend this would have meant participation by the heavily Democratic and union-staffed local government.[42]

Douglas's bill passed the Senate in 1955 with the help of a liberal coalition that included the leading industrialist, Senator Ralph Flanders, a Vermont Republican, and the Committee for a National Trade Policy, an influential group of liberal businessmen who sought to reinforce labor support for free trade through programs to compensate those hurt by broadening competitive pressures. The administration blocked the bill in the House with the aid of the conservative faction of the Democratic party, but the steady, slow increase in the number of congressional Democrats in the late 1950s led both Houses to pass it in 1958 and then again in 1959. President Eisenhower vetoed the measure both times.[43]

Meanwhile, Studebaker's employment had fallen from 20,000 in 1950 to 10,000 in 1954. By early 1956, Studebaker-Packard's precarious existence had become the object of special attention in the Eisenhower administration. As a candidate in 1952 Eisenhower had endorsed the liberal public philosophy that the federal government had a responsibility to counteract serious inflation and unemployment, but as president he followed a neo-Keynesian policy based on the essential soundness of the private forces driving the economy. The government's role was to ensure growth through the macroeconomic tools of balanced budgets and monetary policy. Hence, the justice department approved mergers among the small auto companies while allowing GM to increase its market share above 50 percent. Nonetheless, the administration very much wanted to prevent Studebaker's bankruptcy, apparently for fear of its impact on financial markets and the combined impact of these at the polls.[44]

Studebaker management's strategy at merger with Packard had been to rely on defense contract profits to bridge the company over to its full-line product strategy. But the Eisenhower administration, through former GM President and now Secretary of Defense Charles Wilson, was reducing military spending as part of its policy of fiscal restraint and cutting back its supplier base to fewer large companies, which undercut Studebaker's plan. Paul Hoffman now busied himself lobbying the Defense Department and his good friend Eisenhower for defense contracts. The president was responsive because Studebaker had a good defense production record; moreover, this kind of aid could be considered ad hoc rather than a departure from administration economic policy. The UAW supported these efforts. Local 190 in Detroit, the former Packard local, voted to support Hoffman. The UAW Studebaker department appealed to Wilson to give defense orders to Studebaker-Packard, while Democrats urged greater government spending on the military.[45]

At the same time Studebaker sought to secure more capital from the firm's creditors and/or find another merger partner to perform both these purposes. The banks did want the company to survive somehow, if only because the company's assets were so devalued they would be insufficient to pay back even preferred debt. But First National City Bank, Chase Bank, and Metropolitan Life Insurance Company refused further funds in January and February 1956. The New York Federal Reserve Bank was cool to a loan and eventually said no. The U.S. Federal Reserve would not guarantee a loan, and they blocked any talks between Studebaker-Packard and American Motors.[46]

In August 1956 the Defense Department awarded contracts to

Studebaker, which "sold" them to Curtiss-Wright, a major defense contractor, which also leased Studebaker's two most modern plants. In addition Studebaker sold its subsidiary in California, which had a contract for the Dart missile. As another part of the deal, President Nance resigned, the Packard line was dropped, and elements of the old Studebaker management took control.[47]

With the money thus earned, Studebaker paid off its creditors and launched its new, very profitable compact Lark in 1959. It also earned about $10 million as the marketing agent for Mercedes-Benz. But rather than continue its specialty market strategy, Studebaker managers used its profits to diversify by acquiring a dozen manufacturing companies in the next three years. In doing so, a former Studebaker fleet sales manager argued, they failed to develop markets for police cars, taxis, and luxury designs, one of which proved profitable in the hands of independent producer Avanti.[48]

In late 1963 Studebaker suddenly announced it was suspending all car production. It left behind 7,200 active Local 5 members, a $30 million unfunded pension obligation, and a 9.1 percent unemployment rate in South Bend. Luckily for Local 5 workers the national economy was broadly expanding at the time that Studebaker abandoned the auto business. Not only did the rate of unemployment in South Bend soon decline to the national average, but Local 5 also survived by organizing the companies that bought the old Studebaker plants.[49]

## Conclusion

In retrospect, Studebaker's crisis was not so much caused by high product prices, loose production standards, or a management effort to GMize industrial relations but by a broader political institutional limit on the alternatives available. The root of the problem was postwar failure of the unions to establish either a public commitment to full employment or labor and community roles in industrial decision making. The emergent postwar settlement truncated the vision the UAW and other CIO unions had of an economic system in which labor would directly participate with management in production planning under state supervision. Instead, the unions were compelled to concede the shop floor to management and replace the effort to intervene directly in the structure of the economy with government management of the business cycle.

Of course, there were legitimate strategies of both cooperation and dissent under the postwar system. Legitimate cooperation took place at the highest level of national collective bargaining and economic policy. Union dissent involved participation in the Democratic party to win social reforms to boost growth and insure workers against economic insecurity. However, the latter were not guaranteed success, nor did reform advocates always observe the boundaries of legitimate labor aspiration in directing the economy. The political stalemate in the 1940s continued in the 1950s—exemplified by the distressed areas legislation—and reinforced strategies for private bargains, managerialist solutions, union defensiveness, and "market" outcomes. The companies' orthodox alternative strategy was disinvestment and diversification. Studebaker played out the orthodox Fordist scenario. The postwar settlement provided incentives for Studebaker management to emulate the Big Three's high-volume, standardized strategy with all that implied for the firm's internal work organization. But a strong local union and strong postwar markets masked until 1953 the incongruities of Studebaker's actual market and labor strategies compared to Fordism. When the crisis began management hardly hesitated to adhere to orthodoxy; it protected its leading investors first and foremost and cut labor costs while diversifying into other products.

The Fordist model was implemented at Studebaker in the post–Korean War period, but the cut in labor costs did not save the company. Their real dilemma was the company's lack of crucial prerequisites for either Fordism or flexible specialization. It could not readily implement a Fordist labor policy: first, because of the militant job control unionism of Local 5, and second, because a high-volume strategy was impractical given its relatively small market. At the same time, the political conditions for a flexible-specialist policy were missing, given the federal government's lack of economic planning. Finally, this study suggests that flexible industrial organization requires a vision of alternative work organization by labor and management alike and, even more important, that union politics must encompass and mobilize a broad community which can link the solutions of local problems to a more flexible industrial policy at the national level.

## NOTES

1. For a more complete description of flexible specialization see Michael Piore and Charles Sabel, *The Second Industrial Divide* (New York: Basic Books, 1984), 258–77. Compare William Abernathy, Kim Clark, and Alan Kantrow, *Industrial Renaissance* (New York: Basic Books, 1983); David Friedman, "Beyond the Age of Ford: The Strategic Basis of the Japanese Success in Automobiles," in John Zysman and Laura Tyson, eds., *American Industry in International Competition: Government Policies and Corporate Strategies* (Ithaca: Cornell University Press, 1983); and Peter Katzenstein, *Small States in World Markets: Industrial Policy in Europe* (Ithaca: Cornell University Press, 1985). For a standard view, see Michael Porter, *Competitive Strategies* (New York: Free Press, 1980).

2. Howell John Harris, *The Right to Manage: Industrial Relations Policies of American Business in the 1940s* (Madison: University of Wisconsin Press, 1982). Nelson Lichtenstein, "Industrial Democracy, Contract Unionism, and the National War Labor Board," *Labor Law Journal* 33 (August 1982): 524–30, and "UAW Bargaining Strategy and Shop-Floor Conflict: 1946–1970," *Industrial Relations* 24 (Fall 1985). Katherine Van Wezel Stone, "The Postwar Paradigm in American Labor Law," *The Yale Law Journal* 90 (June 1981): 1509–81. Charles Sabel, *Work and Politics* (New York: Cambridge University Press, 1982). Compare Steven Tolliday and Jonathan Zeitlin, eds., *The Automobile Industry and Its Workers: Between Fordism and Flexibility* (London: Basil Blackwell, 1986).

3. Walter Dean Burnham, *Critical Elections and the Mainsprings of American Politics* (New York: Norton, 1970), and "The Appearance and Disappearance of the American Voter," in Burnham, *The Current Crisis in American Politics* (New York: Oxford University Press, 1982). Andrew Martin, "The Politics of Employment and Welfare in Advanced Capitalist Societies: National Policies and International Interdependence," in Keith Banting, ed., *The State and Economic Interests* (Toronto: University of Toronto Press, 1986).

4. Charles Edwards, *Dynamics of the United States Automobile Industry* (Columbia: University of South Carolina Press, 1965), 24, chart 2, and 112, table 9.

5. Calculated by the author from Edwards, *Dynamics*, 74, table 6.

6. Many sources agree on Studebaker's market strategy, for example "Independent's Day," *Forbes* 69 (June 15, 1952): 18–26, and "Last Stand of the Auto Independents," *Fortune* 50 (December 1954). The suggestion that Studebaker take over Ford is reported in Peter Drucker, *The Practice of Management* (New York: Harper, 1954), 113–14. 1930s profits are reported in Frederick Harbison and Robert Dubin, *Patterns of Union-Management Relations* (Chicago: Social Science Associates, 1947), 108.

7. Studebaker had the first postwar car, Edwards, *Dynamics*, 106. Sales and market share calculated by the author from Edwards. Foreign plants, *South Bend Tribune*, September 3, 1948, Local History Newspaper Clippings

File, South Bend Public Library. Also *Wards Automotive Yearbook 1955*, 119. 1953 design, *South Bend Tribune*, January 25, 1953. Exports, R. A. Hutchinson Papers (vice-president for exports), Box 1, Studebaker Archival Collections, Discovery Hall Museum, South Bend, Indiana. Up-to-date facilities, Edwards, 18, 146–147. *Forbes* 69 (June 15, 1952).

8. Hoffman quote, Harbison and Dubin, *Patterns*, 105. Studebaker was a leading citizen, William Dempsey interview with Eli Miller, April 11, 1983, Discovery Hall Museum. Miller was director of the South Bend Chamber of Commerce for twenty-five years. Involvement in the community, Dubin and Harbison, 119, and *Forbes* 69 (January 1, 1952). "Father-son-daughter teams," *South Bend Tribune*, November 6, 1952, Studebaker Corporation file, South Bend Public Library; Harbison and Dubin, 121, note 11. Also see Albert Erskine, *History of the Studebaker Corporation* (South Bend: Studebaker Corporation, 1924), 105–33. In the pre–World War I era, Studebaker managers were members of the Progressive National Civic Federation. Jack Detzler, *A Decade Dedicated to Reform: South Bend 1910–1920* (South Bend: Northern Indiana Historical Society, 1960).

9. See Robert Collins, *The Business Response to Keynes* (New York: Columbia University Press, 1981), and Harris, *The Right to Manage*. Studebaker's bankers, Glore, Forgan and Co., Kuhn Loeb and Co., Lehman Brothers (Edwards, *Dynamics*, 42), Chase Bank, First National City Bank, and Metropolitan Life Insurance Co., (Minute Book of the meetings of the board of directors, Studebaker Corporation, Studebaker Archival Collections) also were internationalist businesses.

10. Harbison and Dubin, *Patterns*, 114, 134, 138. Robert MacDonald, *Collective Bargaining in the Automobile Industry: A Study of Wage Structure and Competitive Relations* (New Haven: Yale University Press, 1963), 365. "Effects of the N.W.L.B.'s Actions in the South Bend Labor Market Area," Appendix K-9, *The Termination Report of the National War Labor Board* (Washington, D.C.: Government Printing Office, n.d.), 1146. Local 5 Collection, Box 18, Archives of Labor History and Urban Affairs (ALHUA), Walter Reuther Library, Wayne State University, Detroit, Mich. (hereafter ALHUA).

11. Harbison and Dubin, *Patterns*, 108–16, 147, 157, 164–66, 202. Their description, though supported by other opinion at the time, was roundly criticized later, especially by Robert MacDonald whose interpretation of Studebaker's problems has become the accepted one. Harbison and Dubin believed they saw at Studebaker what great results could be accomplished in the organization of work once basic issues of union security and wages were guaranteed. In contrast, MacDonald argued that management gave away the store to labor and paid the price of union irresponsibility and market uncompetitiveness.

In fact, what Harbison and Dubin witnessed was a transitional period in the labor system in which diverse elements intermixed. They highlighted certain practices they hoped would form a new pattern. MacDonald's work reflected the resurgent managerial view of the late 1950s and 1960s, simply ignoring the complex historical and political conflicts that had created the contemporary industrial relations system. (MacDonald's book appeared before Studebaker left the business.)

Other opinion, see, for example, John Sembower, "What's Behind Stude-baker's No-Strike Record," *Industrial Relations* (October 1946), and Glenn Griswold, "Humanized Employee Relations: Studebaker an Example," *Public Opinion Quarterly* (September 1940).

12. James D. Hill, *U.A.W.'s Frontier* (UAW Region 3 Auto Council, 1971). Note the title of this history of unionism at Studebaker. Farmer-labor party, see Janet Weaver interview with Carl Shipley, December 31, 1982, Discovery Hall Museum. Al Rightly of Local 5 was on the board of the Filene Foundation which paid him, as a UAW organizer, to promote the coop movement within the UAW. "Minutes of the March 17–26, 1947 Meeting," UAW International Executive Board, IEB Collection, ALHUA. Also "The New Studebaker Is Nice, but Have You Seen the Local? Rochdale Cooperation in South Bend Has Led to Farmer-Labor Cooperation" (UAW Education Department Publication #126, c.1948), Industrial Relations Collection, Littauer Library, Harvard University. As noted, the political basis for this did not develop.

13. Harbison and Dubin, *Patterns*, 121–25, 156, 177, 160. Loren Pennington interview with George Hupp, May 19, 1972, 17–20, ALHUA. Hupp started work at Studebaker in 1929. He was president of Local 5 from 1946–1947 and after 1948 worked for Studebaker management. Hupp interview, 48.

14. Clerks, Loren Pennington interview with Lester Fox, June 21, 1971, 24, ALHUA. "GM Wage Case Research 1945–7," UAW Research Department Collection, Box 13, ALHUA. The wage structure at Studebaker was high and also compressed, as actual production worker wages were higher and skilled wages were lower than at GM and Ford. Compare MacDonald, *Collective Bargaining*, 271, for wage data from 1954.

15. Harbison and Dubin, *Patterns*, 173. Hupp interview, 50. Fox interview, June 21, 1971, 24. Fox was a second generation union official at Local 5. He was first elected a steward in 1949 and held office until 1964. Harbison and Dubin, 153, note that workers quit early after achieving their rate.

16. Harbison and Dubin, *Patterns*, 170–72. MacDonald, *Collective Bargaining*, 267.

17. MacDonald, *Collective Bargaining*, 358–59, 367.

18. Full line strategy, Edwards, *Dynamics*, 70–73. Studebaker's major dealer in New York at 56th and Broadway went bust, and the company had to create Whiteway Motors to replace it. Studebaker also invested in its largest Los Angeles dealer (Hoffman's son Lathrop Hoffman) to allow him to buy other dealers and maintain market coverage. Minute Book, September 25, 1953, and November 22 and December 17, 1954, and January 20, 1956.

19. Edwards, *Dynamics*, 112, table 9, 166, 76–77, tables 6–8, 157, note 14, and 169. Compare Lawrence White, *The Automobile Industry since 1945* (Cambridge: Harvard University Press, 1971), 50, 292–93, shows that foreign sales doubled from 1954 to 1955 and almost doubled again in 1956. By 1958 they had almost quadrupled the 1956 mark and stood at 8 percent of the

market. Compare also Brock Yates, *The Decline and Fall of the American Automobile Industry* (New York: Empire Books, 1983), 127–28. MacDonald, *Collective Bargaining*, 268–69. New models from the annual statistical issue of *Automotive Industries*, March 15, 1953–1956. "Ex-car," *Forbes* 69 (June 1, 1952): 22. Raymond Loewy, "More Compact Power Plant Key to Better Automotive Design," *Ward's Automotive Yearbook 1955*, 11.

20. Relations between Nance and Hoffman, see Loren Pennington, "Prelude to Chrysler: The Eisenhower Administration Bails Out Studebaker-Packard" (unpublished paper, Discovery Hall Museum), and Alan Raucher, *Paul G. Hoffman: Architect of Foreign Aid* (Lexington: University of Kentucky Press, 1985), 116–19. New management, Edwards, *Dynamics*, 42, 87–88. Many were trained at GM. Hupp says "a lot" of lower level production people were brought, Hupp interview, 76. Concerning crises of 1956 and 1958, see Edwards, and Minute Book, February, March, and May 1956; reorganization, Minute Book, October 4, 1954; management resistance, Fox interview, 49.

21. Minute Book, December 18, 1953. Anna Rosenberg worked "half time" for the Rockefeller brothers, John Hay Whitney, Marshall Field, and Mrs. Albert Lasker. "Anna Rosenberg—She Sells Intuitions," *Fortune* 50 (November 1954).

Her liberal elite credentials also included having been a political confidant of Chester Bowles and William Benton. She was Assistant Secretary of Defense in the Truman administration and, like Hoffman, a member of the first Committee on the Present Danger. See Jerry Sanders, *Peddlers of Crisis: The Committee on the Present Danger and the Politics of Containment* (Boston: South End Press, 1983); Chester Bowles, *Promises to Keep: My Years in Public Life* (New York: Harper and Row, 1971), 229.

22. "Operation '55," A. J. Porta, Vice-President Papers, Box 3, Studebaker Corporation Collections. Also, "Contracts 1937–55," Local 5 Collection, Box 18, ALHUA. *South Bend Tribune*, August 2 and 10, 1954.

23. High training costs, Memorandum of Anna Rosenberg to Paul Hoffman, May 18, 1954, "Studebaker-Packard Corporation II: Labor Negotiations —Misc. 1954" file, Paul Hoffman Collection, Box 152, Harry S. Truman Presidential Library, Independence, Missouri. Hupp interview, 21. Harbison and Dubin, *Patterns*, 170. In 1954 the local agreed to one-way bumping: if the worker cannot qualify, then he can only new bump into an open job. "Minutes of Executive Board and Membership Meetings, 1954," October 14, 1954, Local 5 Collection, Box 10, ALHUA. And they agreed to bump first in their current division, ibid., January 19, 1954. Compare with Steve Jefferys's account of Chrysler in this volume.

24. Testimony before the Joint Committee on the Economic Report, Subcommittee on Economic Stabilization, October 17, 1955, Transcript, 20, UAW Local 5 Collection, Box 1, ALHUA. Meeting with the union, Minute Book, December 18, 1953, and January 14, 1955. Local 5 president Louis Horvath met with Anna Rosenberg "privately," Fox interview, 16. Pressure on the local

leadership, Fox interview, 11, and Loren Pennington interview with J. D. Hill, May 12, 1972, 40–45, ALHUA. Hill was one of the early union organizers, president 1949–1950, and then staff of the UAW Studebaker Department in Detroit.

25. The red-baiting was "vicious," Hupp later agreed. Hupp interview, 64–65. Purge of regional staff, Janet Weaver interview with Raymond Berndt, April 1, 1980, 40–55, Discovery Hall Museum. Berndt became the single most influential person in the Indiana CIO Council. Melvin A. Kahn, *The Politics of American Labor: The Indiana Microcosm* (Carbondale: Southern Illinois University Labor Institute, 1970). Dubin and Harbison note that South Bend was 55 percent Catholic, *Patterns*, 117. South Bend Democratic politics were organized around labor and ethnic groups, especially Poles and Hungarians. John Million, "The Democratic Party of South Bend, Indiana" (paper, political science department, Kalamazoo College, 1965). Harlen Noel was chosen to become the CIO-PAC director in South Bend in 1948 in part because he was Catholic. Author interview with Harlen (H. J.) Noel, June 27, 1984. Noel was from Bendix Local 9, an Addes local. Annual Polish Day rallies regaled crowds with anticommunism for ten years, greeted by "bursts of applause." *South Bend Tribune*, September 10, 1945, and November 26, 1955.

26. In other words the UAW's anticommunist campaign did not win it union or Democratic friends since they themselves were considered extreme.

27. Postwar job control demand, Hupp interview, 9. Job control militancy, see Harbison and Dubin, *Patterns*, 142, 161–63. Janet Weaver interview with Ray Berndt, April 1, 1980, 47–48. One-party South, Pennington interview with Fox, June 21, 1971, 4. Loren Pennington interview with William Ogden, May 15, 1972, 9–10, 78, ALHUA. Ogden was the principal oppositionist. He was originally a coal miner, like his father, and then an early organizer of the local. He was its president 1944–1945, 1951–1952, and 1955–1957. Autonomous departments, Hupp interview, 23–24.

28. MacDonald, *Collective Bargaining*, 262–66, for 1950 negotiations. For similar exchanges, see "Minutes of Meeting Concerning Skilled Trades Policy," September 12 and 24, 1952, Local 5 Collection, Box 12, ALHUA. Compare Fox interview, 17: "why should the workers bite the bullet?" In 1948 the local executive board discussed the company's poor prospects. They sought out president Vance and met privately with him at his home to urge him to tighten up. Hupp interview, 27–28.

Between 1947 and 1953 there was more than one drop of 800 workers from the payroll per year. Robert Gold, *Manufacturing Structure and Pattern of the South Bend-Mishawaka Area* (Chicago: University of Chicago Department of Geography Research Paper, no. 36, 1954). Gold calculated that a drop of 350 was enough to significantly affect the whole area's employment, 103–4. Total Studebaker employment in South Bend was:

21,868 on September 11, 1950
15,638 on September 8, 1952

23,247 on April 6, 1953
16,417 on October 12, 1953.

"Employment by Sex," Automobile Manufacturers Association survey, Industrial Relations Department, Box 1, selected weeks, Studebaker Corporation Collections.

29. *South Bend Tribune*, August 2, 6, 9, 10, and 13, 1954. Fox interview, 12, 21.

30. The "heart" of the union, Fox interview, 12–13. There was major opposition to tighter discipline and the absence of "guarantees" and of company openness. *South Bend Tribune*, August 6 and 11, 1954.

31. "Minutes of Executive Board and Membership Meetings," September 23, 1954, Local 5 Collection, Box 10. Minute Book, March 18 and May 20, 1955. "Grievance Memorandum No. 306," January 6, 1955, and "Grievance Memorandum," January 13, 1955, Industrial Relations Department, Box 1, Studebaker Corporation Collections.

32. "Grievance Memorandum," January 13, 1955, Studebaker Corporation Collections. "Cooperate" with the union, *South Bend Tribune*, January 17, 1955. Compare *South Bend Tribune*, January 20 and 21 and February 9, 1955. *Business Week*, January 29, 1955, 126. Vote reported in "Local 5 Official Bulletins, 1953–55," Local 5 Collection, Box 1. Minute Book, March 18, 1955.

33. Minute Book, May 20, 1955. "Local 5 Official Bulletins, 1953–55," May 23 and June 1, 1955, Local 5 Collection, Box 1.

34. "Local 5 Official Bulletins, 1953–55," July 9, 1955; Minute Book, May 20, July 15, 1955. MacDonald, *Collective Bargaining*, 281. *South Bend Tribune*, July 8, 21, and 29, and August 2 and 4, 1955.

35. *South Bend Tribune*, June 11, 1955. Fox's recruitment, Janet Weaver interview with Fox, March 5, 1979, 16, Discovery Hall Museum. Slate loses, "Studebaker Workers Endorse a 'Get Tough' Policy," *Business Week*, July 16, 1955, 132. "Strike and Strategy," Official Bulletin, August 15, 1955, Local 5 Collection, Box 15. There were thirty-one wildcats counted by the local press from July 1 to September 30. *South Bend Tribune*, November 23, 1955.

36. "Minutes of Executive Board and Membership Meetings, 1955," September 22 and October 10, 1955, Local 5 Collection, Box 10. *Studebaker Weekly News*, Local 5, December 16, 1955, 1–4, Local 5 Collection, Box 15. *South Bend Tribune*, December 13, 1955.

37. *South Bend Tribune*, September 6, November 10, and December 2, 1955. "1956 Working Agreement Ratification Vote," Local 5 Collection, Box 19. *South Bend Tribune*, January 8, 1956. MacDonald, *Collective Bargaining*, 282–83.

38. Minute Book, January 14, 1955. Compare December 16, 1955, and January 20, 1956.

39. Minute Book, November 18, 1955. "1956 Model Difficulties thru 11/30/55," Industrial Relations Department, Box 1. "Work Stoppages from January 1, 1956 to . . . ," Memoranda of February 14 and March 7–9 and 12, 1956,

Industrial Relations Department, Box 4. The company was still fighting over this issue in 1962.

40. Ogden interview, 18, 27, 30–32. Fox interview, Industrial Relations Department, Box 4, 8–9. Weaver interview with Fox, 15–16. Bitterness, Pennington interview with Fox, May 19, 1972, 1. Compare Fox interview, June 21, 1971, 10–11, 15, 17–18, 25–26, 33, 48.

41. Disqualifying, *South Bend Tribune*, August 29, 1958. SUB payments, Pennington interview with Stanley Ladd, July 17, 1972, 58–59, Discovery Hall Museum. Deferring SUB, MacDonald, *Collective Bargaining*, 283.

42. James Sundquist, *Politics and Policy: The Eisenhower, Kennedy and Johnson Years* (Washington, D.C.: Brookings Institution, 1968). Sar Levitan, *Federal Aid to Depressed Areas* (Baltimore: Johns Hopkins University Press, 1964). *Area Redevelopment Hearings*, Senate Committee on Banking and Currency, 85th Congress, 1st Sess., March 6–May 15, 1957, 281–85. *Proceedings*, First Constitutional Convention, AFL-CIO, December 5–8, 1955. Also, *Proceedings*, 1957, 308, and *Proceedings*, 1959, 225–27. After the Democrats swept into office in 1955, seven local leaders joined city and county government, including former president Louis Horvath. "Minutes of Executive Board and Membership Meetings, 1955," December 29, 1955, Local 5 Collection, Box 10.

43. *Redevelopment Hearings*, 646–50, 668, 698f. John Bibby and Roger Davidson, *On Capital Hill: Studies in the Legislative Process* (New York: Holt, Rinehart and Winston, 1967). The Committee for a National Trade Policy included on its board of directors Studebaker's banker, Glore, Forgan partner John Fennelly. "Committee for a National Trade Policy," Box 72, Hoffman Collection. William Batt, the committee's secretary, had been research director of the Democratic National Committee in the Truman years and, after the Congress again passed the distressed areas bill in 1961 and President Kennedy signed it, he became an administrator of the Area Redevelopment Adminstration.

Moreover, the UAW was unable to win higher and more extensive unemployment compensation benefits in Michigan in 1952 and in Indiana in 1954. "Minutes of Executive Board and Membership Meetings, 1954," March 24, 1954, Local 5 Collection, Box 10. To the contrary, the UAW and the Indiana CIO Council had to fight for years to repeal Indiana's right-to-work law, passed in 1957 at the instigation of the Chamber of Commerce. Despite favorable party alignments in the legislature in 1959, Democratic leaders' concessions to rural Democrats foiled repeal. The law was finally repealed in 1965. Kahn, *Politics*, 242. My interpretation of the political conditions differs from Kahn's.

44. The story of 1956 comes from Pennington, "Prelude." William Harris, "The Breakdown of Studebaker-Packard," *Fortune* (October 1956): 139. Eisenhower and elections, "Studebaker Corporation 1956," Donald Montgomery Collection, Box 79, ALHUA.

45. Pennington quotes an entry in Eisenhower's diary following a meeting between Hoffman and the President:

> All day long I have been receiving advice to the effect that all of us must do our best to keep the Packard-Studebaker combine from liquidating, which it seems to be on the point of doing. For more than a year I have been working on this particular matter, especially urging the Defense Department to give this firm some defense contracts, in the items in which it has already established a fine production record.

Hoffman's efforts are discussed in the Minute Book, April 18, July 15, and November 18, 1955, and January 20, March 23, and May 2, 1956. UAW and defense contracts, *Detroit Times*, May 16, 1956. UAW Studebaker Department Collection, Box 1, ALHUA. Democratic demands for greater defense spending, see Seymour Harris, *The Economics of the Political Parties* (New York: MacMillan, 1962).

46. Minute Book, February 27 and March 23, 1956. Pennington, "Prelude," 11. Studebaker's debt was high compared to other car companies, making it sensitive to its creditors. "Independent's Day," *Forbes* 69 (June 15, 1952). One recent study argues that "the key determinant in the incidence of closings and phasedowns is whether absentee owners continue to invest in local plants." Charles Craypo, "The Deindustrialization of a Factory Town: Plant Closings and Phasedowns in South Bend, Indiana, 1954–1983," in Donald Kennedy, ed., *Labor and Reindustrialization: Workers and Corporate Change* (University Park: Department of Labor Studies, Pennsylvania State University, 1984), 63.

47. Edwards, *Dynamics*, 73.

48. Pennington, "Prelude," 15. Edwards, *Dynamics*, 98–103. Also its top managers availed themselves of their stock options and reportedly made $1 million. B. J. Widick, "The Tragedy at Studebaker," *The Nation*, February 17, 1962. After 1953, stockholder equity had been further reduced by over one-third during the years 1954–1959. Edwards, 77, table 8. Theresa Schindler interviews with John Duncan (former Truck and Fleet Sales Manager of Studebaker) and Arnold Altman (former Packard dealer and later president of Avanti), South Bend, Indiana, March 29 and April 4, 1983. Note that the Avanti car was a Studebaker luxury design successfully developed, produced, and marketed by Altman after Studebaker left the business.

49. Suddenness, "End in South Bend: Then There Were Four," *Newsweek*, December 23, 1963, 57. Pennington interview with Fox, 22–23. There was also a furious, brief debate in the Johnson administration about whether to aid geographical relocation of workers or whether to keep skilled labor in South Bend to make it a more viable industrial district. See Federal Records: Council of Economic Advisors, Reel 45, Task Force on Studebaker, Lyndon B. Johnson Presidential Library, Austin, Texas. B. J. Widick, "Studebaker: End of a Dream," *The Nation*, January 6, 1954, 29. About 500 employees, mostly skilled and management, moved. $30 million, Ogden interview, 58. Fox became director of Project ABLE, a joint venture of the U.S. Labor Department and National Council on Aging to train workers over fifty years of age. 1,300 of 3,500 eligible participated; 70 percent finished the program, and

70 percent of these found jobs. *New York Times*, November 14, 1966, 64. Studebaker bought annuities for those sixty and older; for those forty to sixty they paid them 15 cents for every dollar accrued pension credit and nothing for the rest. Ibid., November 28, 1966, 63.

# 9

## Shop Floor Bargaining, Contract Unionism, and Job Control: An Anglo-American Comparison

### STEVEN TOLLIDAY and JONATHAN ZEITLIN

### Introduction

International comparisons of industrial relations systems have historically carried a critical edge. Often foreign institutions are displayed as models by domestic advocates of reform; occasionally, a dominant power such as the United States attempts to export its own institutions as a formula for bringing political stability and industrial peace to its less fortunate allies. From the nineteenth century through the 1920s, the AFL and its sympathizers saw the voluntarist framework of British labor law as the template for the freedom from judicial intervention in collective bargaining they hoped to obtain in the United States; while in the 1930s and 1940s, the liberal arbitrators and labor economists who staffed the federal labor relations agencies sought to promote the spread of the industrywide bargaining procedures they held responsible for Britain's contemporaneous record of industrial peace. Beginning in the 1950s, conversely, British politicians, lawyers, and academics alarmed at the growth of trade union power and the proliferation of unofficial strikes began to look with envy on the legally regulated system of collective bargaining in the United States. They believed it conducive to economic efficiency and orderly industrial relations, and the abortive Tory Industrial Relations Act of 1971 drew heavily on the American model.[1]

A similar perception of Anglo-American differences began to capture the imagination of radical critics dissatisfied with the apparent integration of American trade unions into the capitalist order during the 1960s and 1970s. From this perspective, the British labor scene seemed to embody much of what American radicals found lacking in the domestic trade union movement. American unions, in this view, had lost by the 1950s most of the militant fire of their formative years. The pursuit of economic gains through the process of collective bargaining, it was argued, had led the unions to accept the hegemony of managerial authority in the workplace and largely abandon the struggles for job control that had sparked their early organizing drives. In their quest for written contracts with employers, American unions had acquiesced in the elaboration of bureaucratic grievance procedures, capped in most cases by binding arbitration; they restricted shop floor initiatives and rendered most forms of job action illegal during the life of the contract. Union officials were therefore obliged to assist management in imposing discipline and respect for procedure on their members; meanwhile, the increasing centralization of bargaining and the consolidation of executive power had effectively excluded the rank and file from any substantive influence on union policy.[2]

In this light British industrial relations appeared to present an attractive contrast to conditions at home. In most industries, collective bargaining was highly decentralized, with negotiations conducted by shop stewards elected directly by the workforce and largely autonomous from national union control. Collective agreements were unenforceable in the courts, and there were few legal restraints on industrial action. The stewards were therefore free to take militant action in their struggles against management, using tactics such as slowdowns, overtime bans, and "quickie" strikes; and the result was thought to be effective worker control over such key managerial functions as manning, workloads, and the introduction of new technology. Thus, to many American observers, the example of shop floor bargaining in Britain seemed to signpost a road not taken by their own trade unions, one which might have bridged the gap between the organizations and their members and avoided the malaise apparently afflicting the postwar American labor movement.[3]

In recent years, prominent American labor historians such as David Brody and Nelson Lichtenstein have drawn on this image of the British experience as a foil for their interpretation of the evolution of American industrial relations between the 1930s and the 1950s. In a pioneering essay on the postwar domestication of American labor, Brody argues that the challenge to management control posed by unions at the end of World War II was ultimately contained by the employers, in part because of the development of a sophisticated managerial response, together with the underlying economism shared by workers and unions. Most crucial, however, was the emergence of the "workplace rule of law," in the shape of written contracts, formal grievance procedures, and neutral arbitration; work groups were inhibited from engaging in "fractional bargaining," that is, from employing direct action in pursuit of their job control objectives. "In England, where union contracts did not penetrate down to the factory floor," Brody observes, "the shop stewards carved out a bargaining realm quite independently of the union structure. In America, fractional bargaining could not evolve into a comparable shop bargaining system. The workplace rule of law effectively forestalled the institutionalization of shop-group activity."[4]

In a stimulating study of workplace industrial relations in the auto industry between 1937 and 1955, Nelson Lichtenstein goes further toward proposing the British model of shop floor bargaining as an alternative option potentially available to American trade unionists in this period. Having traced the emergence of powerful networks of shop stewards who contested managerial prerogatives in a number of major auto manufacturing plants during the late 1930s and early 1940s, Lichtenstein continues:

> The wartime struggle over factory discipline seemed to lay the basis for a decentralized system of postwar industrial relations in the auto industry that would incorporate both effective shop-floor bargaining over production standards and company-wide negotiation over pay and other benefits. This system would not have been different from that which in fact came to characterize large sections of British industry in the postwar era. There a militant, semi-autonomous shop stewards movement won a central role in the life of the unions representing car workers. While the Amalgamated Union of Engineering Workers and other national organizations still negotiated periodic pay adjustments, these company-wide arrangements were little more than a platform from which stewards could legitimately seek to win improved conditions in direct confrontations with plant management.

In Lichtenstein's view, three factors explain the failure of these wartime struggles to establish a permanent role for shop floor bargaining in the postwar auto industry. Powerful managements fought to regain control of the production process, assisted by bureaucratic grievance procedures which took shop floor issues out of the stewards' hands and clamped down rigidly on unofficial strikes. The centralization of both collective bargaining and political authority within the UAW further reduced the scope for shop floor activity, as did the spread of automation, which eliminated many of the more combative occupational work groups in the factories.[5]

Although this picture of Anglo-American differences has some real purchase on reality, particularly from the vantage point of the late 1960s and early 1970s, recent developments, contemporary and historiographical, on both sides of the Atlantic suggest the contrast between workplace industrial relations in the two countries is overdrawn and misleading in important respects. In Britain, the onset of recession and monetarist economic policies have demonstrated the fragility of fragmented plant-based organizations, and many of the job controls won by stewards in better times have been rolled back by aggressive managements such as that at British Leyland.[6] Similarly, recent research on the history of industrial relations in the British auto industry shows that 100 percent trade unionism, the construction of durable shop steward organizations, and the erosion of managerial power in the workplace were only achieved in most of the major companies during the late 1950s and early 1960s. And even when shop stewards did achieve significant levels of job control, these were often applied flexibly and cooperatively except in periods of acute conflict.

On the American side, the resurgence of virulent and often successful employer antiunionism even in companies with long histories of union organization casts doubt on the claim that the postwar system of collective bargaining placed no major constraints on management's freedom of action in the workplace. Michael Piore has argued, for example, that the seniority rules, job classifications, and disciplinary procedures specified by most union contracts constitute a system of job definition and control which imposes substantial rigidities on the deployment of labor in the enterprise. During the period when Fordism and Taylorism were the central principles of efficient industrial organization, he suggests, these rules were acceptable and even advantageous to management. But rapid shifts in markets and technology have transformed them into major obstacles to the introduction of more flexible systems of work assignments needed to meet international competition, and contractual job controls have accordingly become a major stimulus to management's quest for a union-free environment.[7]

Piore's views are broadly confirmed by a comparative study of workforce reduction policies in the American and German auto industries, showing that American employers are much freer to lay off workers in response to short-term fluctuations in demand than their German counterparts but much more constrained in the selection of which workers to lay off.[8] An even more striking finding is that of Bryn Jones's comparative study of the British and American aerospace industries: he discovered that under favorable circumstances American unions are able to use the rights provided in their legally binding contracts to gain influence over manning on numerically controlled machine tools comparable to that established by British shop stewards through autonomous bargaining.[9]

The rapidly growing literature on the emergence and development of American industrial unions echoes these discoveries. Many studies document the magnitude of the break marked by the coming of the CIO with the arbitrary shop discipline and pervasive insecurity of the preunion era; and even those writers most concerned with pointing out the eventual containment of the union challenge provide extensive evidence of the practical restrictions collective bargaining imposed on management's freedom of action in the workplace.

In this chapter we discuss two important concepts. First, we present some results from recent research on the British auto industry and cast doubt on the received wisdom about shop floor power in a major mass production sector. Second, we draw on the recent historiography of the CIO as well as on the older industrial relations literature to suggest that the American system of collective bargaining placed greater constraints on managerial prerogatives in the automobile industry and other mass production sectors than generally supposed. Although a comparison between the mass production sectors may understate Anglo-American differences arising from international variations in industrial structure, it is an appropriate focus for assessing the viability of British-style shop floor bargaining in an American context. At the end we return to the original contrast between the two countries and draw some tentative conclusions.[10]

## Britain: Shop Floor Bargaining and Job Control

The picture of shop floor bargaining in the British auto industry used by Brody and Lichtenstein is based on a widespread but largely erroneous view:[11] Union organization strongly established itself in the auto industry by the end of the Second World War, taking advantage of the tightening labor markets of the prewar rearmament boom and the favorable conditions of wartime production. After the war, it is argued, employers were faced with almost insatiable demand and a shortage of labor, and they were prepared to concede high wages and a considerable measure of job control to powerful shop steward organizations in order to achieve continuous and expanding output. By the time that international competition began to intensify in the mid-1950s, employers had largely lost control of the shop floor; and it was only during the recession of the early 1980s that they were able to reestablish control over the entrenched shop stewards.

In fact, this picture is only accurate, with certain qualifications, for Standard Motors and the smaller auto companies in the Coventry area. But these firms produced less than a fifth of British car output during the postwar boom, and in the big producers the situation was very different. Employers maintained their prewar hostility to unions into the 1950s with considerable success. By 1956 Morris Motors was only 25 percent unionized; Vauxhall was well below 50 percent; Ford was in the same range and was notorious for its limitations on shop stewards. Austin fluctuated between 60 and 90 percent unionization during most of the 1950s, but there, too, the shop floor organization had made only very limited incursions on managerial authority during this period. In all these firms, the consolidation of strong shop floor organization occurs only in the late 1950s and early 1960s; at Vauxhall it is arguable whether there has ever been a powerful shop steward organization.[12]

It would be wrong to see these organizations as being built solely from the bottom up by autonomous oppositional action in the workplace. Shop floor militants were able to build limited organization in face of managerial resistance in the 1940s and 1950s, but they were only able to consolidate it effectively when management moved away from confrontation and toward accommodation. The initial union breakthrough in the war period depended largely on the mitigation of employer hostility as a result of government policy, and the belated consolidation of organization in the late 1950s was closely associated with government refusal to support employers who chose confrontation tactics.[13]

This is not to say that management exercised effective control over the workplace in the 1950s. Considerable informal bargaining took place on a day-to-day basis in the workplaces, even where union organization was weak. Pressures for speedy output were urgent, labor was in short supply, and the production facilities were outmoded and undercapitalized. In this situation, in firms with weakly elaborated managerial structures, shop floor supervision had considerable autonomy and the leeway to make concessions and surrender cost control in order to get output and effort.[14] The result was an "indulgency pattern" characterized by leniency and covering up for mistakes, side by side with hostility to unions and insistence on managerial prerogatives.[15] Management was actually prepared to pay high wages to keep unions out of the plant, and wages in weakly unionized firms moved forward at the same relative pace as those in the Coventry firms between 1948 and 1956, although the absolute gap was not narrowed substantially until after the unions entrenched themselves across all firms in the 1960s.[16] Managerial and supervisory discretion and slackness produced a creeping relaxation of custom and practice on the shop floor even without sustained union pressure. When union organization consolidated itself, it was able to rigidify these practices and demand cash bargains for any relaxations of these practices.

Across the auto firms a spectrum of job control developed depending particularly on the history of unionization, managerial strategies, and the structure of wage systems. At the bottom end of the spectrum came firms like Ford and Vauxhall; there day-wage structures denied stewards the opportunities of piecework bargaining, and management maintained a firmer control on the shop floor. From the 1930s, Ford at Dagenham sought to avoid any bargaining on the shop floor. Payment was on the basis of grading and day-rates, and from 1944 these were negotiated solely with national union officials. Stewards received hardly any formal recognition and almost no facilities; in the mid-1960s Ford still insisted that workloads were beyond the reach of negotiation. In the late 1950s and early 1960s this Ford system was put under pressure after Ford incorporated the adjacent Briggs Bodies factory and brought a powerfully organized piecework-based shop steward organization into the company with it. The so-called "harmonization" campaign, a long and finally successful offensive to bring Briggs conditions into line with those of Ford followed. This produced the most sustained shop floor challenge to Ford's right to manage in the form of a running battle of constant short stoppages over workloads. But in 1963 Ford sacked the core of the stewards organization; after that resistance fell away. At Dagenham in the 1960s stewards were not consulted over speed-up, the company was able to move workers around the factory more or less at will, and supervisors pressured individuals into accepting additional tasks on their jobs for the same money.[17]

In the mid-1960s the center of shop floor militancy within Ford shifted to their new plant at Halewood, near Liverpool. The degree of job control won by stewards there was significant, but a detailed study by Beynon has clearly demonstrated the underlying ambiguities and frailty of the stewards' bargaining position. Ford refused to negotiate over manning and individual workloads and rejected "mutuality" in job timing and work allocation. Workloads were the site of a major struggle over job control. One central issue was resistance to the speeding up of the assembly line *during* shifts. Through a campaign of unofficial walkouts, stewards won the right to hold the key that locked the line speeds during the shift. But the company still refused to negotiate about manning levels on the line, and when line speeds were increased they were often able to increase the manning less than proportionately.

Until the mid-1960s the foreman was able to decide unilaterally who was to work overtime and when; only later did stewards begin to get this power out of the hands of the foreman and apply a rota. It was the late 1960s before stewards won the right that work study should not *retime* a job without a steward present, and the initial timings remained unilateral. On layoffs, those to be laid off were generally selected by the supervisors without consultation; only on the strongest sections were stewards able to have them selected by being pulled out of a hat instead. The established controls, as Huw Beynon notes, "did not involve a very radical challenge to management organization of the plant." The struggle to control workloads was "running flat out to stand still." Periodic upsurges won the shifts in the frontier of control that were obtained, but they frequently drifted back again afterwards.[18]

Other than Ford and Vauxhall, however, the big auto firms worked on piecework; within this wage system shop stewards were able to exert their highest degree of control. The Donovan Commission focused on the loss of managerial control and the disorderly structures of industrial relations evident within this system. But lack of management control was not the same thing as the existence of union control. Evidence to the commission showed that the shop steward system under piecework bargaining was fraught with inequity, lack of security, constant haggling, and divisiveness. But it did provide stewards with enormous scope for bargaining and opportunities to show that union organization could deliver the goods in cash terms.[19] By the 1960s stewards were exerting real control over piecework prices, using their knowledge and sectional bargaining power to push earnings and erode the predictability of wage costs for management.

This fragmentation of bargaining had consequences only partially satisfactory to stewards. As a result of prolonged piecework bargaining, chaotic and widespread differentials emerged, with neither managerial nor union rationality behind them. Workers in the same grade had widely different earnings, even in the *same* plant. It was common for a job to be highly rated within one plant's hierarchy of earnings but lowly rated in another. Jobs that were easy to rate-study were often on "tight" prices and had below average earnings, but jobs requiring no more skill or effort might have high earnings simply because they were hard to assess.[20] Although differentials in the U.S. auto industry had become highly compressed by the 1960s, they remained very wide in Britain.[21] Moreover, there was no tendency within the piecework system to change this. Indeed, steward bargaining often sought to maintain those differentials even among semiskilled workers, and workers on individual piecework were ready to tolerate surprisingly wide differentials between similar jobs.[22] The key factor that altered earnings was the frequency and vigor of collective bargaining, especially at the steward leadership level.[23] An immense amount turned on local interpretations of the 1931 National Engineering Agreement, whereby no changes could be made in piecework prices once a job had been assessed unless there was a change in "means or methods of production." In some departments this could be interpreted to limit severely the opportunities for renegotiation, whereas in others stewards were able to take advantage of it to demand complete renegotiation after very minor changes.[24]

In part, the high levels of strike activity in autos in the 1960s arose from the direct use of shop floor muscle as a motor to increase wages. But strike activity is not a real indicator of union strength and control. Often short strikes were "attention getters," a sign of cumbersome grievance procedures and inadequate management structures.[25] But in the mid- and late 1960s they often arose from insecurity issues, such as loss of earnings arising from breakdowns, faulty scheduling, shortages of components, and layoffs.[26] Shop steward organizations were at their weakest in mitigating such an unstable earnings environment, and their weakness on these issues gave management a particular leverage in introducing Measured Day Work (MDW) in the early 1970s, which increased pay stability as a trade-off against the loss of continuous bargaining rights.[27]

Thus, stewards within the piecework frame were unable to challenge inequity and insecurity. They were also unable to develop broader strategic goals. Much of their bargaining advantage in the shops derived from astute manipulation of custom and practice. This, however, should not be confused with unilateral regulation of conditions in the workshops. The rule of custom arose primarily in areas where managerial decisions had hitherto been absent. Its effects were partly random, since the implications of a particular decision were often unclear to both stewards and managers.[28] More importantly, the nature of such gains won through a policy of shop floor opportunism meant that stewards could not think or act strategically. One result was the dissipation of the collective power of the workforce through frequent actions over somewhat tendentious grievances. The extreme decentralization of such bargaining exacerbated sectionalism and compartmentalism and could often foster internal antagonisms; for example, in the late 1960s sectional activity at Cowley often disrupted the work of others over issues not at all clear.[29] This lack of unity was rarely offset by effective companywide Joint Shop Stewards Committees, which were often unable to overcome interunion rivalries within multiunion companies or to develop coherent policies. Over and above the factory level, steward combine organizations remained skeletal throughout the 1960s.[30]

In certain areas where stewards did exercise job control it was often less oppositional and more cooperative with management than often recognized. As a result self-regulation within a piecework system was double-edged, for they played a quasi-supervisory role in work organization to ensure continuity of production, prevent bottlenecks, and maximize production and hence earnings. Such expanded responsibilities soon posed a new set of problems which can be clearly seen at Standard Motors in the 1950s where this role developed furthest around the Standard "large gang" system. Stewards exercised considerable control over the deployment of labor and manning levels. Under MDW this would be the essence of job control, but under payment by results it very much threw the ball into the trade union's court and was ambiguous in its effects. There was a standing temptation to either deman gangs and intensify effort, increasing income, or to discriminate against members of gangs; for instance, by having more members on lower grades within the gang, the proportion of the bonus taken by the higher grades was greatly raised.

Once the system had been in motion for a few years these pressures created internal division and rivalry. Two or more gangs might both lay claim to a lucrative job, or one gang might conspire with management at the expense of another. In 1955 the firm decided to subcontract out the work done by women trimmers on Gang 13 unless they accepted a price at the level tendered by subcontractors. The Gang decided not to defend the women; instead, they agreed with management to kick the women out and create a new women's gang, avoiding the now low-priced job pulling down their earnings.[31] The line between job control and self-supervision was thin, and under piecework stewards might choose to maximize output rather than strictly defend working conditions and rights.

The picture presented here seriously qualifies the commonplace notion of job control under shop stewards in the British auto industry. It developed in a much later historical period than is often suggested and even then required a significant degree of external assistance from the state and management. Job control was highly dependent on the bargaining opportunities of a particular payments system, and, largely because of the way shop floor strategy was shaped by this context, it did little to curb inequities or insecurity; it was based on sectionalism, specific local conditions, and the exploitation of loopholes. Stewards struggled to develop forms of coordination and more strategic control with little success. Even within piecework firms there was a considerable range of job control between the best organized firms such as Standard Motors and the Coventry producers and a range of firms like Morris, Austin, or Rover where shop floor control remained significantly less developed.

## United States: Contract Unionism and Job Control

Bearing in mind these findings on the slow development and limited achievements of shop steward organization in the British auto industry, to what extent did a more decentralized system of shop floor bargaining represent a real historical option in American mass production industry? A number of factors highlighted by recent historical treatments of the rise of the CIO, including those of Brody and Lichtenstein themselves, weighed heavily against this prospect.

The first is the sporadic and often highly sectional character of rank-and-file militancy. The most intense rank-and-file involvement in the upsurges of the 1930s appears to have come during the NRA strikes of 1933–1934, but it fizzled quickly in the face of employer opposition and AFL ambivalence. During the formative years of the CIO itself, many mass production workers had little durable loyalty to the new unions, and after brief periods of mobilization they would soon relapse into apathetic disinterest, leaving the union activist dangerously exposed to management reprisals.[32] Even after unionization, the rash of sitdowns, slowdowns, and "quickie" strikes which hit the auto and rubber plants in the late 1930s proved extremely sectional and divisive, dissipating the collective power of the workforce in a succession of ill-timed stoppages which laid off large numbers of workers over the grievances of isolated work groups and threatened to provoke a devastating managerial counteroffensive.[33] Wartime wildcats raised similar problems for the unions, manifesting themselves in an extreme form during the "hate strikes" against the promotion of black workers to more skilled jobs which erupted at Packard and other Detroit plants in 1943.[34] As in Britain, moreover, the proliferation of sectional bargaining would have produced large and persistent disparities of earnings and conditions among workers both with and between plants, which the egalitarian wage policies and opposition to piecework shared by most UAW activists explicitly sought to prevent.[35]

The unions' need to develop a more unified strategy was rendered more urgent by the vast power and resources of their opponents. Most giant corporations that dominated the mass production industries had accepted collective bargaining only after bitter strikes or under intense pressure from government agencies. It seemed likely that they would try to rid themselves of union organization once the political and economic climate had changed; and it was evident that union strategies would have to be carefully calculated and coordinated if they were to have any assurance of survival. After the war, the enormous bargaining power and strategic capacities of corporations such as GM forced the unions to accept management rights clauses and reductions in steward numbers; and only a relatively centralized bargaining strategy could prevent these companies from playing off one plant against another.[36] Finally, even in those auto firms where strong steward organizations did survive into the 1950s, the competitive pressure exerted by the industry leaders ultimately cut the ground out from under them, either through the firms' demise as at Packard and Studebaker or through the reassertion of managerial authority as at Chrysler.[37]

The overwhelming power of their business opponents was in turn the main reason for the CIO's dependence on support from government agencies. As Brody and others have demonstrated, without active federal government support the CIO organizing drive would probably have suffered the fate of 1919 steel strike; and the War Labor Board's backing was equally essential in forcing collective bargaining on the major holdout firms, such as Ford, Goodyear, Westinghouse, and Little Steel, those the CIO had been unable to subdue before the war.[38] An additional constraint was the resurgence of conservative forces in Congress after 1938, giving CIO leaders ample reason to fear that a wave of uncontrolled wartime strikes would provoke harsh antilabor legislation and administrative restrictions on union activity. Indeed the defense strikes of 1940–1941 and the coal strikes of 1943 paved the way for the passage of the Smith-Connally Act, as the postwar reconstruction strike wave did for Taft-Hartley. From Lichtenstein's own account, it seems clear that the CIO leaders' commitment to the no-strike pledge in the later years of the war stemmed as much from their anxiety to avert a right-wing backlash and the threat of a "labor draft," as from their social patriotism and desire to reassert control over the rank and file. Faced with powerful enemies in business and Congress, the CIO unions could not have gone it alone, as ambitious and opportunistic leaders such as Walter Reuther realized, and a majority of rank and filers who voted reaffirmed their support for the no-strike pledge in the UAW's March 1945 referendum.[39]

If the triumph of militant, autonomous shop floor unionism was not a real possibility in postwar America, how much did the more centralized and contractual collective bargaining which actually prevailed limit management's freedom of action in the workplace? Most historians and industrial relations experts have emphasized management's success in containing and rolling back the union challenge to its control in the immediate postwar years. In the auto industry, for example, corporations such as GM and Ford resisted the UAW's attempts to intrude on their pricing policies and their strategies for responding to seasonal demand, fending off in the process demands for union participation in establishing production standards, job classification schemes, and disciplinary rules. More positive from their perspective, the auto giants extracted from the UAW sweeping declarations of management rights and a significant reduction in the number of stewards and committeemen, as well as draconian powers to punish wildcat strikers. The NLRB and Taft-Hartley further contributed to the reestablishment of managerial control by removing the protection of the Wagner Act from foremen and supervisors, whose nascent unions were quickly smashed. Developments in other mass production industries followed a similar pattern, but few companies were as adept as GM in taking advantage of their revived bargaining power.[40]

Although these developments marked a serious setback to the unions' broader ambitions and help account for management's reconciliation to collective bargaining in most major companies, they should not obscure the magnitude of what had already been achieved by comparison to the preunion era or, for that matter, to the situation in Britain even a decade later. The salient features of workers' experience in the preunion auto factories, as in other mass production industries such as rubber, steel, and electrical goods, had been pervasive insecurity and subjection to arbitrary managerial discipline. Where companies had themselves instituted seniority systems, management retained wide discretion in their administration, and even long-serving workers faced continual bullying from foremen and the threat of instantaneous dismissal.[41]

By the 1940s the seniority systems and disciplinary procedures unions had won in most plants marked a fundamental break with this regime. By 1950, seniority was well on its way to becoming the principal criterion for layoffs and recalls in most mass production industries, and in many cases it had made substantial inroads into transfer and promotion policies as well. In the rubber industry, layoffs were governed by strict seniority, which also applied to promotions where the worker was capable of learning the job within a reasonable period of time. In steel and autos, merit and ability still qualified seniority in layoffs and promotions, but arbitrators had ruled that the burden of proof for deviations fell on management. In the electrical industry, where seniority had become the main factor governing layoffs and recalls for 94 percent of workers covered by UE contracts in 1947, Ronald Schatz observed: "The union seniority systems were less flexible than the preunion company policies. They denied managers most of the freedom they had formerly enjoyed in issuing assignments to individual workers."[42]

In most large companies, moreover, management was no longer free to discharge employees at will. In fact, it could ultimately be forced through the grievance procedure to justify its actions before a neutral arbitrator, demonstrating "just cause" in the form of written rules, clear precedents, prior warnings, and even-handed treatment of individuals; where any of these were absent, the arbitrator was likely to reverse or modify the penalty. Through these contractual means, concluded Neil Chamberlain in his 1947 study of conditions in the auto, steel, rubber, meatpacking, electrical and public utility sectors, unions "have succeeded in sharing a very great measure of authority in the disciplinary control of employees."[43]

Taken together, these limits on arbitrary discharge could have a profoundly subversive effect on shop floor discipline. In the electrical industry, for example, Schatz reports that the coming of seniority and grievance procedures greatly eroded foremen's powers over individual workers. Whereas previously foremen could victimize those who crossed them, workers now felt sufficiently secure to challenge their authority on sensitive issues, such as piecework times and prices, producing extensive wage drift. In each industry he studied, Chamberlain found that the union inroad in the disciplinary area had far exceeded the provisions of the contract, but this clearly depended on effective shop floor enforcement; without detailed studies, it is difficult to say how far it persisted into the 1950s and 1960s.[44]

As collective bargaining became better established, seniority systems and grievance procedures were progressively elaborated and extended to new firms; and the constraints they placed on management's freedom to allocate labor were, if anything, enhanced. In 1960, for example, Slichter, Healy, and Livernash reported that, "many managements . . . are troubled by the inroads of the seniority criterion on the promotion of employees, and more particularly, they are convinced that seniority rules impair the flexibility of assignments needed for efficient operation." The same was true of the classification systems and job descriptions that had become a standard feature of most union contracts during the preceding twenty years. "Few companies," they observed, "ever entered into these programs . . . with the thought they would limit their right to assign work or that they would lead to unrest among employees concerning work assignments. Yet in a surprising number of cases these have been the consequences."[45] Disciplinary procedures, too, continued to constrain managerial discretion; a study of 1,055 discharge cases between 1942 and 1955 showed that management's decision was sustained in only 41 percent, the penalty reduced in 33.8 percent, and revoked entirely in 25.2 percent.[46]

In some cases, unions had also managed to retain or acquire influence over important aspects of the production process. In the steel industry, for example, local rules concerning crew sizes and working conditions were protected by the national contract, and arbitrators had extended this protection to customary practices not recorded in the local contracts themselves. The steel companies' attempt to modify this clause was defeated in the protracted 1959 strike, although individual rules could be modified through technological change or bargaining with the locals.[47] In auto, the UAW had won substantial rest periods for assembly workers at the major companies; the GM contracts specified that workers should be able to meet production standards while working at a "normal pace," and the standards were supposed to vary with the model mix. In the last instance, production standards and health and safety issues were strikeable during the life of the contract, but only after the final step of the lengthy grievance procedure had been completed.[48]

In industries where certain issues were strikeable during the life of the contract, these could be used to pressure the companies over nonstrikeable issues, including managerial prerogatives not subject to mandatory bargaining under NLRB rules. In the auto industry, for example, management at GM, Ford, and Chrysler complained repeatedly throughout the 1950s that production standards and health and safety issues were used to force concessions over nonstrikeable issues.[49] In the electrical industry, local unions took advantage of the collapse of national bargaining and the companies' resistance to arbitration to develop a highly successful strategy of using legal grievance strikes to harass management through short stoppages at well-timed moments. The locals would store up grievances which had passed through the procedure, enabling them to strike at any moment or after 1970 with twenty-four hours' notice. These tactics, Bryn Jones argues, enabled the unions to win control over new technology for skilled workers in the aerospace industry.[50] In the rubber industry, where "fractional bargaining" was particularly well established, James Kuhn discovered that in many plants stewards and foremen were permitted to make "mutual agreements" modifying the operation of the contract in particular shops.[51]

These last observations suggest that the "workplace rule of law" was not in itself so severe a constraint on shop floor struggles for job control as many historians have claimed. Why then did these not play a greater role in postwar American industrial relations? Part of the answer lies, of course, in the power of the corporations and their determination to clamp down on such developments, discounting exceptional cases such as GE.

But part of the answer also lies in the policies of the unions themselves. Sophisticated union leaders such as Walter Reuther were always careful to remain in touch with the mood of the rank and file and sought to incorporate demands over workplace issues, such as production standards, into their bargaining strategy to a limited extent. Less responsive leaders such as Sherman Dalrymple of the URW were unseated by rank-and-file revolts when they imposed harsh penalties on wildcat strikers. But for men like Reuther, these local grievances were always secondary to their larger concern with companywide problems, such as pensions and the guaranteed annual wage; moreover, they were a potential threat to effective central union control. The UAW, therefore, tended to press its locals to curtail their strikes over production standards to avoid interfering with national negotiations. After the 1960s, however, the International responded to growing pressure from below by authorizing an increasing number of local strikes over shop floor conditions—many during the life of the contract itself—which soon dwarfed wildcat stoppages in terms of man hours lost in the industry as a whole.[52]

The contractual system of collective bargaining emerging from the Second World War substantially constrained management's freedom to deploy labor and impose arbitrary discipline in the enterprise through the elaboration of seniority systems, grievance procedures, and binding arbitration. But it also left a certain latitude for shop floor struggles over job control not fully utilized given the centralizing ambitions of both management and unions. In this limited sense, workplace industrial relations in postwar America might indeed have been different, although they could never have conformed to the imaginary model of shop steward power in Britain.

## Conclusion

Reflecting on the British labor scene in 1920, the American economist Carter Goodrich observed that "the greater or less degree" of control is at once impossible to measure and less illuminating than "the nature and policy of the union exercising it."[53] Subsequent commentators on the "frontier of control," however, have tended to regard it as a straightforward index of the shop floor balance of power between labor and management, ranking national systems of industrial relations along a single scale by the level of job control they allow the workforce.

A detailed historical examination of the British and American auto industries—a classic case in point—undermines both such national stereotypes and the underlying conception of job control. On the British side, as we have seen, trade unions and shop steward organization were weakly established for much of the postwar period, and even in their heyday during the late 1960s and 1970s job controls remained partial and defensive; they were often applied flexibly and cooperatively except in periods of acute conflict. In both countries, however, when unions established themselves in the workplace they significantly constrained management's freedom of action, through contractual seniority rules and grievance procedures which enhanced workers' security in the United States and through more decentralized bargaining over manning, workloads, and piecework prices in Britain. These differences in the focus of job control reflect the very different histories of industrial relations in the two countries. But each system entails a complex blend of power and constraint for both unions and management whose precise implications depend in large measure on the bargaining strategies of the contending parties themselves, never more so than in a period of economic and political upheaval like the present.

### NOTES

1. Conservative businessmen and politicians dissatisfied with the Wagner Act also looked favorably on the restrictive provisions of the British Trade Disputes Act of 1927. For information on American perceptions of British

industrial relations in this period, see Howell Harris, "The Snares of Liberalism? Politicians, Bureaucrats and the Shaping of Federal Labour Relations Policy in the United States, ca. 1915–47," in Steven Tolliday and Jonathan Zeitlin, eds., *Shop Floor Bargaining and the State: Historical and Contemporary Perspectives* (Cambridge: Cambridge University Press, 1985). For the influence of the American model on the drafters of the Industrial Relations Act, see Michael Moran, *The Politics of Industrial Relations: The Origins, Life and Death of the 1971 Industrial Relations Act* (London: Allen and Unwin, 1977); and for a British study of industrial relations in the auto industry contrasting American arrangements favorably with the prevailing pattern in the United Kingdom, see H. A. Turner, Garfield Clack, and Geoffrey Roberts, *Labour Relations in the Motor Industry* (London: Allen and Unwin, 1967), especially ch. 10.

2. For representative interpretations of American labor history in these terms, see Stanley Aronowitz, *False Promises: The Shaping of American Working Class Consciousness* (New York: McGraw-Hill, 1973); and Jeremy Brecher, *Strike!* (San Francisco: Straight Arrow Books, 1972).

3. Another important contrast between the two labor movements concerned their relation to politics. Much of the discontent of American radicals with the trade unions stemmed from the latter's support for the Vietnam war and close ties with the Democratic Party. British trade unions, on the other hand, had thrown their weight behind a Labour Party committed to a socialist constitution, and many shop stewards were open supporters of the Communist party or small far-left groups. For a good picture of perceptions of British labor on the American left in the early 1970s, see the special issue on "Class Struggle in Britain," *Radical America* 8, no. 5 (1974).

4. David Brody, "The Uses of Power I: The Industrial Battleground," in his *Workers in Industrial America: Essays on the Twentieth Century Struggle* (New York: Oxford University Press, 1980), 172–214; the quotation is on 206. In an earlier essay on "Radical Labor History and Rank and File Militancy," Brody draws on the experience of the wartime shop stewards movement, together with the importance of craft production, the availability of radical ideologies, and the continuity of trade union organization to explain why ideas of workers' control appeared to have had so much greater resonance in Britain than among the rank-and-file activists of the early CIO: ibid., 146–58.

5. Nelson Lichtenstein, "Auto Worker Militancy and the Structure of Factory Life, 1937–55," *Journal of American History* 67 (September 1980): 335–53; the quotation is on 348. Lichtenstein shows that at Studebaker and Packard the steward system remained intact until the companies' collapse in the late 1950s, as it did at Chrysler to a substantial extent until the 1957–1958 recession; ibid., 359; compare also his "Life at the Rouge: A Cycle of Workers' Control," in Charles Stephenson and Robert Asher, eds., *Life and Labor: Dimensions of Working-Class History* (Albany: State University of New York, 1986), 237–59; Steve Jefferys, *Management and Managed: Fifty Years of Crisis at Chrysler* (Cambridge: Cambridge University Press 1986); and Robert M. MacDonald, *Collective Bargaining in the Automobile Industry* (New Haven: Yale University Press, 1963), chs. 6–7.

In his study of the CIO during the Second World War, Lichtenstein assigns the principal weight in the emergence of contract unionism to two reasons: the formal grievance procedures and provisions for union security imposed by the NWLB, and the CIO leaders' willingness to support the no-strike pledge as a result of their political alliance with the Roosevelt administration and their pursuit of power over the rank and file within the unions themselves. In his conclusions, he returns to the British example: "In contrast to Great Britain, where the post-war prosperity and growth of unionism gave rise to an increasingly confident stratum of shop steward militants, in America the rigidity of the collective bargaining process thwarted the emergence of an independent cadre that could give continuous leadership to the episodic conflict that still unfolded in the workplace." Nelson Lichtenstein, *Labor's War at Home: The CIO in World War II* (Cambridge: Cambridge University Press, 1982), 243–44.

6. For an account of recent developments at British Leyland, see Paul Willman, "Labour Relations Strategy at BL Cars," in Steven Tolliday and Jonathan Zeitlin, eds., *The Automobile Industry and Its Workers: Between Fordism and Flexibility* (Cambridge: Polity Press, 1986). For evidence that British shop steward organization has held up better outside the nationalized sector, see Michael Rose and Bryn Jones, "Managerial Strategy and Trade Union Response in Plant-Level Reorganisation of Work," in D. Knights, H. Willmott, and D. Collinson, eds., *Job Redesign* (London: Hutchinson, 1986); and Eric Batstone, *Working Order: Workplace Industrial Relations over Two Decades* (Oxford: Blackwell, 1984).

7. Piore takes as his point of departure the elaborate internal job structures established by union contracts negotiated at the plant level. "The union imposes on this structure a set of negotiated wages, actually specifying how much an employer must pay for *each* job . . . a set of 'job security' provisions which determine how these jobs are distributed among the workers; and a set of disciplinary standards which limit, in the light of each worker's own particular work requirements, what obligations he or she has to the employer and how a failure to meet those obligations will be sanctioned." Most interpretations of American industrial relations emphasize management's freedom to define the initial job structure. But as Piore points out, "what is often missed in such discussions is that the jobs must nonetheless be defined, the jobs stabilized over a period long enough that they have real meaning, and the employer accept the wages, worker allocation and disciplinary procedures which his job definitions imply." Michael J. Piore, "American Labor and the Industrial Crisis," *Challenge* (March–April 1982): 8–9; and compare Piore and Charles F. Sabel, *The Second Industrial Divide: Possibilities of Prosperity* (New York: Basic Books, 1984), 111–32, 240–46.

8. Christoph Köhler and Werner Sengenberger, "Policies of Work Force Reduction and Labor Market Structures in the American and German Automobile Industry" (paper presented to the conference of the International Working Party on Labour Market Segmentation, Modena, Italy, September 7–11, 1981); and their *Konjunktur und Personalanpassung: betriebliche Beschaftigungspolitik in der deutschen und amerikanischen Automobilindus-*

*trie* (Frankfurt am Main: Campus, 1983). A detailed study of current trends in the U.S. auto industry which supports this view and that of Piore is Harry C. Katz, *Shifting Gears: Changing Labor Relations in the U.S. Auto Industry* (Cambridge, Mass.: MIT Press, 1985).

9. Bryn Jones, "Controlling Production on the Shop Floor: The Role of State Administration and Regulation in the British and American Aerospace Industries," in Tolliday and Zeitlin, eds., *Shop Floor Bargaining and the State.*

10. For a comparative study which highlights the importance of industrial structure in explaining differences in Anglo-American industrial relations, see Bernard Elbaum and Frank Wilkinson, "Industrial Relations and Uneven Development: A Comparative Study of the American and British Steel Industries," *Cambridge Journal of Economics* 3 (1979). The limited existing research on industrial relations in other British mass production sectors suggests a broadly similar pattern to that of the automobile industry: compare on electrical engineering, Ronald Dore, *British Factory-Japanese Factory* (London: Allen and Unwin, 1973); and on rubber, Ian Maitland, *The Causes of Industrial Disorder: A Comparison of a British and a German Factory* (London: Routledge and Kegan Paul, 1983).

11. See Jonathan Zeitlin, "The Emergence of Shop Steward Organization and Job Control in the British Car Industry: A Review Essay," *History Workshop Journal*, no. 10 (Autumn 1980): 122–23; Andrew L. Friedman, *Industry and Labour* (London: Macmillan, 1977), ch. 14; Richard Hyman and Tony Eiger, "Job Controls, the Employers' Offensive and Alternative Strategies," *Capital and Class*, no. 15 (Autumn 1981): 133–34; Peter J. S. Dunnett, *The Decline of the British Motor Industry: The Effects of Government Policy, 1949–79* (London: Croom Helm, 1980), esp. 52–55, 82–85, and 108–14; Richard Price, "Rethinking Labour History: The Importance of Work," in James E. Cronin and Jonathan Schneer, eds., *Social Conflict and the Political Order in Modern Britain* (London: Croom Helm 1982), 196; Keith Middlemas, *Politics in Industrial Society* (London: Andre Deutsch, 1979), 400.

12. Figures on union density derive from work in progress at the Kings' College, Cambridge Research Centre. For the weakness of unions at Vauxhall even in the 1960s see J. H. Goldthorpe, *The Affluent Workers: Industrial Attitudes and Behavior* (London: Allen and Unwin, 1968).

13. These points are argued fully in Steven Tolliday, "Government, Employers and Shop Floor Organisation in the British Motor Industry, 1939–69," in Tolliday and Zeitlin, *Shop Floor Bargaining and the State.*

14. On weaknesses of managerial structures, see Richard J. Overy, *William Morris, Viscount Nuffield* (London: Europa, 1976), esp. 60–66. Roy Church, *Herbert Austin: The British Motor Car Industry to 1941* (London: Europa, 1979), 157–68.

15. For the "indulgency pattern" generally, see Alvin Gouldner, *Patterns of Industrial Bureaucracy* (Glencoe, Ill.: Free Press, 1954), 177.

16. Based on information from Engineering Employers' Federation wage data cited in Tolliday, "Government, Employers."

17. A good account of this is given by Ernie Stanton who was a NUVB

steward at Ford in the early 1960s in Ernie Stanton, *What Happened at Fords*, Solidarity Pamphlet, no. 26, 1967. On the wider background of industrial relations at Ford, see Henry Friedmann and Sandor Meredeen, *The Dynamics of Industrial Conflict: Lessons from Ford* (London: Croom Helm, 1980); Huw Beynon, *Working for Ford* (London: Allen Lane, 1973). On the "harmonization issue" see *Report of a Court of Inquiry* (Cameron Report), Cmd. 131 HMSO, 1957; and *Report of a Court of Inquiry* (Jack Report), Cmd. 1949, HMSO, 1963.

18. Beynon, *Working for Ford*, chs. 5, 6, 7.

19. Minutes of Evidence to Royal Commission on Trade Unions and Employers Associations, HMSO 1965–68 (Donovan Commission) and R.C. Report, 1968 Cmd.

20. Turner, Clack, and Roberts, *Labour Relations*, ch. 5. The classic example of the hard-to-time job is that of grinder where an experienced worker can raise an impressive shower of sparks while barely touching the metal and thus run rings around the rate-fixer.

21. In 1963 in the United States three-fifths of production workers earned between $2.70 and $2.90, a range of less than 8 percent; MacDonald, *Collective Bargaining*, 84–88. To encompass a comparable proportion of British auto workers a range of more than 50 percent would be required: Turner, Clack, and Roberts, *Labour Relations*, ch. 10.

22. William A. Brown, *Piecework Bargaining* (London: Heinemann, 1973), 51–60. At Standard Motors, the best organized auto plant in the 1950s, the "large gang" system had had the closure of differentials as one of its major initial aims. In practice it failed to maintain the initial narrowing of relativities. Price fixing developed on a ratchet system. When a new job came in, the demand was for the price to yield the average earnings of existing work; then, once the gang got the hang of the job and improved efficiency, the earnings moved ahead. But some sections might not get a new job for several years, and gangs working on the oldest vintages had the lowest earnings while those on the newest the most. Once a new job came in it was very often possible to leap-frog to the top of the wage hierarchy. In the meantime, however, despite union bargaining strength, wide inequalities were tolerated for long periods. In contrast to the relatively stable relativities on individual piecework at Austin Motor Co., the Standard gang system had very erratic fluctuations. See Steven Tolliday, "High Tide and After: Coventry Engineering Workers and Shop Floor Bargaining, 1945–80," in Tony Mason and Bill Lancaster, eds., *Life and Labour in a Twentieth Century City: The Experience of Coventry* (Coventry: Cryfield Press, 1986).

23. Eric Batstone, Ian Boraston, and Steven Frankel, *Shop Stewards in Action* (Oxford: Blackwell, 1977), 234–35.

24. Brown, *Piecework Bargaining*, 90; for comparable analyses of the wage structure irrationalities created by piecework bargaining in the electrical engineering and rubber industries, see Dore, *British Factory-Japanese Factory*, 76–94; and Maitland, *Causes of Industrial Disorder*, 74–91.

25. For an example from a Coventry motor firm, see G. Clack, *Industrial*

*Relations in a British Car Factory* (Cambridge: Cambridge University Press, 1967), 61–63.

26. Turner, Clack, and Roberts, *Labour Relations*, ch. 4. See also *14th Report of Select Committee on National Expenditure*, 1975, ch. 9. This was particularly the case at Morris Motors, Cowley. See interviews with Tom Richardson, industrial relations manager at Cowley, 1965–1968, and with Alan Thornett, former TGWU deputy senior steward at Cowley, November 1982. Transcripts in the possesion of the authors.

27. Interviews with David Buckle, TGWU district secretary for Oxford Area, and Bill Roche, TGWU covenor Cowley Body Plant, 1982.

28. Brown, *Piecework Bargaining*, esp. 142–53.

29. For a classic example of this in the early 1970s see S. Johns, *Victimisation at Cowley* (Oxford: Blackwell, 1974). For cases in the late 1960s see the Les Gurl Papers at the Modern Records Centre, Warwick University.

30. Shirley W. Lerner and John Bescoby, "Shop Steward Combine Committees in the British Engineering Industry," *British Journal of Industrial Relations* (1966). On the problems of the BMC Combine Committee, see the papers of Les Gurl, the former chairman of the Combine Committee, M.R.C. Warwick.

31. The Standard system has been described and somewhat idealized by Seymour Melman, *Decision-making and Productivity* (Oxford: Blackwell, 1957), and D. Rayton, *Shop Floor Democracy in Action* (Nottingham: 1977). See also A. Friedman, *Industry and Labour*, ch. 14. For a critical discussion of the situation at Standard see S. Tolliday, "High Tide and After."

32. On the sporadic character of rank-and-file militancy and the weak commitment of workers to the unions during the 1930s, see Brody, *Workers in Industrial America*, 134–35; Lichtenstein, *Labor's War at Home*, 9–14; Ray Boryczka, "Seasons of Discontent: Auto Union Factionalism and the Motor Products Strike of 1935–36," *Michigan History* 61 (1977); and Robert H. Zieger, "The Limits of Militancy: Organizing Paper Workers, 1933–35," *Journal of American History* 63 (1976).

33. Lichtenstein, *Labor's War at Home*, 14–17; Ray Boryczka, "Militancy and Factionalism in the United Auto Workers' Union, 1937–41," *The Maryland Historian* 8 (Fall 1977). Thus Lichtenstein writes, "Uncoordinated and unpredictable—at least to top union officials—these strikes made it difficult for the union as a whole to formulate a general strategy toward management. They proved immediately advantageous to workers who were strategically located in the production process, but they could destroy solidarity among the larger group, especially when a strike in one department produced a layoff in another. Finally, these strikes threatened the union's entire relationship with the company. They undermined the managerial incentive to continue recognizing the union, and during the 1937 recession, when the union stood on the defensive, they were used by management as occasions to eliminate shop floor militants." Lichtenstein, *Labor's War at Home*, 15.

34. Ibid., 121–27.

35. On wage drift and shifts in relativities generated by piecework bar-

gaining at Studebaker, see MacDonald, *Collective Bargaining*, 123–25; on the UAW's egalitarian wage policy and its opposition to piecework, see ibid., 90, 105–33, 148–59, 206–36.

36. Howell Harris, *The Right to Manage: Industrial Relations Policies of American Business in the 1940s* (Madison: University of Wisconsin Press, 1982); Brody, *Workers in Industrial America*, 183–88; Lichtenstein, *Labor's War at Home*, 219–30.

37. MacDonald, *Collective Bargaining*, 259–84, 317–29, 346–67.

38. "The Emergence of Mass Production Unionism," in Brody, *Workers in Industrial America*, 82–110; Harris, "The Snares of Liberalism."

39. Lichtenstein, *Labor's War at Home*, 47–51, 56–63, 95–96, 157–71, 182–202. On the central role of congressional conservatism, see Richard Polenberg, "The Decline of the New Deal, 1937–40," and David Brody, "The New Deal and World War II," both in John Braeman, Robert H. Bremner, and David Brody, eds., *The New Deal: Volume One, The National Level* (Columbus: Ohio University Press, 1975). Compare also Harris, "The Snares of Liberalism," who argues that

> "responsible unionism" *paid off*. During the war, unions observing the no-strike pledge, not pressing the full weight of their bargaining power, obtained institutional security of income and membership, a recognized status in the plant or firm, liberalized fringe benefits, some extensions of joint consultation and bargaining, and arbitration-terminated grievance systems which denied employer demands for unilateral authority at the same time as they confined unions and their members within the language of contract and time-consuming, legalistic procedures. It is not self-evident that "irresponsible unionism" would have secured more than this, given the willingness and ability of Congress and the administration to strike at non-complying unions in a variety of harmful ways.

Ibid., 183.

40. Brody, *Workers in Industrial America*, 173–95; Harris, *Right to Manage*, 67–89, 139–58; Lichtenstein, *Labor's War at Home*, 221–31, 241–45, and "Auto Worker Militancy."

41. On preunion conditions in the auto plants, see Roger Keeran, *The Communist Party and the Auto Workers Unions* (Bloomington: Indiana University Press, 1980), 28–59; and Frank Marquart, *An Autoworker's Journal: The UAW from Crusade to One-Party Union* (University Park: Pennsylvania State University Press, 1975), 6–39. On the electrical industry, see the excellent study by Ronald Schatz, *Electrical Workers: A History of Labor at General Electric and Westinghouse, 1923–1960* (Champaign, Ill.: University of Illinois Press, 1983). The references in this chapter are to his 1977 University of Pittsburgh Ph.D. diss., esp. 67–69, 77–87, 120–22, and 134–36.

42. Neil W. Chamberlain, *The Union Challenge to Management Control* (New York: Harper and Bros., 1948), 78, 81, 270, 281; Schatz, *Electrical Workers*, 127–33; the quotation is on 131–32. Seniority had also become

an important factor in promotions at GE and Westinghouse, although here aggressive local bargaining was needed to enforce contractual provisions.

43. Chamberlain, *Union Challenge*, 79–80, 270–71, 292–93, 309–10; the quotation is on 79–80.

44. Schatz, *Electrical Workers*, 133–39. Foremen also lost the right to assign overtime, although they retained some power over piecework allocation and some influence over promotion. For Chamberlain's findings on the informal extension of union powers in the disciplinary area, see the passages cited in note 43 above.

45. Sumner Slichter, James J. Healy, and E. Robert Livernash, *The Impact of Collective Bargaining on Management* (Washington, D.C.: Brookings Institution, 1960), 106–9, 139–41, 252–53; the quotations are on 140 and 252, respectively. The authors also found that in many cases seniority had become a constraint on managerial discipline and even in some instances on management's right to subcontract work, as a result of decisions by arbitrators. As one industrial relations director told them, "It's bad enough to be saddled with the seniority rules we know about, but now we find seniority can be used to support almost any kind of restriction the union dreams up." Ibid., 141. For a more critical view of seniority in the late 1960s, see Richard Herding, *Job Control and Union Structure* (Rotterdam: Rotterdam University Press, 1972), 17–28, 145–57; and for contemporary evidence of the constraints placed by seniority rules on the deployment of labor in the auto industry, see Katz, *Shifting Gears*.

46. Slichter, Healy, and Livernash, *Impact of Collective Bargaining*, 657; compare also Orme W. Phelps, *Discipline and Discharge in the Unionized Firm* (Berkeley: University of California Press, 1959), esp. 138–40. Although these figures show that management was especially successful in dismissing workers for "incompetency and/or inefficiency," a more recent case study of a Ford engine plant shows that charges such as "careless workmanship" or "excessive scrap" had higher than average rates of redress. Carl Gersuny, *Punishment and Redress in a Modern Factory* (Lexington, Mass.: D.C. Heath, 1973), 43.

47. Brody, *Workers in Industrial America*, 195–96; Herding, *Job Control*, 31–34, 133–39; Jack Stieber, "The Work Rules Issue in the Basic Steel Industry," *Monthly Labor Review* 85 (1962).

48. Herding, *Job Control*, 28–30, 124–32, for an account emphasizing the weight of bureaucratic delays and pressure from the international in curbing production standard strikes.

49. MacDonald, *Collective Bargaining*, 316, 325–26, 337–38; compare also Slichter, Healy, and Livernash, *Impact of Collective Bargaining*, 673–74, 758. In the 1950s, Ford charged that "since 1949 not a single negotiation of an authorized strike notice has been restricted to the so-called strikeable issue. In almost every instance the strikeable issue has been insignificant in the negotiations which we have been forced to undertake with the union to avoid an actual walk-out or to end the walk-out which has already taken place." Quoted in MacDonald, *Collective Bargaining*, 337–38.

50. James W. Kuhn, "Electrical Products," in G. G. Somers, ed., *Collective Bargaining: The Contemporary American Experience* (Madison, Wis.: The Industrial Relations Research Association, 1980), 251–61; Jones, "Controlling Production on the Shop Floor."

51. James W. Kuhn, *Bargaining in Grievance Settlement* (New York: Columbia University Press, 1961), esp. 174–76.

52. For gains made in contract clauses and grievance procedures dealing with production standards in the auto industry during the 1950s and 1960s, see Herding, *Job Control*, 29. For evidence of the calculated flexibility of Reuther and his associates in incorporating demands from below into their own program, see Jack W. Skeels, *The Development of Political Stability within the United Auto Workers Union* (Ph.D. diss., University of Wisconsin, 1957), 334 ff.; Jack Stieber, *Governing the UAW* (New York: John Wiley and Sons, 1962), 153–55; William Serrin, *The Company and the Union* (New York: Alfred A. Knopf, 1973), on the treatment of the "30 and out" demand during the 1970 GM negotiations; and Lichtenstein, *Labor's War at Home*, 146–57, 194–97, 214–15, and 221–29. On the wildcat strike issue and the dismissal of Dalrymple in 1945, see ibid., 197–201; and for the UAW's changing line on local strikes, see the discussion in Nelson Lichtenstein, "Reutherism on the Shop Floor: 1946–1970," in Tolliday and Zeitlin, *Automobile Industry*.

53. Carter L. Goodrich, *The Frontier of Control: A Study in British Workshop Politics* (1920; rev. ed., London: Pluto Press, 1975), 253, 260.

# Notes on Contributors

STEPHEN AMBERG teaches political science at the University of Texas, San Antonio. He is currently revising his MIT dissertation, "Liberal Democracy and Industrial Order: Autoworkers under the New Deal," for publication.

STEVE JEFFERYS teaches economic history in the faculty of Management and Business at Manchester Polytechnic. He is the author of *Management and Managed: Fifty Years of Crisis at Chrysler* (Cambridge University Press, 1986) and the forthcoming *Suitcase Soldier: Fifty Years in Auto* (with John Anderson).

THOMAS KLUG teaches history at Marygrove College in Detroit. He is completing a dissertation at Wayne State University on the history of employers' management strategies in Detroit from the late nineteenth century to 1933.

WAYNE LEWCHUK is a member of the department of economics and the Labour Studies Programme at McMaster University. He has published papers in the *Journal of Economic History* and in *Business History* and is the author of *The British Motor Industry, 1895–1980: The Roots of Industrial Decline* (Cambridge University Press, 1987).

NELSON LICHTENSTEIN teaches history at The Catholic University of America. He is the author of *Labor's War at Home: The CIO in World War II* (Cambridge University Press, 1982) and of a forthcoming biography of Walter Reuther (Basic Books).

STEPHEN MEYER directs the Labor Studies Program at the University of Wisconsin-Parkside. He is the author of *The Five Dollar Day: Labor Management and Social Control in the Ford Motor Company, 1908–1921* (State University of New York Press, 1981) and a forthcoming study of labor and management at Allis-Chalmers.

RUTH MILKMAN teaches sociology at the University of California, Los Angeles. She is the editor of *Women, Work and Protest: A Century of Women's Labor History* (Keegan-Paul, 1985) and author of *Gender at Work: The Dynamics of Job Segregation by Sex during World War II* (University of Illinois Press, 1987).

STEVEN TOLLIDAY is a faculty member at the Harvard Business School. He is the author of *Business, Banking and Politics: The Case of British Steel, 1919–39* (Harvard University Press, 1987), and with Jonathan Zeitlin is coeditor of *Shop Floor Bargaining and the State: Historical and Comparative Perspectives* (Cambridge University Press, 1985) and *The Automobile Industry and Its Workers: Between Fordism and Flexibility* (Polity Press/Basil Blackwell, 1986).

JONATHAN ZEITLIN is a lecturer in the department of history, Birkbeck College, University of London. In addition to the collections he has coedited with Steven Tolliday he is the author of numerous articles on labor history and industrial relations and coeditor with Royder Harrison of *Divisions of Labor: Skilled Workers and Technological Change in Nineteenth Century Britain* (University of Illinois Press, 1985).

# Index

A. O. Smith Corporation, 84
Abernathy, William, 4
Absenteeism, 23
Addes, George, 201
Adler, Paul, 73
Aerospace industry, 223
Affirmative action, 139, 147
Aldren, A. J., 115
Allis-Chalmers, 85
Aluminum Castings, 62
Amalgamated Society of Engineers (ASE), 26, 32
Amalgamated Union of Engineering Workers, 221
Amberg, Steven, 12, 13
American Auto Trimming and Painting, 62
American Car and Foundry Company, 47
American Federation of Labor (AFL), 101, 106, 107, 110, 219; federal labor unions, 106, 110, 193
American Federation of Labor-Congress of Industrial Organizations (AFL-CIO), 201, 206
*American Machinist*, 84, 89
American Motors Corporation, 91, 197, 206, 207
American Protective League (APL), 59
American system of manufacture, 78
Americanism, 159
Americanization: immigrants, 9, 55, 56, 57; production, 31, 32
Americanization Committee, 56, 57
Anderson, John W., 104
Anderson, Lisa, 130, 138
Andrews, Jack L., 106
Anna Rosenberg and Associates, 198
Annual model change, 3

Anticatholicism, 159
Anticommunism, 109, 110, 118–19, 201
Antiunionism, 103. *See also* Open shop
Apprenticeship, 78
Argyll, 27
Army Ordnance Department, 85, 86
Arrol Johnston, 32
Assembly line, 2, 3, 4, 5, 6, 17, 20, 21, 24, 32, 33, 35, 42, 132, 157, 226
Associated Equipment Company, 35
Atlanta, 145
Austin, 33, 34, 224, 229
Automated machines. *See* Automation; Machinery
Automation, 3, 9, 84, 86, 87, 88, 89, 200, 222; cost of, 88; department at Ford, 88; displacement of labor, 90; government funding, 85; hysteria of 1950s, 94; reduced production costs, 89, 90; social impact of, 91–93; social premises of, 85; upgraded skills, 86
*Automobile Engineer*, 27
Automobile Industrial Workers' Association (AIWA), 101, 110, 111, 113, 116, 117, 118
Automobile industry: defeminization, 129; economic status of, 1; Great Britain, 12, 17–36 *passim*, 219–36 *passim*; Japan, 4, 17; luxury producers, 24, 25, 26, 75, 208; mass producers, 25; parts production, 133–34; post-war expansion, 141; shakeout, 91, 197; structural change, 13–14; Sweden, 17, United States, 1, 17–36 *passim*, 219–36 *passim*; West Germany, 4, 17, 223
Automobile Manufacturers Association, 178

247